THE CORNKISTER DAYS

THE CORNKISTER DAYS

Portrait of a Land and its Rituals

by

DAVID KERR CAMERON

LONDON
VICTOR GOLLANCZ LTD
1984

First published in Great Britain August 1984
by Victor Gollancz Ltd,
14 Henrietta Street, London WC2E 8QJ
Second impression October 1984
Third impression December 1984

British Library Cataloguing in Publication Data
Cameron, David Kerr
    The Cornkister days.
    1. Farm life—Scotland   2. Scotland
    —Social life and customs—19th century
    3. Scotland—Social life and customs—
    20th century
    I. Title
    941.1081   DA818

    ISBN 0-575-03492-0

Typeset at The Spartan Press Limited, Lymington, Hants
and printed in Great Britain by
St Edmundsbury Press, Bury St Edmunds, Suffolk.
Illustrations originated and printed by Thomas Campone, Southampton

Some years ago I wrote a book called *The Ballad and the Plough*, a folk history of life around the old Scottish farmtouns. As I did so I became aware that another story ran in parallel: that of the life of the fields and the work routines of the old farming countryside. This was the backcloth against which the farmtoun folk lived out their days; its seasons and rituals governed their lives, and ultimately their destinies. Here now is that story, the story of a landscape all but lost before the onward march of agri-business and agri-technology. With *The Ballad and the Plough* and *Willie Gavin, Crofter Man*, a recollection of the North-east Lowlands crofting experience, *The Cornkister Days* completes a trilogy and a portrait of an old farming landscape.

ACKNOWLEDGEMENTS

This is a book of many voices. So intertwined is the culture of the North-east Lowlands with its countryside that it would have been inconceivable to omit the work of its poets and writers. Wittingly and unwittingly, they were the observers of the scenes, moods and seasons of the older landscape, earlier recorders of that ceaseless conflict of men with the soil. I have acknowledged the sources of their words wherever I have used them; I am deeply indebted to all of them. In particular, for generously allowing the use of copyright material, I should like to thank Flora Garry (for permitting me to quote from her work); The Aberdeen University Press and the Charles Murray Memorial Trust (for allowing the inclusion of work by John C. Milne and Charles Murray respectively); the Bailies of Bennachie; John Stewart Collis; Mr Gavin Muir and Chatto and Windus; and publishers Paul Harris, Faber and Faber, Oxford University Press, Thomas Nelson, Century and Robert Hale. Excerpts from the work of Lewis Grassic Gibbon are reprinted by permission of Curtis Brown Ltd, London, on behalf of the estate of James Leslie Mitchell © Ray Mitchell 1967.

Henry Stephens' *Book of the Farm*, first published in 1844, ran to later editions. The two outstanding sources of the old bothy balladry are John Ord's *Bothy Songs and Ballads* and Gavin Greig's *Folk-song of the North-east*.

The photographs have been gathered from several sources, individually acknowledged. My thanks are due to all those who helped me to locate them, and in particular to John A. Fraser, secretary of the Clydesdale Horse Society, and Douglas M. Spence of D. C. Thomson.

D.K.C.

CONTENTS

ILLUSTRATIONS

Unacknowledged photographs from the author's collection

I

Introduction: The Land and the Folk

THEY ARE GONE from the land, those men I once knew. They had
the old speak and grizzled, five-day beards. They were wiry and
argumentative and the years had honed them in bone and sinew.
They stood near the end of their days, sunk in the heavy folds of
their sleeved waistcoats and in the threadbare corduroys that were
the traditional costume of their class, and swore to you through
tobacco'd teeth that their beasts were the finest in the parish, their
oats without parallel, and that their *neeps*, their turnips, were still
fattening in the drill long after the New Year.

They were, some of them, men of piercing gaze and scarifying
wit, respectful neither of man nor beast, the laird included. They
ran their small farmtouns through the early, depression years of
the century with an iron grip that kept *fee*'d man and fattening
beast in thrall to the seasons. And if they cared so little for
appearances it was only that they had long put aside all semblances
of vanity. Some were brawny men, whose ponderous movement
belied a nimble wit and a native shrewdness. Some were so frail of
stature it seemed that only the burning fire of their love for their
"parks" kept them alive. Strange their ways may seem to us now
these long years after. Yet once, like the generations before them,
they imposed their will and a pattern on the farmtoun landscape of
Scotland's North-east Lowlands. Their lives turned with the
seasons; only the land possessed them.

Theirs was the society of the Clydesdale horse and the hired
man. It was a society of folk dominated by hard work and the six-
monthly Sacrament Sunday though, for all that, the man who
travelled the stallion round the spring touns crept quietly into the
maidservant's bed and was not made unwelcome.

Its folk were never the dull stoics of Jefferies' English landscape
— "not facile at expressions . . . the flow of language denied to
them". Most, in fact, were damnably contentious, loquacious even
within the limits of their own known world, and not a few lifted

their horizons beyond it. They were part of a rural society more complex than might now be supposed, one of strange subtleties and almost undetectable nuances: that of the *fee'd loon*, the wandering cottar, the crofter, the tenant farmer and the land-owner, in that relationship of rising order. Its stresses and divisions were at times fearsomely real and sometimes desperate.

The cottar in his tied cottage was a man always at the mercy of his master's goodwill and the crofter man, for all his talk of liberty, hardly less vulnerable, his freedom a sad, illusory thing, since he was so dependent on the neighbouring big toun for the heavier working of his land. The farmtoun tenant, in his turn, came constantly under the scrutiny of the Big House, where his moral and political stance as well as his agricultural performance could be called into question as the end of his lease drew near. Only the laird dwelt in some peace of mind, though that too would be shaken as the fortunes that had maintained a gracious lifestyle finally began to ebb and the mansion's occupants became aware that the old social order was foundering.

It was not a polite society. Far from it. Greeting was coarse and often abrasive. Its folk did not praise highly; few were masters of the facile phrase or skilled in that fulsomeness that oils the wheels of self-interest. If that made them more awkward, maybe it also made them more honest, their friendship a finer thing. Their mischief, like their music, was home-made, often pointed and sometimes malicious. A too-persistent suitor, for instance, threatening to queer the pitch for a more favoured contender, would anonymously and hurriedly be sent a discarded pair of grandmother's steel-rimmed spectacles—to let him see that he was not wanted. If he had any sense of what was good for him he took the hint. Forsaken lasses were as philosophical about the broken bands of love, and rarely long forlorn:

> Oh, I'll put on my goon o' green,
>   It's a forsaken token,
> And that will let the young men know
>   That the bands o' love are broken.
> There's mony a horse has snappert and fa'en,
>   And risen and gane fu' rarely,
> There's mony a lass has lost her lad,
>   And gotten anither richt early.

There's as guid fish into the sea
　　As ever yet was taken,
I'll cast my line and try again,
　　I'm only ance forsaken.
Sae I'll gae doon to Strichen toon
　　Where I was bred and born,
And there I'll get anither sweetheart,
　　Will mairry me the morn.

Sae fare ye well, ye Mormand Braes,
　　Where aftimes I've been cheery,
Fare ye weel, ye Mormand Braes,
　　For it's there I've lost my dearie.

The song was one of the most popular round the old farmtouns of
Buchan and still sung in the cottar's house of the 1930s.

It was a society, more than now, with its "worthies" — its
eccentrics who slotted comfortably into no convenient slot but
often travelled the countryside in idleness or in pursuit of some
useful trade: the selling of besoms, the mending of pots or cane
chairs. In the outliers, those haunted touns that existed away at
the Back of Beyond, out of sight in the landscape and somehow
forgotten, there dwelt stranger folk still who in time grew at
variance with the world and with themselves. Whole families
were raised who had a different outlook on life. Their steadings
fell into a bad state of repair and their fences rotted, for they
were folk who had little need for demarcations. Some in time
had to go from home into a more protective environment;
others continued in their ways, harming no one except, maybe
finally, themselves.

Overwhelmingly though, it was a society based on the plough
that was its most potent symbol, the imagery of its turning furrow
analogous to the years unfolding, a poetic and moving metaphor
for the life-journey itself. Men walked the furrow-bottom, holding
the stilts in a close and solitary relationship with the soil, the
silence broken only by the quiet creak of harness under strain, the
muffled hooves of a Clydesdale pair and the mesmeric hiss of
stubble as it tumbled into the furrow. It was an all-enclosing world
and at its centre stood the ploughman.

In a countryside whose minstrelsy still enshrined a little of the

sweetness of life there were lasses who sang their independence of
rich wooers and their love of "The Ploughman Laddie":

Oh, I've been east, and I've been west,
　And I've been in St Johnstone;
But the bonniest laddie that e'er I saw
　Was a ploughman laddie dancin'.

It's I've been east, and I've been west,
　And I've been in Kirkcaldy;
But the bonniest lass that e'er I saw,
　She was following the ploughman laddie.

She had silken slippers on her feet,
　Her body neat and handsome,
She had sky-blue ribbons on her hair,
　And the gowd abeen them glancin'.

"Faur are ye gaun, my bonnie lass,
　And fat is it they ca' ye?"
"It's Bonnie Jeanie Gordon is my name,
　And I'm following my ploughman laddie."

"I'll gie ye gowd, love, and I'll gie ye gear,
　And I'll mak' you my lady,
I'll mak' ye ane o' higher degree
　Than following a ploughman laddie."

"I winna hae your gowd nor yet your gear
　And I winna be your lady;
But I'll mak' my bed in the ploughman's neuk,
　And lie down wi' my ploughman laddie."

The men who held the stilts of the farmtouns' ploughs were hardy
men. They cycled the country roads early and late, drunk and
sober, their wavering ways lit by the gas-carbide lamp whose
essential and often explosive ingredient was bought in tins from
the village cycle agent's, with irreproachable logic often an
extension of the shoemaker's shop. With stockmen and unfortunate *orra loons*, they filled the squalid bothies of the touns and the

cottar houses of that far countryside. The bothy ballad was their song, set to the scraich of a wild fiddle or the clumsily-buttoned notes of a melodeon and the rhythmic thump of heavy, tacketed boots. Their song was their own story and the story of the Lowlands farmtouns, satirically rendered. Away from the plough, they sang of it, giving themselves a greater glory than they had. Now much of their repertoire is the stuff of rural history, pinpointing in the bygoing the beliefs and back-breaking work rituals of the old farmtoun life.

It is likely that they had need of their fragile glory, for theirs was a comfortless existence. The crews of unmarried horsemen, as the ploughmen of the North-east were called, lived rough, for a farmtoun bothy was a drear and cheerless place devoid of warmth and often of human kindliness — and maybe not even watertight, into the bargain. They were fed without ceremony and sometimes with an ill grace in the toun's kitchen or cooked their own monotonous oatmeal-based diet on the bothy fire. Reflecting on bothy society, the region's greatest writer, Lewis Grassic Gibbon, a man bound closely by childhood ties to the country life, sees in his essay *The Land* only the bitter servitude of the life:

> As I listen to that sleet-drive I can see the wilting hay-ricks under the fall of the sleet and think of the wind ablow on ungarmented floors, ploughmen in sodden bothies on the farms outbye, old, bent and wrinkled people who have mislaid so much of fun and hope and high endeavour in grey servitude to those rigs curling away, only half-inanimate, into the night.

For once, perhaps coloured too much by his politics, Gibbon's view seems too severe, for there was often a camaraderie in the old bothy life, as old men will tell you, that more than relieved its tedium and at worst gave a concerted front against the poor conditions.

But it was never a life of luxury and the cottar's case was scarcely better. And for much of the time it could be worse. He had his perquisites (his agreed quantities of oatmeal, milk and potatoes) but with his tied cottage and a numerous family to feed he was even more trapped in the system. His diet was as deeply committed to the endless permutations of oatmeal and water and rustic ingenuity and he wore the same kind of tackety boots he had worn as a halflin. Like his bothy-housed colleagues he went to the farmtoun's barn each Saturday night after *lowsing*-time for the only thing the farmer never grudged him: the straw with which he regularly filled them to comfort his feet against the hardship of wearing them. The old straw he removed from them was thrown, in passing, into the midden: by then it was nearly as ripe as the dung anyway. At home his cottar house was a bare citadel to the thrift of a careful wife who assiduously put patches into every family garment — and between times hooked rag rugs to cheer a world of bare stone floors and the chill of the linoleum square. If their union, as many did, pre-empted the preacher, it rarely in the end precluded him. They paid tailor, watch-mender and souter at the six-monthly terms of Whitsunday and Martinmas if they decently could: sometimes instead they just left the district.

For it was a feckless, rootless society, one re-orientated yearly and half-yearly by the catharsis of the feeing fairs — hiring markets like the notorious Muckle Friday of Aberdeen's Castlegate and those held in nearly every small town of the region with the necessary inn and a place to stand. There, towards the end of May and November, and at the cottars' markets held earlier, the *fee*'d men of the farmtouns offered themselves to the highest bidder. New engagements were negotiated, hands shaken, drams taken. The pattern of the day, like so many other aspects of the life of the touns, is accurately depicted in the words of the bothy ballads, in this case the long saga of "South Ythsie":

> As I went down to Ellon Fair
>   Ance on a day to fee,
> Likewise an opportunity
>   My comrades for to see.
>
> And steerin' thro' the market
>   An auld neebor chanced to see;
> And when I stept up to him
>   He asked was I to fee?
>
> He told me he was leavin',
>   Likewise his neebor tee;
> He said the grieve did want a hand,
>   And he thocht that I would dee.

He stept up unto the grieve,
 Says, "Here's a man to fee,
I think he'll suit ye very weel,
 If wi' him ye can agree."

He told to me some of the work
 That I would have to do;
He said I would have little else
 But cart and hold the ploo.

He asked at me my wages,
 What they were gaun to be;
So in a short time after
 Wi' him I did agree.

The ballad highlights the kind of introduction and mutual recommendation that went on in the markets. And it pinpoints, yet again, the important role of the grieve, the farmtoun's bailiff. He ordered the toun's days: it was he who made the "bargain" (though the farmer himself often accompanied him) and chose the labour crew that would carry a toun through the following six months: the bothy lads who would drive its Clydesdale pairs and muck its feeders' byres.

Most were hard men, their will prevailed. As late as the 1920s and 1930s a horseman could still be sent from the toun for lagging without due cause in the binder bout (maybe so that his arrival opposite the field gate would conveniently coincide with *lowsing*-time). And a man coming home a day late to take up his Term Day *fee* would hardly have time to throw his bike against the bothy wall before being shown the road from the toun. There was no appeal, and practically no unionisation.

But for all its rigours, its hard work and poor conditions, there was an endless stream of country boys who could not wait to be part of the life, maybe because they knew of no other. None was more keen than the lad of John C. Milne's delightful poem, "The Orra Loon", which provides a splendid litany of all the jobs that fell to the youngest member of a farmtoun's crew — and an instant Doric run-down on the dietary delights that awaited him:

I'll sup ma chappit-tatties, stovies, yavel-broth and kail,

Skirley, saps and yirnt-milk, and mair than I can tell;
On Pess-day I'll get twa big hard-boiled eggs instead o' saps,
On Friday fin the van comes I'll hae bonnie curran-baps,
And fyles the cadger-cairtie will bring herrin fae the sea,
Fin I am aince the orra loon at Mains o' Pittendreee.

So much for dreams: the reality was something else again, and
Milne, the country boy who became an academic, would not have
been unaware of it. Few touns kept a board as varied or greatly cared
what their *fee*'d men ate. Let another North-east poet, the incom-
parable Charles Murray, in his "Dockens afore his Peers" pin down
even more precisely the fate that awaited the *orra loon*'s female
counterpart, that maid of all work, the servant-lass:

. . . syne we hae the kitchie deem, that milks an' mak's the maet,
She disna aft haud doon the deese, she's at it ear' an' late,
She cairries seed, an' braks the muck, an' gies a han' to hyow,
An' churns, an' bakes, an' syes the so'ens, an' fyles there's peats to
                                                                    rowe.
An' fan the maiden's friens cry in, she'll mask a cup o' tay,
An' butter scones, an' dicht her face, an' cairry ben the tray.

Yet still they went, knowing and unknowing — boys and girls
grievously lacking education (but not native wit) — from the school
desk to the *feeing* market in their best clothes, gauche and un-
worldly, and into the bothies of the touns and their kitchen beds,
to become part of the farmtoun society.

It is a life reflected in poem and legend, song and story,
interwoven to an exceptional degree with the cultural expression of
the region, deeper and all the more trustworthy for being in the
sometimes difficult Doric. Gibbon, with that special reverence he
felt for folk who were his own, drew the link between their lives and
the land:

Those folk in the byre whose lantern light is a glimmer through
the sleet as they muck and bed and tend the kye, and milk the milk
into tin pails, in curling froth — they are The Land, in as great a
measure.

He sees their "apartness" in the larger frame of society sharply:

. . . this Autumn's crops, meal for the folk of the cities, good heartsome barley alcohol — would never be spread, never be seeded, never ground to bree, but for the aristocracy of the earth, the ploughmen and the peasants. These are the real rulers of Scotland: they are the rulers of the earth!

And how patient and genial and ingenuously foul-mouthed and dourly wary and kindly they are, those self-less aristos of Scotland. They endure a life of mean and bitter poverty, an order sneered upon by the little folk of the towns, their gait is a mockery in city streets, you see little waitresses stare haughtily at their great red, suncreased hands, plump professors in spectacles and pimples enunciate theses on their mortality and morality, their habits of breeding and their shiftlessness — and they endure it all!

And it is possible, now, to see Murray, Milne and more recently Flora Garry for what they are: superb observers of the northern country scene with a deep understanding of that demented relationship between men and the soil.

The land of the farmtouns is a countryside remarkably well recorded, not least in that vast repertoire of song, the bothy ballads, written often by the bothy men themselves as they guilelessly disclaimed their crude art . . .

> Now I am not a poet,
> Nor yet a learned man,
> But I will sing a verse or twa,
> And spread them as I can.

. . . yet left us a most marvellous inheritance. When Gavin Greig, the great schoolmaster-collector of the ploughman's songs, died in 1914, he had collected some 3,000 ballads sung in the North-east corner of Scotland. Only now is his work being fully analysed and assessed, but one thing is sure: many were of bothy origin.

It is one of the curious ironies of fate that the other great champion of the ploughman's song — and one of its greatest exponents — should be a farmer, a rich one at that and therefore a member of the class the ballads most consistently attacked in their thumping, rhythmic metre. His name was John Strachan; he was born into what Hamish Henderson of that cultural reservoir The School of Scottish Studies has called "the great heartland of traditional balladry" in 1875, as the farmtouns neared the end of their great boom years. The well-educated son of a farmer and horse-dealer father, John knew a good beast when he saw one — and a good ploughman, too, for that matter for he was in constant demand for the judging at shows and ploughing matches. Oddly, he was himself the embodiment of much of the ploughman's own devil-may-care character and philosophy: he spoke the Doric broadly, played the fiddle and liked dancing. A well-built man, he had a taste for fancy waistcoats and almost certainly enjoyed his role of being "a bit of a character".

He kept his own shelt, the fastest in the district, and drove his own phaeton, disdaining the services of a strapper and claiming always that it took him only three minutes from the parish kirk of Tarves to his nearest toun of Craigies, a three-pair place of some 300 acres, two and a half miles away.

Today his broad Doric, clinically encapsulated on tape, is in the BBC's Sound Archives in faraway London, a strangely alien voice amid the tangled traffic flow of the capital, dusted off now and then to reflect the quality of the old rural life.

John would have liked that for he was a sociable man always willing to sing at concerts. He was good to his farmtoun men and fond of a dram. He had, too, a kind of droll face-saving wit that stood him in good stead, and there is a story they tell still in that bare countryside about John and the crofter man.

John at the time had a guest from the South staying at the farmhouse and was taking a walk with him at "denner-time" — the midday work break of the touns — when they met John's tractor and bogey with a full load of swedes and driven by one of the balladsinger's workmen who had a neighbouring croft.

John and his visitor stood on to the road verge to let the tractor and its visibly embarrassed driver go past.

"Surely, John," the guest finally exclaimed, "that man isn't stealing a load of your swedes?"

"Losh, no!" John assured him instantly. "He will likely be bringing me back a load o' his ain yalla neeps." It was not that John liked always to think the best of folk, more that he didn't like them to be seen getting the better of him.

As a farmtoun figure he would become significant on several

counts. He was a part of the great touns era for he farmed not only Craigies (locally always pronounced Craggies) but a number of other touns, including the more renowned Crichie, near Fyvie, to which he ultimately became more devoted.

Again, he exemplified the dynastical drive of much of the Northeast Lowlands' farming, with its spread of one-family control over many touns. Its reign had a classic pattern: touns were found for sons, for the husband of a daughter who had found favour. Slowly the family stretched its tentacles through a parish, accruing and aggregating, the old man a patriarchal figure, feared or loved — but always consulted — in the biggest toun, an Abraham at the head of his tribe.

But John Strachan was an important figure in quite another way: more than most he carried the culture of the great touns into the future at a time when it seemed it would founder. He took the old bothy songs of his young days across the cultural waste that befell them towards the end of the farmtoun era — from a time when every child of the touns grew up with a melodeon and a mouth-organ and maybe a jew's harp in the house — and into a new acceptance of their worth.

He had help, of course, in keeping the ballads alive. Just over the hill from Craigies, in the little town of Oldmeldrum, there had lived another man whom many considered "the king of the cornkisters", as the bothy songs were called. His name was Willie Kemp and his folk had a hotel there which my great-grandfather regularly visited (though there is no record of him having an ear for music). Willie, too, has been preserved by the astute Corporation and, like his more illustrious countryman, is occasionally reincarnated to give authentic voice to those songs that dird to the tramp of Clydesdales' feet. By the 1930s such men were singing of a way of life on the brink of change.

In a curious way the cottars, like the farming dynasties, had perpetuated the ties of blood with the land. Cottar bairn followed cottar father into the stable and the byre: what else was there? But now the closed social bonds that had long characterised the farmtoun society and made distinctions even within the confines of the toun itself began to disintegrate.

The touns had trapped people, bound them by obligation and duty and sometimes all but destroyed them, like the lass of Flora Garry's poignantly moving "Bennygoak":

Och, I'm tire't o plyterin oot an in
Amo' hens an swine an kye,
Kirnin amo' brookie pots
An yirnin croods an fye.

I look far ower by Ythanside
To Fyvie's laich, lythe lan's,
To Auchterless an Bennachie
An the mist-blue Grampians.
Sair't o the hull o Bennygoak
An scunnert o the ferm,
Gin I bit daar't, gin I bit daar't
I'd flit the comin' term.

The lass's problem was an old one:

Bit ma midder's growein aul' an deen
An likes her ain fireside.
'Twid brak her hert to leave the hull:
It's brakkin mine to bide.

Not even Gibbon, whose prose grows out of the land, at one
with its rhythms, conveys so well the plight of damaged folk. Flora
Garry's work, too, springs mainly from the dour countryside.
Implicit in it is the terrible and moving love of the soil. The land
was like that: its folk lived in that deep enthralment, like the beasts
in the field almost, a part of the cycle of things. It was a love harsh
and heartbreaking that put men at naught against the flow and fade
of the seasons.

The small touns in their way were more typical and more
tyrannical. Most were a modest hundred acres or so, worked by
two horsemen and a bailie (a stockman) and the farmer himself.
Their plight was dire as they rode out the depression years.

Like the crofts that knitted the folds of the cultivated land and
took the edge of the moor and the bare hillside, they shared a
landscape studded with history and a new countryside conjured
into being largely by the Improvement pioneers: men of the
calibre of Grant of Monymusk, Cumine of Auchry and the laird of
Pitfour with its gilded palace. Their new single-tenant steadings
had risen out of the farming revolution to be lapped by the swell of

their newly-margined fields. Behind them, still plainly remembered, was that time of great socio-agrarian change that had largely eclipsed the old subsistence farming and begun the reign of a commercial agriculture. Their rise, and the emergence of the professional farmer, would sweep away the laird's ancient privileges and in time all memory of the old farmtoun clusters bound by mutual obligation and the spell of the traveller's tale. The momentum set in train would peter out only in the late 1800s, though even then there would be hopeful crofter men, spurred by their spurious dream of independence, still breaking ground from the hill. The horse-plough, the prime implement of the new touns, would connive with enclosure to alter entirely the fabric of rural society.

Territorially the land of the ballads spread north from the Vale of Strathmore to Moray; it ranged from the hugely fertile to the grudging, stony uplands. Behind its cliff-hung smugglers' coast — the hinterland now of the oil that is the sea's new riches — it ran bare and windswept across its seaboard plain for the shelter of the Highland hills. Much of it at first had been unpromising but under its bleak skies there came men to meet the hour, men who briefly brought a touch of adventure into farming, as much explorers in their way as Columbus or Cortez. They had their rewards but only a few got rich.

It was a landscape in which, as yet, neither science nor engineering had seriously distanced man from the soil; in which the work patterns of the touns still stretched out of the past from that time when the oxen had forsaken the plough. They would continue beyond the holocaust of World War Two to a time when the tractor would completely oust the Clydesdale pairs. It was a land above all where all life moved against the tapestry of the year, the immutability of the seasons, absorbing their rhythms and their immemorial rituals: ploughing, harrowing, sowing, reaping, threshing and the tending of livestock. It had a soul and a pulse-beat, a dreichness that was not unlovely. Sometimes it stole the heart.

II

The Laird and the Landscape

WHEN THE DOUR Dr Johnson, wit and critic and a man with especially little good to say of the Scots, was passing north in 1773 on his celebrated tour to the Highlands with his friend and biographer James Boswell (without whom precious little might ever have been heard of him), he saw on the eastern seaboard a landscape that confirmed his worst fears. The land had a bareness that plainly offended the old warrior of London's Gough Square. And even the ebullient Boswell, it seems, was cast down by his country's inability to please the eye. Coming up from Montrose, he noted that they "had the Grampian Hills in our view, and some good land around us, but void of trees and hedges. . . ." His elderly companion complained: "The country is still naked, the hedges are of stone. . . ." And even leaving the gracious elegance of Slains Castle, where he was attentively received and taken to see the fearsome Bullers of Buchan, he growled: "I have now travelled two hundred miles in Scotland, and seen only one tree not younger than myself."

There was as yet little to strikingly suggest that the countryside of the North-east Lowlands was on the brink of unprecedented rural upheaval and already well embarked on a tide of vast agricultural improvement. It is odd, however, that neither of the London pair sensed change in the air for they paused at Laurencekirk and went on to Monboddo House to meet Lord Monboddo (posing as "Farmer Burnett" in a rustic suit and a little round hat) and have a farmer's dinner of "admirable soup, ham, peas, lamb and moor fowl". The tedious sage's distemper was in no way mellowed by the meal or Lord Monboddo's entertaining talk. "I have," said the great man churlishly, "done greater feats with my knife than this."

Yet soon all would be transformed, not only at the Big House itself but in the surrounding countryside. The London travellers may not have been apprised of it but the improvers were at work:

the margined field would become the common ground of agricultural usage, the single-tenant farmtoun the revised unit of farming settlement instead of the ancient run-rigs and the old hamlet clusters — the farmtouns of the earlier medieval landscape. The boundaries of the fields would be set by stonewall dykes. There would be hedges too, of beech and quickthorn.

The lairds created the landscape; where they did not, they created the ambience that allowed it. They took the chance too, in their related desire for social self-aggrandisement, to move the croft and the cot-toun from the castle door. Yet the era of Improvement would be their finest hour, before or since, for what had they done earlier but lead the folk into feud and foray and divide them in their loyalties to kirk and state? Unlike their English contemporaries they were largely untrammelled by straitening laws on enclosure: the laird was practically his own law in the final abolition of the run-rigs.

The first real stirrings of improvement had begun almost with the dawn of the 1700s. The times threw up courageous men with the strength of English farming convictions; by the last quarter of the century their improvement would have gained a general momentum and become the launch-pad for the rebirth of rural society.

What gave it its impetus? The Industrial Revolution, of which it was part, for one thing; men like Sir Archibald Grant, for another. Grant was a prince among improvers in the north, though he had countrymen of near-equal calibre and foresight at work from the Mearns up to Moray — lairds such as Cumine of Auchry, Barclay of Ury as well as Lord Gardenstone and the Earl of Findlater. They were a quite remarkable group. Later would come others who would absorb their legacy, both lairds and commoner folk. Villages would multiply on the North-east plain that Dr Johnson's eye had so abhorred, like knots in ill-made brose.

The North-east Lowlands is a land of castles, evidence of old contentions, of standing stones and cairns, a landscape redolent of past deeds and dark encounters, most of them bloody. It has borne the impact and ebb of events and past civilisations to which we no longer have the key. Monymusk was a place already touched with history when Grant made his first acquaintance with its 10,000-acre estate; its hall and farmtoun, inextricably intertwined, were but a rickle of old *biggings*.

His father, Sir Francis Grant, advocate and judge, a man of whom it was said that he "kept a quiet heart in a troubled time" and who sat as Lord Cullen as a Senator of the College of Justice in Edinburgh, had bought it in 1712 from Sir William Forbes, whose debts by then were catching up with him. It was the home of the Monymusk Reliquary, a small casket said to contain a bone that had once been St Columba's, a fact that points up its place in the monastic past.

Malcolm Canmore, they say, on his way through to quell the wild men of Moray in 1078 paused here briefly, and in the hope of God's help in his bloody errand drew out the ground plan of a kirk with his sword-point on the earth, promising to build it should the battle go with him. So Monymusk got its venerable church. And as though that were not enough, Gavin Douglas, later translator of Virgil's *Aeneid* into Scots in the 1500s, was once its dominie; John Skinner of "Tullochgorum" fame, in Grant's own time, the school's assistant master.

The squalor of the estate depressed the father but not the eldest son, who took over in the year after the ill-fated Fifteen rebellion. Sir Archibald, as a Westminster MP, was a member of that oldest of farming clubs, the House of Commons, which he left under something of a cloud in 1732. Thereafter he devoted himself wholeheartedly to the cause closest to his heart: agricultural improvement.

His Monymusk acres straddled the River Don; his programme followed the practical sequence of (a) general improvement of the estate, (b) home farm innovation as an example, and (c) the initiating of improved methods and techniques among his tenantry, though there was undoubtedly overlap in all three. He drained, enclosed and planted trees at a pace and on a scale the like of which the country had never seen: about 50,000,000 during his lifetime, beginning with the still-famous Woods of Paradise in 1719 and stopping only with his death. A fellow-improver said of him, "no other man ever existed on the globe who planted so many trees". It may have been true, and that, by itself, might have been a fitting enough tribute for any man.

But Grant's passion took hold like a contagion. Lairds fell over themselves in their desire to clothe the landscape that had so disenchanted Dr Johnson. Says William Alexander, author and rural historian of the North-east, in his *Notes and Sketches Illustrative of Northern Rural Life in the Eighteenth Century*:

The Earl of Fife and General Gordon of Fyvie planted largely, General Gordon as many as 3,000,000 trees in a single enclosure. James Farquharson of Invercauld, in the years from 1750 to 1806, is said to have planted 16,000,000 firs and 2,000,000 larches on his property in Braemar, through which he constructed more than twenty miles of roads. Towards the close of the eighteenth century, the cultivation of timber trees seems to have become an object of very general attention as testified by the statement of the writer [Dr Anderson] that "there is scarcely a private gentleman in Aberdeenshire who owns an estate of £500 or £600 a year who has not planted many hundred thousand trees."

What Grant imported into his northern lands, as did his few contemporaries, was the agriculture of the south: techniques and men and machines to complement them. He encountered passive resistance if not outright rebellion and where persuasion, example and intimidation failed he fell back finally on eviction. It was, after all, to become a damnably common remedy, and if the numbers were much fewer than those of the tragic Highland Clearances, the hardship was no less. He was a harsh man who loved church music and he was never mealy-mouthed when it came to telling his tenants what he thought of them and their antiquated methods. It was a time, generally, when many of the tenants on improving estates stopped praying for their landlords. But those Grant considered "suitable" tenants were rewarded by the security of longer leases than those of the five- or seven-year run that had previously been given, and it would be niggardly now to minimise his achievement personally or his influence regionally — or even nationally.

When he started his "agricultural revolution" the Monymusk farmtouns were (in his own words, for he left a copious record) "ill-disposed and mixed, different persons having alternate ridges and not one wheel carriage on the estate, nor indeed any one road to allow it". Of the poor *biggings* of the folk (never mind the stock) he added: "The farmhouses and even the corn mills and the manse and the school were poor leaking huts which were pulled to pieces for manure, or fell themselves almost each alternate year."

From the start, Grant had begun "to enclose and plant and provide and prepare nurseries. At that time there was not one acre upon the whole estate enclosed, nor any timber upon it but a few elms, sycamore and ash about a small kitchen garden adjoining to

the house and some straggling trees at some of the farmyards, with
a small copse wood not enclosed and dwarfed and browsed by
sheep and cattle."

Nearly 50 years later, the preacher John Wesley, visiting
Monymusk in 1764, saw "on every side the wild dreary moors . . .
ploughed up and covered with rising corn. . . . Ground as well
cultivated as in England". Grant would have been happy with that
verdict; when he died aged eighty-two, in 1778, he had transformed the Monymusk estate into a showcase for the new farming.
There is, alas, no great burden of proof that he was esteemed or
greatly loved.

He was indeed ahead of his time. He worked, it seems,
surprisingly undisturbed through troubled times. There had been
the folly of the Fifteen and its attempt to restore a Stewart to his
rightful throne — that dreadfully mismanaged rebellion for which
the Old Pretender had stepped ashore, drab and uncharismatic,
at Peterhead too late: the squib had gone out. There followed the
last throe of the Forty-five, equally doomed, a fine and quixotic
irrelevancy on the chequerboard of history that still spreads its
romantic aura over the Highlands. And with the defeat of
Culloden all was changed: ties of blood and fealty sundered in the
mist of Drummossie moor.

Yet, whatever its cost and humiliation (and they were considerable) it could have been a time when men, freed of old alignments,
turned their faces purposely to the future. Alas, harsh government
measures had the reverse, repressive effect. In the North-east
Lowlands, says the Rev. J. B. Pratt, that authority on things past
relating to Buchan, with a hindsight on history that is closer than
ours by well over a hundred years, farms lay a-wasting from the
want of men able, or willing, to take up their leases.

For all that, there *were* men in this time of rebellion and re-
adjustment who were not idle: improvement would grip them too,
as it had Grant. Joseph Cumine, however, was out of a slightly
different mould, a man of wider vision even, for he was inspired by
the deeds of such improvers-extraordinary as John Cockburn of
Ormiston, like Grant an MP (it seems almost to have been a
prerequisite), who took over his lands in the south about the same
time as Monymusk got its improving laird. Cumine, coming into
possession of Auchry in moorland Monquitter, followed Cockburn's grand, if blighted example and took the rural revolution a

step further in the North-east in 1763 by founding the village of Cuminestown — a consumer outlet for the produce of the new-style farming.

Auchry, to the east of Turriff, for any good crow was not an hour distant from Monymusk; in terms of terrain it was worlds away. Grant's land was a fertile haugh, Cumine's was a bare Buchan parish. The Laird of Auchry, like his peers, planted trees by the thousand, enclosed the land and drained it and refurbished the Big House but he is best remembered now from the village that bears his name. Its beginnings were not auspicious. Said an early reporter:

> He planned a regular village on a moorish part of the farm contiguous to the church. For a while he suffered in silence the sneers of his neighbours who called his scheme wild and impracticable, but these temporary sneers soon gave way to lasting esteem.
>
> He first prevailed upon a small number of people to take feus and assisted the industrious with money. Settlers annually flocked to Cuminestown (at first known as Redstone). . . . Soon there were seventy-five feus occupied by a set of industrious honest and active feuars.

Linen was spun by every family for the merchants and "1,000 pairs of cargo hose at 1/– per pair are annually sent to market". Every second house had its loom and there were also several big weaving sheds housing looms.

Cumine was a man with a dream, and maybe his weavers' village deserved a better fate: though initially a success its industrial life-span was cut short and in decline before the 1800s were well begun. Gradually the click of the shuttle was stilled. Yet he had his imitators; indeed the Earl of Fife had anticipated him with the "new town" of Newmill a few years earlier — with even less success. Today Newmill looks back with less pride on its brief industrial past as a "new town" than on the fact that it gave the New World a great journalist in the person of James Gordon Bennett, founder and first editor of the *New York Herald* (later the *Herald–Tribune*).

The years of fevered change saw also the emergence of the Earl of Findlater's New Keith. As Lord Deskford (up to 1764) he had introduced new methods on the Banffshire family estate in his father's reign, bringing home an English grieve to show tenants how to grow turnips, potatoes and sown grasses. He planted 11,000,000 trees and by 1752 had organised a bleach field at Deskford and later set up a factory producing linen and damask at Cullen, where he lived the last years of his life in Cullen House, dying in 1776. His textiles venture fared no better than those of the other "new towns" of the region and fell before the forces of greater manufacturing resources.

Up in the Spey valley, before 1800, the Duke of Gordon pushed the old Fochabers from his gate to a new site that kept it at a seemly distance. Back in Buchan, New Deer would be "raised" by James Ferguson of fabulous Pitfour, MP for Aberdeenshire, a man who worked tirelessly to rearrange the landscape and who drove turnpikes and hedges through Buchan's acres like there was no tomorrow. Born in 1734, as Grant was just getting into his stride, Ferguson too was the eldest son of a law lord — one who had courageously once defended Jacobites thrown into Carlisle's jail in the Forty-five — and in the southern capital was on nodding acquaintance with Boswell who described him enigmatically as "remarkable for a manly understanding and a knowledge of both books and the world".

New Deer was born in 1805, as a crofter-township, along a bare ridge of land in a place once known more romantically as the Field of Bog Myrtle. The fields sloped down to east and west of the one long street, a drab development that hardly extended the planner's skills and one, alas, that became damnably common in that area. Out of that poor beginning though would grow a countryside of wide and smiling fields and an admired agriculture.

Before he died in 1820 Ferguson had founded several villages, including the "new town" of Mintlaw, dug a canal through his own property, and as his obituary said — it was as though Johnson's ghostly whisper were still heard in the land — "planted many hundred acres which promise to rescue the district of Buchan from the reproaches of future travellers and has enclosed whole farms with hawthorn hedges".

At the house of Pitfour itself he indulged a whimsical talent for grandeur by building a 45-acre lake in the grounds and, at their west end, a miniature of the Temple of Theseus in Athens, complete with 34 Doric pillars in granite. And he sprinkled statues through the policies of Pitfour as though it were the Tuileries Gardens. Indeed, there seems to have been a liking for style and ostentation in the rich Pitfour blood and when James died, his brother George succeeded only briefly before Pitfour came to the latter's illegitimate son, also George, who lost no time at all in carrying on where his uncle James left off, building great stables, a racecourse, and an imposing pillared frontage that made the mansion house the speak of Buchan and beyond and turned it into a gilded palace employing a hundred servants. Truly, they knew how to live, those folk of Pitfour.

But they were stirring times and other men too left their mark on the land of the ballad touns. Down in the red-soiled Mearns, where Burns' folk had farmed before they left for Ayrshire — and where Dr Johnson had met with the eccentric judge Lord Monboddo — the rage for progress was no less. Like-minded men were as assiduously sweeping aside the immemorial run-rigs. Looking back as the century turned, George Robertson in his *General View of the Agriculture of Kincardineshire* (published in 1807) would say of the Mearns scene of the 1760s or thereabouts:

. . . there arose in this county a constellation of *cultivators*, which dispelling the mist that till then obscured the horizon of agricultural science, threw out all at once such a splendid light over the labours of husbandry as has not been exceeded, and perhaps hardly equalled even, to the present day.

There is no evidence that Mr Robertson was an excitable man, and extravagant though it is — quite the most splendid statement perhaps by any of the reporters of the time — it was almost justified. They were considerable figures, the Kincardine improvers. The most lustrous of the cluster perhaps was Robert Barclay of Ury, Norfolk-trained, who heired into the estate in 1760. His inheritance was mostly marshland and moor. That cultivated was poorly farmed and badly laid out and the mansion house hardly had a tree to hide it. There was not a single tree, it is said, on any other part of the estate.

Over the next 30 years or so Barclay would plant somewhere around 1,000 acres with timber. He drained prodigiously, removed 100,000 tons of stones from the land, much of which went into the making of old-style stone drains, the remainder, if you can call it that, going into the making of eight miles of policies' roads. The creation of fields of cultivable land, draining, trenching and lifting off stones cost up to an estimated £40 an acre. Three hundred of the acres reclaimed had been heath and bog and his bill for lime alone was £6,000. Barclay could countenance such expenditure for he had come home from Jamaica with a fortune in his pocket. Besides introducing the methods strongly advocated by his friend "Turnip" Townsend, he managed the by now almost obligatory "new town", Stonehaven, as the century closed.

Hard on Barclay's heels came Lord Gardenstone, yet another Scottish judge and a most curious man who slept with a pet sow in his room, laying his clothes on the floor for its comfort, an odd habit even for a man so dedicated to agricultural progress. His other indulgence was snuff, which he consumed in prodigious quantities not from the customary snuff-mull but from a special leather pocket spliced on to his waistcoat. Dean Ramsay, whose childhood countryside lay nearby, in his delightful *Reminiscences of Scottish Life and Character*, says of him:

He was a man of energy, and promoted improvements in the county with a skill and practical sagacity. His favourite scheme was to establish a flourishing town upon his property, and he spared no pains or expense in promoting the importance of his village of Laurencekirk. He built an excellent inn to render it a stage for posting. He built and endowed an "Episcopal" chapel for the benefit of his English immigrants, in the vestry of which he placed a most respectable library; and he encouraged manufacturers of all kinds to settle in the place.

So much for the town. His efforts on the Johnston estate, purchased in 1762, were just as extensive and Gardenstone devoted every available penny to enclosing his tenants' fields and building them new farmhouses, and dressing his own land. Misguidedly, like so many others, he put his trust in textiles to counterpoint the countryside's farming activity.

Besides Barclay and Gardenstone there were in that galaxy of Kincardineshire improvers many others determinedly pushing forward: among them Sir William Nicolson of Glenbervie, a Mr Graham of Morphie; and a Mr Silver of Netherley, who imported lime for his work of reclamation and due to a complete lack of roads had to bring it all from Stonehaven on creels and sacks on the horses' backs. There was Baxter of Glassel and John Innes,

Sheriff-Substitute, who held the Durris lands and, says William Alexander in his *Northern Rural Life*:

> effected a number of improved farm-steadings and cottages and reclaimed at great cost 451 Scots acres, sub-dividing and fencing it, besides enclosing over 2,500 acres. He planted 740 acres of muir ground and built about 50 miles of stone dykes; and all this in seven years, the result being to increase the rental from £1,000 to £2,500.

Lesser men aped their betters. Says Henry Grey Graham in *The Social Life of Scotland in the Eighteenth Century*: "Young lords and law lords, lairds great and small, took to planting and pruning as formerly they had taken to hunting and drinking. . . ."

Cumine's early ideas so fired the mind of James, the second Urquhart laird of Byth, nearby, that in 1764 — a year after Cuminestown was born on the moor – he took the farmtouns of Old, Mid and New Gully into his possession to feu them out in small parcels of land for the village of New Byth, sweeping away the old cot-toun of Byth in the process. In doing so he raised the rental of the Byth lands, at one deft stroke, to nearly five times what they had been 30 years earlier.

Grant, too, had his disciples, not all of them so astute. When the former Forbes' lands of Lickleyhead, in the shadow of Bennachie and not far distant from Monymusk, came finally into the possession of Thomas Gordon about 1776, he took *all* the farms into his own hands, causing upheaval among the local population and doubtless considerable hardship. Says the *Old Statistical Account*, which enshrines so much of the history of improvement under the manse pen:

> Carts from Aberdeen were hired to bring lime to Inverurie and Mr Gordon's own horses and oxen went to Inverurie and brought it to Premnay. The fields were enclosed and planted with hedgerows and thoroughly limed. Proper houses and other necessary buildings were erected and the lands after being several years in the proprietor's hands were let out to different farmers.

Clearly Mr Gordon was not a man to do things by halves. Alas, there was a hitch. Again, the *Old Statistical Account* and the shrewdly well-informed manse hand: "The expense of improving the lands at such a distance from a seaport has hurt the fortune of the intelligent and public-spirited gentleman who improved them." It adds, blandly, showing more native wit than Mr Gordon had done: "It may here be remembered that it is more prudent for a landed gentleman to improve one farm and let it and afterwards to improve other farms in succession than to attempt improving the whole at once."

Poor Mr Gordon. For all his goodwill and reforming zeal (we will not speak here of profit, though it was possibly in his mind) he had made one serious and inexcusable blunder: by such wholesale improvement he had flooded the market with farms and had finally to reduce rents to a ruinous level to find tenants for them.

In the low country of Udny, "Bonnie Widney" of ballad fame and a place where it is said you could be sure of finding the best kind of dairying wife, Mr Udny of Udny House came to notice as an innovator and improver and by 1780 was making a mark with "neat enclosures, thriving hedges and commodious offices, presenting such a picture as made the traveller loath to prosecute his further journey over the many barren, outlying acres." The commentator, significantly, was a farmer from the lusher Lothians in the south. It was Mr Udny, with the zeal of a present-day football manager, who managed to persuade another southerner, James Anderson, to come north into a more hostile land and into the farmtoun of Monkshill.

Anderson was quite tireless, and soon his adopted countryside reflected it. And not only his countryside. Says William Alexander: he was "a man of liberal education, he had studied chemistry in Edinburgh under Dr Cullen and, in 1780, received the degree of LL.D. at Aberdeen. Twelve years before he had married Miss Seton of Mounie, by whom he had thirteen children. He was a contributor to the first edition of the *Encyclopaedia Britannica*, and wrote the first report on the agriculture of Aberdeenshire. . . ."

Part and parcel of the early general fervour, between 1758 and 1765, had been the think-tank of Gordon's Mill Farming Club, whose members met fortnightly (in fact, more comfortably at the inn close by the mill) on the fringe of what is now Britain's oil capital: the Tillydrone district of Aberdeen. They were a motley crew, with the improver Cumine of their number and six of them academics escaping the bounds of Aberdeen University. Conviviality mingled with discussion of such serious and practical problems as the relative ploughing costs with oxen and horses, implement improvement, manuring and liming, the sowing of grasses and clovers, sheep management, winter herding and, of course, enclosure. And even at that early time, they were debating that closest of all northern farming relationships: the black bullock and the turnip.

For all that, the start of general change was delayed until near the end of the century and in 1780 the improver was still rather a rarity among the Scottish gentry. The pattern of progress, therefore, was not uniform: between one estate and its neighbour there might be a time-warp of 50 years or more in the farming methods. The agricultural revolution, for example, seems to have so much bypassed Leslie on Gadie-side in the Garioch uplands, that the minister-writer of the *Old Statistical Account* is nearly beside himself with disappointment. He gives the local farmers their characters in no uncertain way (certain maybe that they will never have the time to read him) and about as bluntly as Sir Archibald Grant had derided *his* tenants about a half-century earlier:

> The same methods of tillage and cropping . . . still prevails which was practised perhaps 200 years ago. With the advantage of excellent soil, a tolerable climate and rents by no means extravagant, the farmer toils on from day to day, harasses and perplexes himself, and after all with difficulty procures the necessities of life for himself and family.
>
> An obstinate attachment to old-established practices too much prevails and neither precept nor example will induce them to alter their plan. . . .

Not everyone liked what was happening: not the small farmer completely without the capital to let him manoeuvre, without the *siller* to buy lime or to pay for drains to be dug or dykes to be built. Not the dispossessed for inevitably, as always, eviction was part of the process of change as the old farmtoun clusters were dispersed. There was dissent from time to time, dykes broken and plantations damaged, though nothing on a scale to equal the activities of the Galloway Levellers, or the mobs of the English enclosure riots.

A new pattern of settlement was born in the countryside, often on the foundations of the old touns but as often on the bare acres of the moor — the new villages, the "new towns" of the lairds, centres of community and consumer market-places. Those settled there, in time, would cross the psychical frontier between the old life and the new. And the work went on relentlessly as land was claimed from heath and marsh.

There were observant eye-witnesses to those days of momentous reconstruction. One of them was Christian Watt, a Broadsea fisher-lass who took her creel round the landward farmtouns and as far in-country as Deeside. Life and the toll that the sea took of her menfolk broke Christian finally and she spent the last half of her long life in Aberdeen's Cornhill mental asylum. There she wrote a moving journal — her memoirs, only recently published. In them, *The Christian Watt Papers*, with so much else, she recorded the transformation of her own landscape:

> . . . the whole world changed. It was not gradual but sudden like lightening [*sic*]. Whole gangs of men came in to reclaim the land, they ploughed bogs and stanks, everywhere was the smell of burning whins. Suddenly huge big parks were marching up the side of Mormond hill, so greedy did they become for land. Around Cairnbulg and St Combs, what had been large tracts of bents suddenly became farmland. You could make a good bit of money at drystane dyking if you had the skill, for all the parks were enclosed.

In Kennethmont parish in the Garioch, reported the Rev. William Minty, in the 1830s, things proceeded apace:

> Several hundred acres of marshy ground have been completely drained and now produce weighty crops. Many acres of moorland, upon which the appearance of ridges was still visible, showing that they had at one time been cultivated, have again been brought under the plough. . . . Many of the houses of the farmers are now built of stone and lime instead of turf and covered with slates instead of straw. . . .

His contemporary in Strathdon, the Rev. Robert Meiklejohn, in his *New Statistical Account* report of 1839, was as well pleased with the way things had gone:

Few parishes have undergone greater change. . . . The vast improvement of the country by reclaiming and planting of waste lands, the drainage and the enclosure of fields and general introduction of the improving system of husbandry; the opening up of the strath by a turnpike road through the centre of the parish and the formation of good cross-roads with stone bridges over the different streams; the elegant and commodious residences of the proprietors, and the comfortable slated dwelling-houses and substantial farm offices of the tenantry are some of the obvious marks of the progress of cultivation.

There were folk alive still in the 1890s who could recall the old landscape and measure how far it had come. They could remember the peat moss and the bog as once it had been, the roads passing over the high ground, with no bridges and the rivers to ford at the shallows, that a level field had been a rarity. Theirs was the last memory of it, though long after the old cultivation had retreated from the land its faded pattern — the lost kingdom of the run-rigs — would still faintly be seen, unexpectedly revealed by the shadows of pale evening sunlight or by the drift of snow in the wind.

As the 1800s closed, and after nearly two centuries of astonishing farming progress, an old man, looking back on his life as bothy *loon*, farmtoun horseman and labourer on the land, would reflect quietly on what had been gained:

As I look around me at the vast amount of reclaimed land . . . I take off my hat to our forbears who from the Forty-five onwards turned bog and moor into these smiling fields, trenching, draining, and enclosing, working early and late in all weathers, waging a hard warfare with Nature, but winning for themselves and their descendants that grit and indomitable perseverance that characterises the natives of the North-east. . . .

His tribute was to the toil of the men whose sweat had done the impossible. Impressive though that was, however, it would not have been accomplished without the vision of the early improving lairds — and that despicable device, the improving lease. What before had been an open, hedgeless landscape — its only enclosures the gardens of the Big House, where the gentry retired from the bucolic gaze — had become a canvas for the regrouping of rural society and the advance of a different kind of farming.

In the fields of Angus and the lower Mearns and in parts of Moray it would be fine farming by the grace of good soil; on the barer ground of Banffshire and in the wilderness of Buchan, it would be by the will of men.

III

End of an Idyll

THERE WAS A saying in the old countryside that you could tell the
worth of a farmtoun by the number of its stone dykes, and even
that "crack toun" of Drumdelgie "up in Cairnie", near Huntly,
subject of probably the best-known of all the bothy ballads, would
not have come kindly out of such an assessment. During the high
tide of the Scottish touns' prosperity from about 1840 to 1880,
when it was farmed by a family named Grant, eleven miles of
drystone dykes (stone walls) were built round its hard-worked
acres and there was still enough rubble left for another four miles
of boundaries — all that without counting all the land-cleared
stones that had gone into the building improvement of the toun
itself.

The belief, of course, was that where those stones had come
from there were plenty more. Very few of the North-east
farmtouns would have come out well from such a judgement, for
all their acres were hardily won. Improvement had brought with it
a clearing of stones from the land the like of which had never been
seen before — or even remotely contemplated. It bewildered the
mind: men went home from the stone-clearing and had night-
mares about it. Said one, caught in the maelstrom of the work:
"After a hard day's clearing what with tired muscles and aching
hands, I have been unable to enjoy refreshing sleep at night, but in
a feverish dream repeated the work of the day."

In the early part of the 1800s Aberdeenshire in particular made
quite dramatic strides forward, inciting comment from that great
improver, Lord Cockburn, on the magnitude of the task, and the
determination of the folk: "A stranger to the character of the
people would have supposed that despair would have held back
their hands from even attempting to remove them."

In fact, the stone-clearing continued in some areas up till the
end of the 1800s and even beyond. That dairying pioneer of the
region, James Keith, looking back on 50 years of farming life,

would recall that when his toun of Old Craig in Aberdeenshire was "taken in" it had 8,800 yards of drystone dykes, each yard of dyke representing two or three cartloads of stones, each load a ton or more in weight. The arithmetic is staggering: 26,400 tons, all collected from the land and by every conceivable means, including the portable tripod crane, and carried to the side of the field.

There were times when the abundance of field stones was more than an embarrassment, leading to the construction of the so-called consumption dykes just to get rid of them. On the estate of Glassel in the Mearns, their concentration was prodigious and resulted in dykes up to sixteen feet wide, hundreds of yards long. But the most conspicuous dyke of its kind is that at Kingswells, on the western fringe of Aberdeen, built by Alexander Jaffray, once factor for Grant at Monymusk. It was an astonishing 30 feet wide, six feet high and 500 yards long. (They finally put a path on top of it and today you can walk it — an ancient memorial to those hardy men whose brawn created the "smiling fields".)

So the rubble stones were gathered from the parks and sledged-off to await the dyker or transported to the steading to be ready for the mason. Hedges, hawthorn and beech (mainly for the Big House policies), appeared to march by the burn and the moor. Neither dyke nor quickthorn changed the contours of the land, but they changed the countryside. What they did — not instantly, since enclosure was slow, haphazard and fraught with bankruptcy — was to abet the transformation of society. In such things, Dr Johnson's "hedges of stone", lay the subtleties of change. The drystone dyke, the hawthorn hedge and the deep and muddy ditches that ran with it through the land were essentially the parameters of the new society, more demarcating, making sharper than ever, and often brutally so, the divisions between the landed and the landless, tenant and the dispossessed. Stone walls were a severance of the future from the past. Yet little hindered the steady onward march of progress. Slowly the communal holding of land was eroded. Out, in time, would go that farming society that had included such formidable figures as the estate hen wife and in which the tenant gave duty and obligation to the laird: some days with his plough and with his sickle or time at the turnip-hoeing besides tribute in kind.

Along with the new crop rotations, enclosure would eclipse the old shieling system of summer pasturing that took the flocks and the families out of a township for months on end — away from the

burgeoning but unfenced fields into the exile of the hill grazing
while the crops ripened. Once, before Grant's time, in the 1600s,
the cattle from Monymusk had been driven as far as the Cabrach,
over 30 miles away, to be fattened there before being offered to the
English graziers. The shieling, however, was primarily for the
domestic animals and the herds went with them. The peripatetic
Pennant, journeying north in 1769 up Glen Tilt for Braemar — on a
road "the most dangerous and the most horrible I ever travelled" —
encountered just such a colony in the hills and took the opportunity
of refreshment: goats' whey. He found:

> a cottage made of turf, the dairy house where the Highland
> shepherds or graziers live with their herds and flocks, and during
> the fine season make butter and cheese. Their whole furniture
> consists of a few horn-spoons, their milking utensils, a couch
> formed of sods to lie on, and a rug to cover them. Their food
> oatcakes, butter or cheese and often the coagulated blood of their
> cattle spread on their bannocks. Their drink milk, whey, and
> sometimes, by way of indulgence, whisky.

Such dairyhouses, as Pennant reports, were common to most
mountainous countries; they were indeed almost contiguous with
the old peasant agriculture. Ultimately the shielings might become
separate units and survive as new farmtouns. Descending to
Braemar, he found "the country almost instantly changed, in lieu of
dreary wastes, a rich vale, plenteous in corn and grass".

Another, related, casualty of enclosure would be the herd *loon*: it
made him redundant finally, and severely diminished the Scottish
song book, not to say the repertoire of the bothy singer, of the folk
melodies associated with him. In the poetry of the region too the
herd received an inordinate amount of attention.

Maybe the reason was not far to seek. Many of the songs of the
herding days were written by men looking back from the last
milestones and its joys, in that interval of early adolescence when
most had their first *fees* as herds, may therefore have been
exaggerated. All the same, most of the songs have a poignancy and
are more genuinely moving than the over-sentimental songs with
which they are usually grouped.

Some tell not only of the joy of that time but of its companionship,
of something idyllic; others dwell on the kind of dalliance that could

give a herd lass a bad name, since often two herds were employed:
a girl for the cows and a boy for the rest of the cattle. That led to the
kind of situation reflected in "The Herdie":

> Then frae the fauld I drove out my nowte,
> So merry as they gaed friskin' about,
> They licked their sleek sides as they fed on the sward
> When I lived the life of a jovial young herd.
> When wee Jenny used to be keepin' the kye,
> Oh, wha were sae happy as Jenny and I?
> We gaed down to the burnie on yon hallow green,
> And puddled till we were baith wet to the e'en.
> Yet fan I min' fu she priend up her cottie
> To catch the quick minnen that swam through the pottie,
> And that I the better might help her to ca',
> I took aff my breekies and flang them awa.
> When baith had been tired and dubbed to the chin,
> We halted to dry our wee duds in the sun,
> To the sunshinie side o' the dykie we'd flit
> And tummle owre goudie frae the head to the fit.

It should be said here that the age at which children began herding
was usually about ten, and often earlier, so the kind of behaviour of
the lass hoisting her petticoat and the lad peeling off his trousers
was a purely practical consideration when it came to catching
minnows in a deeper pool of the burn. However, herds got older:

> Once on a fine summer's evening,
>   A young couple I did spy,
> 'Twas a young man and a maiden —
>   A-courting among the kye.

> And aye as he kissed her and caressed her,
>   And aye as he bade her comply,
> Bonnie lassie, think o' yer sweetheart
>   And leave off keeping the kye.

There was, on the evidence of the bothy ballads, a great deal of that
alfresco kind of thing in the old landscape, not to say, apparently, a
great many voyeurs. Love blossomed on the lea as surely as it did

in the old *hairst* rig, and in "Bogie's Braes" it is the shepherd lass
herself who looks back, lamenting on the idyllic days of such
country love:

> By Bogie's streams that rin sae deep,
> Fu' aft wi' glee I've herded sheep:
> I've herded sheep, or gathered slaes
> Wi' my dear lad on Bogie's Braes.
> But waes my heart thae days are gane,
> And fu' o' grief I herd my lane;
> While my dear lad maun face his faes,
> Far, far frae me and Bogie's Braes.
>
> Nae mair at Huntly kirk will he
> Atween the preachings meet wi' me —
> Meet wi' me or when it's mirk
> Convoy me hame frae Huntly kirk.
> I weel may sing thae days are gane,
> Frae kirk and fair I come my lane;
> While my dear lad maun face his faes,
> Far, far frae me and Bogie's Braes.

Not everyone was happy to go herding. It could seem aimless and
boring and its loneliness played on the imaginative young mind:
Edwin Muir, the Orkney poet and writer, a fearful bairn herding his
father's cows, kept glancing over his shoulder in case a tiger should
be creeping up on him. Where there was no companion, the herd
might well find his own distraction in whittling with the pocket
gully, as did the poet Charles Murray's famous herd *loon*.

> He cut a sappy sucker from the muckle rodden-tree,
> He trimmed it, an' he wet it, an' he thumped it on his knee.

And there were touns, beyond doubt, where the herd lad's lot was
one of acute misery, as in "The Herd Laddie's lament".

> My feet . . . are hacket and sair,
> An' my shune and my stockings they winna repair,
> An' I've nae money left to buy new anes wi'
> That my feet might be hale on this bleak whinny lea.

Though it rains and the win' blaws bitter and caul',
I've nae cloak about me to keep out the caul',
An' my duddies, though drippin', they ne'er get a dry,
For there's nae fire allow'd in the laft where I lie.

The claes I hae on me are a' worn dune,
They're maist as far through as my stockings an' shune;
An' ae leg o' my breekies is aff by the knee,
An' can bring me nae bield on this bleak whinny lea.

The folk that I'm servin' are scrimpin' an bare,
An' there's few o' their dainties that come to my share,
But the grun' o' my stamack that aften I feel
Gars their aul' mouldy bannocks aye taste unco weel.

It is likely that this picture of the herd's hardship is much nearer the grim truth. Folklorist Helen Beaton, looking back in *At the Back o' Benachie* to the old lifestyle of the 1880s in her own Aberdeenshire uplands, quotes traditional lines that confirm it:

He feeds the nowt an' keeps their hooses clean,
Wi' watery nib and nives as caul's a stane,
His duds o' breeks are fairly split in twa;
The knittal brak's ahin, an' doon they fa'
Amo' the sharn.

Whatever happened, the "herd laddie" seemed destined to lose his trousers!

The upland herd's fashion was neither of his own or any other time, just whatever was bequeathed him, his Sabbath coat a hand-me-down that the travelling tailor altered to make it fit where it touched him. For his herding, says the admirable Mrs Beaton, "he had also a 'plaidie', which was made out of an old hame-spun plaid, or piece of blue or brown duffel which was also home-made. The 'plaidie' was kept by the farmer, and might with luck be worn by several herds in successive years".

Herd lasses did little better; Mrs Beaton, noting that "women did much of the herding in those days", says:

A buxom young lass was to be seen taking her turn at tending the cattle, clad in dark blue hodden 'vrapper', which was a garment resembling a maid's raincoat, covering the upper part of the body and other outward covering none, not even 'hose nor sheen', as she followed the nowt over stone and stubble, and when it was time to 'how, how' — that is to say, call the beasts home — mounting on the bare back of her pony and driving the other beasts before her. Many a rural love tale dated from those herding days.

Such then was the stark poverty of the old countryside, a poverty that drove folk to send their children out herding at the earliest age. It would take the Education Act of 1872 finally to bring all the young herds regularly behind a school-room desk, a fact that underlines the slow and often haphazard advance of enclosure and indicates too that it was never the swift measure the social history books suggest.

Most probably because the small farmtouns could not afford the time or expense of dyking or hedge-building, open pasture remained, and the need for learning had always to be balanced against the family's economic straits. Its value was not discounted but in the circumstances, few country bairns would grow up without some experience of the task. Herding indeed was the old country dominies' biggest headache, for their pupils tended to come to school only in the end of the year, when the beasts were housed. For Charles Murray's whistle-whittler and for every other herd *loon*:

> . . . the snaw it stopped the herdin' an' the
>   winter brocht him dool,
> When in spite o' hacks an' chilblains he was shod
>   again for school.

The dominies' despondency is understandable: by then the herd had forgotten whatever little he had learned the winter before.

It was among the crofter families that the need to earn was most acute: their children could wield a stick and poke it into the ribs of a laggard *stot* almost the moment they were able to run after it. They were children who were never very privileged anyway, and who prospered only when they left home since nothing in life was ever so bad again. Mostly they left school at the earliest possible moment. Their chance came with harvest-time, as stand-ins for the touns' regular herds who were recruited, like every other able body, for the heavier work of *hairst*. It was good policy for a toun to engage a strong lad as herd so that he would be able to pull the "smiler" — the harvest rake. Thus freed from his usual duties, says Mrs Beaton, finally dispelling all idyllicism, the herd "had to rake after the scythes, with bent back and probably trembling legs. In a mochy mornin', when the harvesters were snug in the barn drawing thatch or twinin' ropes, the herd might be seen on the top of a cart tramping wet tares or pulling a few early neeps for the kye or holin' and gathering potatoes, so that his work was never over from morning till night." And when his day did finish finally, like the later *orra loon* of a toun, he was the victim of the horsemen's rough humour in kitchen and *chaumer*.

He was paid in coin, clothes, meal or peat according to the most urgent needs of his folk, who usually lived nearby and were often dependent in one way or another on the goodwill of the toun that employed him. For his family it was often a bonus just to get somebody else to feed him. His breakfast, like the horsemen's, was brose (or about a good toun, possibly porridge) and milk followed by a slice of white bread or oatcake *breid*, and he might, provided he stayed on the right side of the kitchen maid, set away to the pasture with a piece of oatcake and cheese in his pocket. When he came home at night it was to. . . .

> A dish o' guid brose wi' the kail and the says
> A herdie was needin' jist aff o' the leas;
> The kail and the says and the drappie o' ream
> Wad set me a-sleepin' as seen's they were deen.

The herd's job was one of variable status. Some even went to market with their master to drove home the stirks he might buy. It was a role that absorbed the unfortunate as well as the poor. The herd of the old countryside — there were 5,000 in 1750 within the Synod of Aberdeenshire — figured in the poll lists and is described by William Alexander in his *Northern Rural Life* as

> not seldom a grown-up person of the male sex; perhaps someone who had been lamed of a hand or arm, or who was of more or less deficient intellect. And his mode of living was apt to be

dependent and precarious; "herd in summer but begs his meat in winter" and "herd on charity, his winter maintenance being gratis" are definitions of this official that repeatedly occur. In any case, the herd was an indispensable functionary.

His responsibility in the community was indeed greater than his years or intelligence might suggest. He carried a club, a throwback possibly to the time when his task was as much protection as herding. Thus John Ord, the Glasgow police inspector who, like Gavin Greig, saved so many of the countryside's old songs, in *Bothy Songs and Ballads*:

> The herd boy carried a club, having engraved thereon a mystic figure which somewhat resembled a fancy knot, and was known as the Meltie-Bow. This figure, it was understood, was able to prevent the club from doing a serious injury to an animal if it by chance was struck on a vital part. The following characters, known as Jocky and his Owsen, were cut in notches on the club, viz.: — II I III V II II IV I I III X II II, followed by a figure supposed to represent Jocky himself.
>
> This is how the notches were read by the initiated. Twa afore ane, three afore five, first twa and syne twa, then four comes belyve, noo ane and then ane, and three at a cast, double ane, and twice twa and Jocky comes at last.

If the symbols had a mystic significance once, the past, alas, has veiled it. And the herd had something else besides his club, enshrined not only in nursery rhyme but in the verse of the parochial poet:

> Herdie, herdie, blaw yer horn;
> A yer kye's amo' the corn.
> Here aboot or far awa'
> A the herds I ever saw,
> Willie Duncan blakes them a'.

In this rhyming send-up of an erring herd the name, in the style of many of the bothy ballads, could be changed to suit present company. "Blakes a' " in old regional dialect means simply "beats all".

Beasts on good pasture were unlikely to stray far; on poor grass, on the other hand, there was incitement for an old cow to try the ripening corn in the adjoining rig, and herds who lost control would bring the farmer's wrath on their heads or reproof even from royal lips. Reprimand for a little girl herd of a Balmoral croft who got carried away in play and let her beasts stray came from a passing lady, none other than the holidaying Queen Victoria herself.

It was fencing, added to the drystone dykes and the hedgerows, that finally superseded the herd *loon*, and in time there died on country lips and in the bothies all those songs that commemorated him and a task that had united generations of country children. They were not the poorer for losing it, but maybe our culture was.

Such times, of course, brought new characters to the fore in the gallery of rural craftsmen, a new élite: the dyker, the ditcher and the hedger. All were figures of some standing and maybe, for all we know, some unpopularity. In 1791, as the first stirrings of widespread change began to awaken the North-east, Milton of Rothiemay by Deveronside just north of Huntly had no fewer than four dykers in its overall population of a hundred.

The dyke idea itself was not new, only its permanence and indestructibility. It stretched out of the past. Feal (turf) dykes had long kept the cows from the crops at night or while the herd went to his supper by forming temporary enclosures or *faulds* on the outfield, thus ensuring an adequate "mucking" in the bygoing. Now the stone dyke of Celtic time was reborn in the skill of families of men, each with an eye that could hold the line of the work while the selective hand unerringly grasped the right stone. It was not the technique that was difficult, only its mastery and the elusive art of locking stone upon stone so that its singular insignificance built in the plural into a thing of pride. A good dyke, as the craftsman built it, was usually two-faced with a "heart" of loose, less bondable rubble-stones, its outer sides tapering to meet at two-thirds the intended height to be crowned finally by heavier stones. Embellishment added up-stones as the gateway to the field with iron hingepins on which a wooden gate could be hung. Generations of gates rotted in the smirr rain of the region but the gate stones lingered on. . . .

Yet dykes varied in their construction; not all were on the grand scale. Small places built their own and some, doubtless, were hurled together in good imitations, to keep up with the times, by the farmtoun folk themselves. The craftsman's dyke, with its wide coping stones, could foil the most persistent old ewe and keep her in the purdah of her intended field; in fact, not too many of the walls that marched the Lowlands plain or the uplands were truly of that calibre and many needed, latterly, to be crowned with fencing to prove an impregnable barrier.

The quickset hedge was hardly a novelty — except maybe on the bare acres of Buchan — only the use it was put to. Its usefulness had been advocated as early as the time of the abbeys' dominance of agriculture in an Act of Parliament of 1457 compelling all freeholders to (a) plant trees near their steadings (something the improvement farmtouns faithfully copied); (b) plant hedges round their fields; as well as (c) planting out broom parks to provide winter fodder. William Mackintosh of Borlum, the Jacobite rebel, languishing in prison with little else to think about beyond Improvement, was a champion of hedges as early as 1729, seeing them then as a means of improving the quality of livestock (by the curb on indiscriminate crossing) and linking them also with the making of hay and pointing out the shelter benefit they might afford to sheep.

The hedge had advantages: properly tended it was an effective stockguard; and it offered shelter not only to the beasts of the field but to the cottar waiting at the roadend in a blatter of rain for the once-a-day bus into town. The planting, on a high bank thrown up from the excavation of the ditches that embraced it on either side, was the easiest part of it. The true hedger's skill was to turn living wood into a boundary of extraordinary strength by "laying" the hedge, a kind of thorny basketry with treacherous shoots and branches that gave it, periodically, a fresh start in life.

It was an exercise on the side of nature and ecologically pleasing.

The use of the paling-wire fence came later, from the mid-1800s. It gave nothing to the countryside, only the impermanence that was its chief virtue (and given the climate of the region, it was never around for long anyway). Initially it had a fast rate of obsolescence few of the small touns could afford: it rusted to hell in no time as its posts rotted away in the mist. Again Helen Beaton, on the reasons for the delay in fencing the fields:

It took some time for the farmers to get reconciled to such fencing, as at first it was iron, and difficult to bend, also it got rusty very quickly. But later galvanised wire was introduced and has remained the chief method of fencing ever since. Barbed wire has also been used, but owing to its destructive sharp points, it is not used freely by many farmers unless necessity compels.

The galvanised wire fence would largely usurp the role of the hawthorn hedge and the drystone dyke in the fields if not within the close bounds of the Big House. It was an almost-instant barrier the farmtoun's horsemen themselves could erect in the slack of summer. Posts raw from the sawmill strode the fields carrying their spaced strands of wire threaded through retaining staples and tightened round an end "strainer" post as taut as the strings of the old smith's fiddle. And whatever the reservations of the upland touns, those of the North-east plain had not the slightest hesitation about the use of *pikit* wire.

It came as a godsend and just in time and they strung it round the countryside with a reckless abandon, the perfect deterrent against any straying livestock. It had a further use: it greatly discouraged trespass in the fields and in particular the short cuts taken across them by late-for-school children. Duck hurriedly between its *pikit* strands and it could take the arse out of your best *breeks* with an unparalleled suddenty and almost surgical precision.

Still and all, the paling-wire fence was a poor structure against the living green of the hedgerow or the sombre dignity of the stone dyke. Yet it was the hedges that became unloved. Though they possibly fared better in Mearns and Angus, in Aberdeenshire in the 1920s and 1930s they sank into decline and neglect. They were hacked into some semblance of shape by well-meaning men who no longer commanded the true hedger's skills. They shrank in status to become shelter belts more than stockguards and now needed the underpinning of the wire fence to do their work effectively. It is likely that in those sad depression years their upkeep had become an economic liability few of the old touns could afford, though for many years yet they would march with the turnpike road to the greater glory of summer and enliven with their bright red haws the melancholy days of winter.

The dyke too lost ground to the faster pace of the fence-post and the paling wire. That was progress. But nothing could detract from its quality of dour endurance or its links with the landscape of the past. It had risen from the land itself as it was trenched and broken in from the peat bog and the moor. It carried memories of earlier men. There are few now in the craft, for good dykers were always working towards their own redundancy. Today though their work can still be seen and wondered at, unchanged from the day they left it. The men, alas, were less enduring.

IV

Patterns of the Year

THEY STOOD CLOSER to nature, those men of the old Scottish farmtouns, and maybe closer to God. We cannot say now, one way or the other, for they spoke little of such things, calling quietly in at the tailor's (their elder's) shop in the village for their communion tokens as they passed through with a drove of *stirks* from the station or with a load of corn to the mill. Come Sacrament Sunday the traffic on the kirk road would be noticeably heavier than normal as folk who had not been from home in weeks took their bikes from the shed and their clips from the dresser drawer.

It is not unlikely that in the one the farm men saw at times the presence of the other, for theirs was a long continuity with the land and its seasons, a life lived in the shadow of its moods — a history, often, of generations in a close bondage with the soil. They worked with nature, coaxing her, taking sly advantage, turning her in on herself, bitterly sharing her disappointments. Their inheritance of skills and country wisdom was something that passed down in the blood like curls or a cleft palate; the yearly pattern of the parks impinged deeply, marking their days. Their speak — the old dialect of the region so riddled with broad unruly vowels — reflected that. It dated events from the rituals of the fields so that almost all conversation in that slow countryside was punctuated by a characteristic reflective pause and the pinpointing of memory in such phrases as "It was the back o' the hyowin' " or "It was last backend. . . ." Promises and entrapments were similarly qualified: "Gin we'd the hairst put past. . . ." The calendar on the kitchen wall was an irrelevance; it had no dominion in their lives except maybe for its Term Days of May and Martinmas.

Their poets and writers, and sometimes their bothy ballads, encapsulate that union of spirit and countryside, a harmony of soul with the seasons — none more so than the somewhat underrated Murray, who wrote far distanced from his native Donside, and, maybe because of it, retained in the eye still the clarity of its

images. Spring, summer, autumn, winter . . . he crystallises for
us now their impact on the old rural community. His "Spring in
the Howe o' Alford", for instance, is a hymn to the days of
seedtime and the first warmth of the year:

> There's burstin' buds on the larick now
> A' the birds are paired an' biggin';
> Saft soughin' win's dry the dubby howe,
> An' the eildit puir are thiggin'.
>
> The whip-the-cat's aff fae hoose to hoose,
> Wi' his oxtered lap-buird lampin',
> An' hard ahint, wi' the shears an' goose,
> His wee, pechin' 'prentice trampin'.
>
> The laird's approach gets a coat o' san',
> When the grieve can spare a yokin';
> On the market stance there's a tinker clan,
> An' the guidwife's hens are clockin'.
>
> The mason's harp is set up on en',
> He's harlin' the fire-hoose gable;
> The sheep are aff to the hills again
> As hard as the lambs are able.
>
> There's spots o' white on the lang brown park,
> Where the sacks o' seed are sittin';
> An' wily craws fae the dawn to dark
> At the harrow tail are flittin'.
>
> The liftward lark lea's the dewy seggs,
> In the hedge the yeldrin's singin';
> The teuchat cries for her harried eggs,
> In the bothy window hingin'.
>
> Nae snaw-bree now in the Leochel Burn,
> Nae a water baillie goupin' —
> But hear the whirr o' the miller's pirn,
> The plash where the trouts are loupin'.

The hopes of the old farmtouns were sown from those "spots o' white", the seed sacks set at intervals down the length of the new-tilled corn parks. They would be answered long months later in the onslaught of harvest — the *hairst*, as they always called it — as they reaped a bounty on what they had sown, or settled bitterly to long protracted days of disappointment. The only thing sure about *hairst* was its uncertainty.

Another exile, later in time, more famous and fresher in the memory, returned briefly to his native landscape as the days of the old farmtoun era drew to a bitter close. It was the fall of the year of 1933 as Lewis Grassic Gibbon looked again through a Mearns window on the fields that lay so close to his heart. He understood the trauma of a northern *hairst* and wrote of it movingly in his essay, *The Land*:

Autumn of all seasons is when I realize how very Scotch I am, how interwoven with the fibre of my body and personality is this land and its queer scarce harvests, its hours of reeking sunshine and stifling rain, how much a stranger I am, south, in those seasons of mist and mellow fruitfulness as alien to my Howe as the olive groves of Persia. It is a harder and slower harvest, and lovelier in its austerity, that is gathered here, in September's early coming, in doubtful glances on the sky at dawn, in listening to the sigh of the sea down there by Bervie. Mellow it certainly is not: but it has the most unique of tangs, this season haunted by the laplaplap of the peesie's wings, by great moons that come nowhere as in Scotland, unending moons when the harvesting carts plod through great thickets of fir-shadow to the cornyards deep in glaur.

These are the most magical nights of the land: they endure but a little while, but their smells — sharp and clear, com-mingled of fresh horse-dung and dusty cornheads — pervade the winter months. The champ and showd of a horse in that moonsprayed dark and the guttural "Tchkh, min!" of the forker, the great shapes of cattle in the parks as you ride by, the glimmer far away of the lights of some couthy toun on the verge of sleep, the queer shapes of post and gate and stook — Nature unfolds the puppets and theatre pieces year after year, unvaryingly, and they lose their dust, each year uniquely fresh. You can stand and listen as though for the lost trumpet of God in that autumn night silence: but indeed all that you are listening for is a passing peewit.

It is quite superb, echoing that strange heartache that haunts the exile. Probably in no other piece of his writing does Gibbon so deeply demonstrate his love and understanding of his own countryside or how deeply, once, it enfolded men in the cycle of nature and the pattern of the year. Yet the land of Gibbon's *hairst*, as of Murray's spring, was as we have seen relatively new.

If enclosure had given it dykes and hedgerows, that was only a part of the story. There coalesced in that time of fevered excitement, the late-1700s, an entirely new concept in farming, as actively pursued by that race of pioneering lairds who daily pushed agriculture through all known barriers. Its keynote was to be not only the revision of the farming unit but with it a bold alliance of new crops and rotations, the most revolutionary being the elevation of the lowly turnip to a lordly status and the serious cultivation of grass. Together these factors would change the look of the countryside and quilt it with fresh colours. The air hummed with ideas so that even the most diehard traditionalist must have sensed change and, however unsettling, known it to be inevitable.

There were bold men in the lower ranks of rural society who knew an opportunity and when to seize it. As Arthur Young, first Secretary to the Board of Agriculture, and a kind of minor Cobbett, said of another countryside but in the same context:

For the individual farmer the main advantage of enclosure was that instead of having a holding made up of fragmented plots scattered through the open fields he occupied a farm consisting of one compact block of land (or at most a few such blocks) over which the rights of other farms to pasture their stock had been abolished. After enclosure he could freely choose (or, if a tenant, ask the permission of his landlord) to convert land to its most profitable use, break up the old weed-ridden pastures, and put worn-out arable down to grass. He was no longer tied by the restrictions of communal husbandry and could adopt whatever practices seemed most likely to swell the output of his farm.

The horizon indeed was wide and the future beckoning. The patterns of the old run-rig agriculture would fade from the land and it is easy now to scoff at the limitations in-built in their communal organisation. It would be foolish to do so, for if the shift to the boundaried field and new cropping cycle was obviously right, the old system in its time had its own unquestionable logic and communal viability. All social considerations apart — and these were many and fundamental — there were several things that inhibited a healthier agriculture. Not least was the lack of dung: its dearth had a chain effect for it limited the amount of land that could be manured, the corn that could be sown, and necessarily the yield that could be expected. In these straitened circumstances poor folk did what they could: they dunged the infield, the arable ground (sometimes also called the "croft" or "intoun" land) that lay close round the farmtoun cluster, one-third of it each year. This one-third patch was expected to give in the first instance a crop of bere (poor, old-style barley) and in following seasons, without further incitement, to bear two crops of oats — all of this in continuous rotation. There were communities where they restarted the cropping cycle after the normal two yields of oats; others, it seems, where they seemed intent on entering *The Guinness Book of Records*. In Banffshire one field might carry up to fourteen crops of oats in succession, and there were even more extravagant demands made, it is said, with these "robber rotations". As one early Buchan minister exclaimed: "While the heritor only plows where he cannot get grass to grow any longer, the tenant sometimes plows as long as corn of any kind will grow." It was a practice that could lead only to exhaustion of the ground and miserable yields of only three times the seed sown were average.

Beyond the "intoun" land was the outfield, not the simple marginal expanse you might suppose but a part of the system that played its own complementary role. That extraordinary man of many parts, Dr Anderson, reporting on the farming of Aberdeenshire in the late-1700s, throws an illuminating light on its peculiarities and operation in that county:

That part of the farm called the outfield is divided into two unequal portions. The smallest, usually about one-third part, is called folds, pronounced faulds; the other larger portion is denominated faughs. The fold ground usually consists of ten divisions, one of which each year is brought into tillage from grass. With this intent it is surrounded with a wall of sod the last year it is to remain in grass, which forms a temporary enclosure that is employed as a penn for confining the cattle during the nighttime and for two or three hours each day at noon. It thus gets a tolerably full dunging, after which it is plowed successively for oats for four or five years, or as long as it will carry any crop worth reaping. It is then abandoned for five or six years during which time it gets by degrees a sward of poor grass, when it is again subjected to the same rotation.

The system meant that about half the folds were in grass, half in oats. The faughs were a northern refinement; they got no dunging of any kind, were roughly ploughed up on the same half-and-half basis as the foldo and bore poor grass and even poorer oats in the same sort of ratio.

On average, about a quarter of the total land area of a toun would be infield ground; in Aberdeenshire, where things were always worse, perhaps only one-fifth. When Grant took on his life's achievement of transforming Monymusk he found that a husbandman holding 26 acres would only have six of them as intoun crop — a vivid indication, if one were needed, of what improvement had to overcome and the base from which it would move.

Of Scottish farming, Professor J. E. Handley, observing the same 1700s' landscape in his *Scottish Farming in the Eighteenth Century*, says:

Methods of raising crops had remained unaltered for centuries, standards of farming had deteriorated since the battle of Flodden, and the piratical practice of forcing the soil to give a return until it was exhausted, without any attempt to make good the virtue that it lost in the process or even permitting it an interval of rest, to recuperate, had resulted in a steady decline in the quality of the land. By the end of the seventeenth century much of this land had reverted to its primitive state. . . .

Yet bad though it undoubtedly was, the Scots peasant's agriculture was probably no worse than his counterpart's south of the Border or elsewhere in Europe. It had stretched from the Middle Ages, uninterrupted in its limitations or strange excesses. Its basis was the run-rig; it was old in the land and fell, for the purpose of drainage, with the slope of the ground. It was the landscape still of Slezer's *Theatrum Scotiae* of 1693. That equality might reign, the rigs were re-allocated yearly, two- or even three-yearly, though annually seems to have been most usual.

It was a system that locked the countryside in the old pattern, unable to move in the rigidity enforced by the communal activities of ploughing, sowing and harvesting; it gave not an inch to individual whim or inspiration. Little could happen until the ancient mould was broken — until the days of the run-rig and rundale ended. From that moment progress began, and in some cases its first stirrings had already occurred, for into it there had already stepped those bold men of the 1700s, the improving lairds, intent on momentous transformation.

In some places, the run-rigs had already been bulked to give permanent land-holding in an intermediate stage that obviously gave a man more incentive. In others, the land that would be claimed had previously been under cultivation and had fallen back to the waste in the dreadful famine years of the early 1700s. In the failure of crops then tenants had been forced into destitution, their landlords at times into debt and penury. Farming folk, if they emerged at all from that time, did so without the money to take up leases and such was the want of tenantry that lairds were forced into offering substantial inducements, such as an oxteam or milk cow, in order to fill their touns.

But there were also large tracts of ground that had never felt the plough-point or a husbandman's foot. Hardy men would claw their acres from the moor in a herculean marathon of labour that in its scope still manages to astound belief. A man seized a mattock and began a dynasty — the long association of a family with a holding of land. In time the two would become inseparable, and typifying that North-east Lowlands experience is Flora Garry's lines, in "Bennygoak", the prelude to the farming dream:

> It wis jist a skelp o the muckle furth,
> A sklyter o roch grun,
> Fin granfadder's fadder bruke it in
> Fae the hedder an the funn.

Granfadder sklatit barn an byre,
Brocht water to the closs,
Pat fail-dykes ben the bare brae face
An a cairt road tull the moss.

They are the rough spare words of a stark spare countryside that
never spoke well of itself. (Understatement was such an ingrained
habit that you could well be lulled into believing that things were
never as bad as they were.)

Such then was the new farming settlement in the countryside
that James Ferguson transformed. It was settled not only by the
farmtouns but also by countless crofter men, an even hardier
breed. They took a patch of the heath or hillside and poured their
sweat into it, their pattern of cultivation a microcosm of the
farmtouns' work. Their conquest was often of the rough ground
not on the lairds' charters and begat them the deepest of
improvement ironies for by showing their land's worth they
became captive on the laird's rent-roll.

So much for the land and the forces that shaped it. The thing
that gave it colour was new crops burgeoning in the fields. The
future of the farmtouns was bound to those rotations, as vital in
their way as the outfield *faulds* or the intoun crop. They absorbed
the elements of the new agriculture — winter keep, turnips and
hay, and outlawed fallowing — and put the plough round the
farm.

They would sustain the farmtouns through their heyday and
they stood the old crop cycles on their head. Each field had become
part of the whole; the outfield and permanent pasture faded before
the advance of temporary grass. It was called ley farming and in its
grass years it had a fine in-built pause, an organ-stop in the recital
of the year, that could be lengthened according to need. There
would come a time when the old touns would be thankful for that.

Something like it had been part of the country's earlier monastic
farming but had been lost in the dissolution of the abbeys. But if
the touns' rotation had similarities, it came from a farther
countryside. Like the Norfolk system on which it was based, it
combined cash crops with fodder production and incorporated
with them stock (and, importantly, their manure) in a fine-knit
circle of fertility in which the turnip flourished like a native and
ushered in the era of the feeders' byre. Few things in farmtoun life

fell together with such harmony. The basic sequence was: oats/ turnips/oats/hay/grass/grass. The lying in grass could be extended almost indefinitely, alas with a rapid decline in grazing quality. Farmers would no more have thought of deserting the rotation than they would have thought of leaving their gudewives. It so interlocked that Arthur Young most pertinently observed: "Every link of the chain of Norfolk husbandry has so intimate a connection and dependence that the destruction of a single one ruins the whole." The same would be said of the rotation of the north. It seemed perfection and undoubtedly there were men who could foresee nothing else for as long as the sands of time would run.

So was set the pattern of the farmtoun year. Each spring refurbished a landscape that had lain cold and dreich under winter's furrows. The parks took on a new intensity; they were more sharply etched by the line of greystone dyke and dark-twigged hedgerow. Seedtime when it came brought a fresh brown on to nature's palette — the tilth that instigated the sequence and slowly faded under braird and burgeoning green.

The quilt of the farmlands did not greatly change. . . . It brought familiar colours and rearranged them. Only their place on the chequerboard differed as the stubble gave way to the indispensable turnip, the old turnip park sprang grain and last year's ley shaded slowly to corn-gold.

If the spectrum was limited, that was ordained by the immutable cycles, by the unbending rotation. It was the pattern of the year, constantly rewoven by the summer of the *hyow* and the hay, the autumn of harvest, the winter of the plough and the incessant threshing and carting of turnips. When winter fell it was on bare parks where only the turnips still sat regal in the drill, outlasting patience itself, their frost-blasted shaws the last speck of green left over from the riot of summer. It was an ending of a kind; a mist of melancholy gathered on the fields and closed in on the touns.

V

The Ploughs of Winter

IT ALL BEGAN with the plough: it was the bow drawn slow on the fiddle strings, a prelude to the long orchestration of the farmtoun year. The plough was old in the land; its ritual spanned cultures and millenniums. Symbol of peace and settlement, it was greater finally than the sword that so ceaselessly sought to usurp it. Even in time of strife the plough prevailed, more powerful than the mere tug of history and sometimes almost unaffected by it. Ultimately it united men more than philosophies.

Winter long the ploughs of the old farmtouns drew their lonely furrows on a bare landscape, first in the stubble, later, as the year turned, on the ley — the grassland — where the earth was dark and rich and furrow fell upon furrow with an evenness that soothed the eye and in a perfection that made the old men nod when they left their winter firesides to lift their staffs from the lobby and take a turn on the road. Long away from the plough, they knew "guid wark" still and maybe it warmed their countrymen's hearts to see it. They would know their legacy was secure.

It had always been so round the touns of that northern countryside: the role passed down as the strength left the plough arms but the connoisseur's eye remained, undimmed and as sternly critical as it had always been. The man *lowsed* from the long *yoking* of his working life would stand on the cold endrig catching his death, watching the young ploughman who had usurped him. The skill of the "ploo park" fell easily down the years from those grizzled men to the callow halflin who had but newly bought his first cut-throat razor at the *feeing* fair — more in hope than in any urgent need of it.

It was mainly in the plough that the touns judged the worth of a man in a life where, beyond question, none was hampered who had not trod the groves of academe. For the ploughboy's academy was the stable and his exam-sheet the plough-rig. Most came naturally to the plough's work, knowing nothing more, expecting nothing

less. Most now underplay the demands of the task and the skills
involved. Listen to an old horseman, long distanced now from the
work of his youth:

> Wi plooin', if ye made a richt beginnin' ye couldnae gang wrang.
> There was naething til't. Ye jist cam' til't. . . . When ye were a
> loon aboot a toun, ye were aye gaun tae be a horseman. Ye'd be
> hame fae the school . . . well, mony a time maybe ye wid hae gane
> roon' tae where the horsemen were a workin' in the ploo, ye
> ken. . . . Ye'd be watchin' his ploo . . . he'd maybe gie ye a haud
> o' the ploo. Ye'd seen ither folk daen't. Ye jist kent fit tae dae. . . .
> It wis jist . . . automatic. . . .

The pipe tobacco is no longer thick black twist but a sophisticated
ready-rubbed, feeble by comparison but more socially acceptable.
But the reflective puff or two takes him back for a moment:

> Och aye . . . the horse, onywye, kent foo fast tae go. . . . A pair o'
> experienced Clydesdales kent they were plooin'—kent better nor
> the young horseman whiles, fit they'd tae dae.

Even so, many of the halflin lads of the farmtouns, those young
teenagers given to the flamboyance of broad bonnets and a loud
opinion of themselves and barely able to scratch their names on the
bothy wall, eventually carved out a reputation in the end-of-year
fields. A man might rise to match status even and champions came a
pound or two dearer in the *feeing* market. James Edward Ransome
— his name a familiar one in the bothy-talk— put it all rather neatly
in his pamphlet *Ploughs and Ploughing*, and maybe not only in the
cause of wooing customers. Writing in 1865, to explain the art of
using "the most useful and most general of all agricultural implements", he considered that the ploughman himself, though he
might not have had the benefit of a fine education, "had an
implement to study and work to perform, which requires years of
patient daily toil to master and become proficient at" (happily his
ploughs were more graceful than his prose). Most of the horsemen
of the single-tenant touns in fact brought a new artistry into the
fields.
   It was a skill honed by contest. By the late 1880s, the Highland
and Agricultural Society's medals were being awarded at 150

ploughing matches throughout the country. Contestants brought
their ploughs and their own claques to the field and competition
alarmingly heightened the blood. There was argument and
contention: what *was* good ploughing? Henry Stephens, in his
Book of the Farm, had no doubts and ruled succinctly on its
obvious characteristics:

> The furrow-slices should be quite straight. . . . They should be
> quite parallel as well as straight, which shows that they are of a
> uniform thickness; for thick and thin slices lying upon one
> another present irregularly parallel and horizontal lines. They
> should be of the same height, which shows that they have been
> cut of the same breadth; for slices of different breadths laid
> together at whatever angle present unequal vertical lines.

Ploughing match judges knew as much, though they might not
always see work of such excellence. They were usually brought in
from outside the local community and, having given their
decision, might have to leave under cover of darkness and by the
back roads.

Short men, folk said, could not be good ploughmen — though
that never stopped them winning their share of the medals and
prizes. Stephens was as uncertain about the suitability of tall men:
"Tall men, in having to stoop constantly, lean hard upon the stilts;
and as this has the tendency to lift the plough up, they are obliged
to put the draught bolt higher to keep it in the ground."

Old ploughmen, on the other hand, knew a few tricks too many,
especially when it came to lightening the work:

> Some ploughmen habitually make the plough lean a little over to
> the left, giving it less land than it would normally have, and to
> counteract the consequent tendency to a narrow furrow-slice
> move the draught-bolt a little to the right. The ploughing with a
> lean to the left is a bad custom, because it cuts the lowest end of
> the furrow-slice with a slope, which gives the horses a lighter
> draught than when turning over a square furrow-slice. Old
> ploughmen, feeling infirm, are apt to practice this deceptive
> mode of ploughing. The plough should always be level upon its
> sole, and turn over a rectangular furrow-slice.

The action of the plough indeed was threefold: it cut deep-rooted weeds; buried top growth (to provide humus); and offered up the soil to the weather. The mechanics were simpler than Stephens might lead one to imagine: it sliced the soil — the stubbles of autumn, the leys of winter and the *neep grun* of late spring — both laterally and vertically, to throw the resulting furrow unceremoniously on its back against its neighbour of the previous bout at an angle (to please Stephens) of 45 degrees.

Such then was the simple geometry. It was in its execution, in its patterns, and in its place in the immutable sequence of the seasons, that the ploughing stirred the heart as did few other phases of the year. Thus Flora Thompson in her classic, *Lark Rise to Candleford*:

> There were usually three or four ploughs to a field, each of them drawn by a team of three horses, with a boy at the head of the leader and the ploughman behind at the shafts. All day, up and down they would go, ribbing the pale stubble with stripes of dark furrows which, as the day advanced, would get wider and nearer together, until, at length, the whole field lay a rich velvety plum-colour.

If it is a heightened, poetic vision, English and very much of the writer's beloved Oxfordshire, it is in essence a ritual that differed little from that which transformed the winter fields of the ballad touns — except that the Scottish ploughman guided his own Clydesdale pair from between the plough-stilts. Yet those rumbustious bothy songs which record so much of the farmtoun life and pay due homage to the "ploughman lad" are sadly silent about the poetry of ploughing. The young horseman of the touns, it is likely, thought little of such things; the only music in his ears was the raucous screech of the gulls as they birled and wheeled behind him, demented in their gluttony. The work went on with a fine and comforting inevitability, like the will of God and with the blessing of centuries. Furrows sleek from the plough, with the mouldboard's gleam like a bloom still on them, fell together with a mesmeric grace, in unquestioning order.

It cannot be said that the old horsemen revered the plough, as long ago the emperors of old China did: they took hold of the plough stilts once a year so that they would not get too much above themselves. The horsemen of the old farmtouns walked behind the plough every winter working day of their lives and were never in danger of forgetting their lowly existence. For though there were touns, where affairs were less desperate, that could countenance a day or two's grace in the stable or in some time-filling steading chore, there were as many harsh ones that sent their horsemen, heavy-overcoated, to the plough in everything bar blind smoor.

In the chill North-east Lowlands landscape the ploughs held sway from mid-October, and maybe before, until the end of April. They started on the stubble almost as the rakings left it to continue through the end of the year and move, with the New Year, into the old grassland, coming finally to the ploughing of the "clean land" as soon as the turnips could decently be got off the face of it. That order was unrelenting, and in other ways too a thread from the past spun down: for all its artistry, its divergence from the days and tenor of the crude ox-plough, the ploughing of the farmtouns echoed the pattern of the run-rigs.

The farming year began on the faded stubble — a broad brown thread that ran the length of the field and back again; a double furrow thrown in on itself (to keep the soil level). In the later ley, the start was little more than a *scrat*, double fine lines of two-inch deep mini-furrows maybe twenty inches apart. It had a name that first pass of the plough across the land: the *feering*. It took a second bout, deepened by adjustment of the plough wheel, of five-inch depth before the plough in its third "round" sank in to its true working depth: six inches for land coming out of ley, seven to eight inches for what would be the "clean land" and the turnip ground. The hand that "set up" the *feering* was the ploughman's own, though his props, the divots raised for guidance on the stubble, might be set or supervised by the grieve and "paced out" from the dyke to ensure its equidistance the whole length of the field. Only the stubble provided any problem for the *feering* was traditionally raised in the *mids* of the previous ploughing, usually discernible, even on the ley. Turnip ground was easier still, for here the *feering* could follow the line of the drill, a method all but infallible even for the rawest halflin.

So, with its alternating *feerings* and *midses* the pattern of the plough persisted beyond one year and the next, in a continuum of cultivation that set this autumn's furrows contra to those of the year before. Only at the start of a new cycle of rotation, with the "clean land", could change be countenanced and a decision made as to the width of the plough-rigs for the following six years or so. That pattern of the ploughing was sacrosanct, the "gathering and skailing" of furrows extending even to the endrigs, the headlands, the ploughing that finished the work and enclosed the field like the border on a cottar wife's knitting. Here, unwritten but unvarying, the tradition was that the furrows of the "clean land" or turnip ground turned away from the dyke or hedgerow, while those of the stubble and ley lay towards it. The endrigs — the *fleeds* as the old farmtoun men often called them — were necessary for the turning of the plough and its Clydesdales and were usually of four yards' (fifteen or so furrows') width. But there was nothing mystical about the alternating of the furrows, either on the *fleed* or in the rig: the practice merely ensured that the soil did not "bank up" at the dykeside or move slowly with the years across the field.

The ploughing was always with the lie of the land; the need for drainage dictated it so, and it was that, too, that determined the width and number of the "rigs", the work-strips assigned to each ploughman. On what had been *neep grun*, in the 1920s and 1930s, a "rig" might encompass 26 drills' width, at three furrows to the drill, 78 furrows.

The work began from one side of the field — there seems to have been no cut-and-dried preference — with each horseman setting up his own *feering* in a previous year's *mids*: four rigs, perhaps, gradually broadening as each "gathered" clockwise to the *feering*, to knit together the whole furrowed pattern. When two men's rigs had closed to within, say, six feet of each other, one horseman would move away to set up a new *feering* while his bothy colleague stayed to "close the work", i.e., take out the new *mids* (about two feet wide) which would finally link their adjoining pieces of ploughing, his Clydesdales walking on the ploughing to turn the final furrows. The *mids* was a trickier piece of work than the *feering* and in the match-rig it was what toppled many a champion when the crown seemed already on his head.

The method thus had a system, a cohesion that cleverly linked one rig to its neighbour as work progressed and yet again demonstrated the method-study that marked so many of the farmtoun tasks. Though seldom seen, round-and-round ploughing was not unknown: it would be done, changing the pattern entirely, only where a field was large, level and well-drained. Here the work began round the edge of the field, anti-clockwise since the ploughs threw their furrows to the right. The work closed to the centre of the field, leaving a strip from the gate, which was ploughed last.

In round-and-round ploughing the horsemen followed their foreman's furrow in stable order, with seldom more than 25 yards between them — so that the "fourth" would not be left too far behind at *lowsing*-time. Here the rule was to take the plough out of its furrow at *lowsing*-time so that it would not impede re-yoking should a man be sent elsewhere in the afternoon. In the rigs, the custom was to put the plough into work for a yard or two away from the endrig, leaving it pulled back in the furrow to give the Clydesdales an easier start.

Though the advice to the young ploughman in the match-rig might be discreet, *sotto voce*, with a nod and a conspiratorial wink, far different were the grieve's demands about his own toun, where artistry often came a poor second in the bossman's mind to the driving need to get through the work.

"Pit on mair lan' " (Put on more land), the ploughman might be peremptorily told as the grieve sought a wider furrow: the lateral adjustment was made where the yoke hitched to the plough bridle. Once, before the moveable plough-point became universal in the 1930s, his ears might have burned from succinct assessment of his character and the savage imprecation that he should instantly "Pit on mair yird" (Put on more earth), i.e., keep the plough into the ground to increase the depth of the furrow: this necessitated a vertical adjustment. Good though a man was, praise was always poor stewardship.

There was a protocol in the plough, as there was about nearly everything round a farmtoun. Where three or four pairs of Clydesdales took the field — and that was at every moderate-sized toun — the foreman (the first horseman) set the pace while his bothy colleagues followed him, each in his own rig, in ranked order. It was sensible never to fall too far behind the foreman, and even more so not to press too hard on his heels, and that was easy enough where the ploughman's pair was biddable and had maybe been longer at the plough than the ploughman himself. But where both Clydesdales and ploughmen were young there could be problems, especially where the foreman believed in "haudin' in", holding back his pair in the plough.

Not all the old ploughmen believed in that. Come the 1920s
there were just as many who thought it was no hardship on the
Clydesdales to let a pair "walk withoot hingin' " — walk without
holding back. What was never in doubt was the astonishing
number of plough points a young horseman and a high-strung
Clydesdale between them could break during a *yoking*. And in the
ballad-toun country there was no shortage of damnably stony
fields, nor of farmtouns with poor-quality ploughs. Bad horses and
bad ploughs came often together, as obviously they did at "Guise
of Tough", that oddly-named toun in the Alford uplands. They
were a gift to one bothy lad with a waggish talent and a blunt
pencil. Having "gone home" at the Term, November 28, the
traditional half-yearly feeing time for hired help, he records:

> On the followin' mornin'
> I gaed to the ploo,
> But lang, lang or lowsin' time
> My pairie gart me rue.
>
> My ploo she wasna workin' weel,
> She wadna throw the fur,
> The gaffer says, "There's a better ane
> At the smiddy to gang for."
>
> When I got home the new ploo
> She pleased me unco weel,
> But I thocht she would be better
> Gin she hid a cuttin' wheel.

It was with such lines that the bothy lads indicted a toun for its
poor equipment when it might have been unwise to complain to
the grieve.

Beyond the artistry and painstaking symmetry of the match
field there was by no means great consensus among the farmtouns
on what was good ploughing, though most touns liked to see their
ley furrows sculpted and unbroken and with that bloom of
perfection that the mouldboard for a day or two left on them. They
had good reason: there was a belief that such furrows shrugged off
the winter rain while the furrow's thinness enabled the frost to
penetrate. Yet there were, even then, farmer men who wanted

their furrows broken; they were the revolutionaries who would usher in a more modern husbandry, rebels in their time though today without a taint of obloquy against their names. Others again were pernickety about depth, constantly advocating their horsemen to take "mair yird". One year, in the mid-1930s, Major James Keith, that farming frontiersman of the ballad country also with extensive farming interests in England, surprised the horsemen of his Mains of Cairnbrogie toun by appearing suddenly in the "ploo park" to issue each of them with a small folding rule. The implication was plain: they would plough the seven-inch depth he wanted if they wished to stay much longer about his toun. Keith was also a champion of the short-mouldboard plough, preferring the American-made Oliver, a whim that put his horsemen at a strong disadvantage in the local match field, something "the Major" characteristically and immediately rectified—by sponsoring a class for such ploughs.

The farmtoun ploughman's day was one of continuous dialogue with his pair broken only, when he had the chance, by a shout to a colleague in the adjoining rig, or over the endrig dyke to a passing bairn or a comely tink. Out of the grieve's sight he might stop for a moment on the endrig to kindle his stumpy Stonehaven pipe before coiling the reins again round his wrists, spitting on his palms and regripping the plough-stilts. They were great spitters-in-the-palms the old farmtoun men, and could hardly take hold of anything without doing so — unless it was the kitchen maid.

There are bothy ballads, some of them looking back to an even earlier time, that sing of such things and tell us about the Scottish ploughman's day (and his nights). One in particular, "The Ploughman", lingered long in the farmtoun bothies:

> Now that the blooming Spring comes on,
>   He tak's his yokin' early,
> And whistling owre the furrowed field
>   He goes to fallow fairly.
>
> When my ploughman lad comes hame at e'en,
>   He's aften wat and weary;
> Cast aff the wet, put on the dry,
>   Come to your bed, my dearie.

Then up wi't noo, my ploughman lad,
And hey, my merry ploughman;
Of a' the lads that I do ken,
Commen' me to the ploughman.

If the song records the ploughman's lot, it also indicates his popularity with the lasses. It was one revised at different times and by different hands, among them Lady Caroline Nairne, composer of such jaunty Jacobite airs as "Charlie is my Darling", and even by Burns. It is easy now to forget that the Ayrshire poet was capable, when not being paraded through the fashionable salons of Edinburgh, of turning a furrow with the next man. Away from the gentry's adulation, he was aware of the ploughman's contentment:

A country fellow at the pleugh,
His acre's tilled, he's right ineugh.

The horse-plough drew the ploughman into a closer harmony with the soil. It was a relationship enunciated by John Stewart Collis, a man who had never held a farm implement until war took him out of the scholarly life and into the realm of agriculture. He fell completely under the spell of the land and he is eloquent about the plough. He describes in *The Worm Forgives the Plough* the simple pleasure kindled by handling that implement. The field, he says, is a laboratory, unable to realise its potential without the help of man. The instrument of liberation, he says, is the plough — a symbol that outlasts temples and palaces, creeds and philosophies. He describes his own first acquaintance:

. . . at length the time came when I stood on the field with a plough and two horses. It lay on its side for it was extremely like a ship out of water — a ship with a great fish's fin for a keel. An awkward bulk to handle until it was launched into its proper element, the earth.

He articulates the ploughman's skill, what every bothy lad experienced when he put his hands on the stilts:

All the body is engaged, and all the mind, while eye keeps watch on the horses and the plough, fascinated by the way the solid soil leaps up into a seeming fluid wave to fall immediately into stillness again in your wake — a green wave rising when on ley, light-brown on stubble, grey on stony ground. It falls and falls away, this little earthy breaker, until quite soon you see that a section of your field has turned colour completely, and you say to yourself — "I've ploughed that much." The eye is severely engaged indeed, and yet there is time, and a great inclination, to glance round at the scene as a whole — at the seagulls snow-flakingly following, at the cloud figures, at the sunset as the day closes. I could look down from a certain high field in Dorset into a deep vale which was often filled with sparkling light while we were in shadow. One late afternoon the clouds so gathered that one field below alone received the sun: one lanterned ray enlightened it, filled it completely, not going over the hedges but just down upon that green field only — as if the finger of God were pointing to one page which I must con for truth. I could not con it, being otherwise engaged, but was glad to see the print was there; and glad also, many a time, to glance up as the cold winter day closed down, and see the sunset blooming like a rose, and the tree-top tracery write its hieroglyphics on the lofty scroll.

The farmtoun ballads, homespun in the bothies, sadly, convey little of such things. Strange they would have thought it, those bothy *loons*, that an Irish intellectual should speak of their art. Theirs was a simpler song.

Confessing his enjoyment of working with the tractor and the three-furrow plough, Collis, in his cosmic consciousness, saw the old horseman's task much more deeply:

. . . nothing can really compare with the simple, strenuous horse work. For one thing there is no other physical work to compare with it. . . . And, fascinating as the machine work is, you do not hold the plough. But it is just this *grasping* of the handles of the plough, both arms stretched out fully and often putting out full strength, that somehow is the very top-notch of satisfaction. . . . Then your feet are upon the earth, your hands upon the plough. You seem to be holding more than the plough and treading across more than this one field: you are holding together the life of mankind, you are walking through the fields of time.

It is likely, though they never said so, that some of the old farmtoun horsemen felt something of the kind as they ploughed their lonely furrows. Poor cottars and bothy *loons* though they were, many were better men, more knowledgeable and articulate, than they ever let on. Some made songs or melodies that would pass down for those who sought to know and understand their ways. Some managed to take their accordions and melodeons out of the bothy and on to the dance-hall dais. Some were bright and quick, with the gift of the gab, as any old kitchen maid could tell you; and often damnably handsome and persuasive (and she could tell you that too). If you doubt it, look again on the haunted "film-star" face of Ramsay MacDonald, in 1924 Britain's first Labour premier. There is the oft-told story of him being taken as a young boy to the top of a northern hill by his mother, a former servant-lass, who pointed to a distant figure at work in a furrowed field.

"Yon's yer father," she told him.

It may be true. And if it is, the young boy's plight was no different from many another's. For slow-stepping though they were, the horsemen in the heyday of the ballad touns fathered between them an inordinate number of bairns, on both sides of the blanket. More important, however, is the legacy they passed down: the land we see before us today and the still-enduring patterns of the plough on which the farming year unfurls.

VI

Harrowing Time

AUTUMN MELLOWED THE old touns. The shortening days drew the horsemen early home from the plough to steadings hazed and softened in the last of the afternoon light. The *fa' o' the year* the old folk called it, that time of pause as the days slid slowly into long nights by the fire with the wind at the door and folk went *furth* only as necessity or the need for a dram drove them. It was a time of lanterns, of bobbing lights in the farmtoun night far and away so that looking out to the hill before bedtime you might see Hilly making his captain's rounds of his toun — a last tour of the *biggings* before trusting his head to the pillow — or watch Mains's new bailie going home to his cottar-house from a last look in the byre.

November could bring the first dusting of snow to the parks, lingering at the dykesides and cresting the dark furrows; "waiting for mair", folk said. And so it would be: the cold breath of winter long on the land, the parks quiet and still. Then the ploughs sat lone and forlorn, turned in from the endrigs and crouched in the furrow, breast and share locked in the ground. Snow feathered stilt and cross-stay. Wind and frost chilled a strange statuary along the burn banks and blew drift-forms of weird and fluid fantasy through the bare hedgerows. For all that, it was a world, suddenly, of astonishing beauty.

Old men clung to the fire; horsemen unyoked from the plough and unsettled by idleness moved cautiously in the silence of the winter-wrapped toun cowled in corn bags, like monks in a cloister, as drift blattered on the bothy skylight and blanketed the lantern pane.

For six weeks together, and maybe for longer, the ploughs would be rested as the year turned. Only the lengthening days brought a sigh that the worst was past, and as seedtime drew on small-toun men who had not given anybody a civil word all winter long spoke almost kindly to their wives and stepped jauntily into their morning stables, jovial with the thought of it.

It was the awakening of the year.

So, too, the poets saw it — and not only Murray with his delightful evocation of that quickening in nature that set all the countryside about its business, mingling the rebirth of all economic and social life with the upheaval in the fields. Another, looking back on the lonely landscape of his childhood and the spring sowing in particular, in his moving *An Autobiography*, the record of a dreich young life, would recall the feeling that the farmtoun spring awoke in the soul:

> About that time of the year the world opened, the sky grew higher, the sea deeper, as the summer colours, blue and green and purple woke in it.The black fields glistened and a row of meal-coloured sacks, bursting full like the haunches of plough-horses, ran down each one; two neat little lugs like pricked ears, stuck up from each sack. They were opened; my father filled from the first of them a canvas tray strapped round his middle and strode along the field casting the dusty grain on either side with regular sweeps, his hands opening and shutting. When the grain was finished he stopped at another sack and went on again. I would sit watching him. . . . The sun shone, the black field glittered, my father strode on, his arms slowly swinging, the fan-shaped cast of grain gleamed as it fell and fell again; the row of meal-coloured sacks stood like squat monuments on the field. My father took a special delight in the sowing, and we all felt the first day was a special day.

The child was Edwin Muir. He draws us into a more mystical past and a task uniting the centuries and the generations. The scene was one enshrined in the mind of every rural Scottish child of his time and even later, powerful in its imagery, in the link it provides with an older landscape. The sight was still common enough a generation later in the quiet uplands of the ballad country, and on Lowlands crofts right up to World War Two. the memory now is of old, sinewy men as dour and enduring as the land itself (and poorer, even, than Muir's own folk would have been) striding the fields in those lonely outposts where a strange and protracted agriculture consecrated the old ways and where the hopper and the scythe, each in its turn, still resurfaced yearly. Common too to all crofting childhood was that general thankfulness that pervaded the

Toun crews: bothy burlesque, *above*, at supper time for the visiting photo-grapher's benefit and to emphasize the rough lifestyle of the farmtoun men. The diet was brose, made by mixing oatmeal with hot water in the wooden caups. Each man here has his own individual flagon of milk. *Below*, later and more sedate and "framed" by a big harvest shelving, a typical group of the early 1920s at Kirktown of Slains, in Aberdeenshire, with broad bonnets, melodeon and the little kitchen maid in the middle.

Horse of pride: *left*, the perfect sire and father-figure of the Clydesdale breed in the 1920s, Willie Dunlop's famous stallion Dunure Footprint. His fee was 120 guineas and his prowess was proverbial.

Code for the road, *right*, as the ploughman plods his weary way home at the end of the day seated on his nearside beast, his land horse and usually the more intelligent of his pair.

Below right, a day away from the plough and one to remember: strength and a docile grace are reflected here in an ornately-harnessed and heavily-ticketed show winner of the later 1920s.

Days in the plough: winter-long the workaday ploughing, *above*, was the main farmtoun task, continuing about some touns even as the snow fell. It was about the turn of the year that the young horsemen got a chance to show their skills at ploughing matches round the countryside. *Below*, a young contender and his well-turned-out pair of the 1920s pause momentarily for the camera. It was a day when a man passed over in the ploughing might go home consoled with a prize in the harness class.

Once, the sower was a symbolic figure striding the spring fields: his work began the sequence that ended months later in the crescendo of harvest. The grain seed was scattered one-handed from the sowing-sheet, *right*.

The shoulder-slung hopper, *far right*, made it two-armed work but either way the task demanded a metronomic mastery of pace and timing. The hopper faded from the toun fields with the arrival of the broadcast-sower and the corndrill. Only the old crofter men, without capital, kept faith with it.

Harrowing time: three Clydesdales are yoked here in the harrows, that quintessential tool of springtime, to tear down the grey furrows of winter. The scene brought hope to the heart and inspired the ballad singers.

Checking the seed: one of the rare pictures, *above*, of Donald McKelvie (right), the Arran grocer whose genius gave Scottish (and English) farming a whole new range of potato varieties. He began his experiments with potatoes he found sprouting in his wife's kitchen basket. *Below*, the moment of commitment as the seed potatoes are painstakingly placed in the bottom of the drill. It was a job, in the 1890s, that brought sun-bonneted women into the fields.

The potato-planting, *above*, got a little easier with the years as some touns allowed the seed to be dropped rather than placed in the bottom of the drill. It was less back-breaking. Some tasks, however, did not change and the sheep-shearing, *below*, still brought the kind of yearly struggle epitomized in this turn-of-the-century encounter between the hand-clippers and a bewildered ewe.

The end of the farmtoun day: mellow sunlight bathes the scene and lends a delusory enchantment as the horsemen come home from the fields.

croft kitchen when the seed was in. It was like a blessing on the house.

It fascinated the mind that old spring ritual, even that of the douce man of letters, the sage of Chelsea, Thomas Carlyle, who, captive to the mesmeric grace of the sower and Border bairn that he was, responded with uncharacteristic exuberance:

> Now hands to the seed-sheet boys,
> We step and we cast, old time is on the wing
> And would ye partake of harvest's joys
> The corn must be sown in spring.

The "seed-sheet" was the precursor of the hopper — the canvas tray of Muir's memory, the *happer* of the farmtoun countryside — a linen sheet from which the sower cast the seed-corn.

Stephens, nearer that time, is as usual highly informative:

> In former times the sower by hand in Scotland was habited in a peculiar manner. He sowed by one hand only, and had a sowing sheet wound round him. The most convenient sheet is of linen. It is made to have an opening large enough to admit the head and right arm of the sower through it, and a portion of the sheet to rest upon his left shoulder. On distending the mouth of the doubled part with both hands, and receiving the seed into it, the loose part of the sheet is wound tight over the left hand, by which it is firmly held, while the load of corn is supported by the part of the sheet which crosses the breast and passes under the right arm behind the back to the left shoulder.

The cost of such a sheet was about two shillings in Stephens' time; the sower's rate of work he estimated at about sixteen acres for the then-standard ten-hour day. The *happer* when it came must have been a godsend to men so diabolically swaddled. It also increased the daily area: on Stephens' reckoning, to twenty acres.

Such, once, had been the in-come of spring. With it often enough in that northern landscape had come the "thigging" that Murray refers to, when the poor — the old croft folk working the barest cultivable margins of the land — without seed corn and with barely the will to scatter it, went round the bigger touns begging the grain with which to sow their stony, hillset fields. It was a practice so usual and necessary as hardly to be considered a disgrace, only the natural outcome of things: those with nothing begging from those who might have a little to spare after a moderate harvest. Seed would be given willingly where coin (with all its other temptations) might have been withheld.

The reality of the farmtouns' spring work and its relentless pace though was something different, and we catch its indelible echoes in the bothy ballads and in one in particular, "Harrowing Time", long sung by men like John Strachan to the dirding thump of that even better-known favourite "Drumdelgie".

> Cauld winter it is noo awa,
>   And spring has come again;
> And the cauld, dry winds o' March month
>   Has driven awa the rain.
>
> Has driven awa the dreary rain,
>   Likewise the frost and snaw;
> So our foreman in the mornin'
>   He's ordered out to saw.
>
> The rest o' us merry ploughboys
>   We a' maun follow fast;
> We're told by our hard master
>   There is no time to rest.
>
> We're told that we must be a-yoke
>   Each mornin' sharp by five;
> And quickly owre and owre the rigs
>   Our horses we maun drive.
>
> We drive them on to twelve o'clock,
>   Syne home to dinner go;
> And before the end of one short hour
>   The farmer cries, "Hillo!"
>
> Till the farmer cries, "Hillo, boys,
>   It's time to yoke again,
> See that ye get it harrowed oot,
>   For fear that it comes rain."

Murray's verse and Muir's prose may have their heady images but for the old folk who once worked the ballad touns it is that gravelly voice from yesterday that evokes the raw edge of a farmtoun spring.

When the onslaught of seedtime began it was usually with the blessing of a scouring late-March wind that lacerated the cheeks and nipped at the fingers. All the same it was the kind of drying wind — a *drooth*, they called it — that the parks and the touns had been waiting for. Now the fields were alive with folk, figures slow-motioned for as far as the eye could see. Shafts of watery sun glinted on harness, dust trailed the harrows; there was suddenly, unspoken, a conspiracy of men with nature. False starts were made by inexperienced grieves too anxious to please their masters but always there came that moment of consensus, a feeling that flitted down the howe and through the countryside like a contagion, a tide that gathered its own momentum.

They say that once, away down in the mists of Argyll and far, far from the northern touns, the old men of the land had a strange and near-pagan way of gauging the approach of seedtime. They would set little sticks into the ploughed ground, leaving them there for a day or two. Then they would pull them from the earth, sniff them with great concentration before quietly replacing them — or holding them joyously aloft with a shout that the earth was "in rut".

If the old farmtoun men ever heard of such things, it is likely that they took a quiet bit smile to themselves. For them, the moment was something felt in the soul, smelt in the air — a thing born of long understanding of the soil. In Buchan's bare acres, as elsewhere, it was a final judgement taken through the gouging heel and the scuff of the toecap of a tackety boot and maybe not infrequently on a walk through the Sunday quiet of the parks. What was never in doubt was that the "spring wark", when it began, was in earnest.

It was a time of tooth and untender claw. The grubber, the heavy cultivator, ripped across the land, overthrowing the long reign of the stubble furrows. Clod and sod were unceremoniously riven from the long sleep of winter by strong curved tines that could come shatteringly to a halt as they hit hidden stone. It was the kind of tiring work, a day behind the grubber, that sent a man home at night convinced that one of his legs had foreshortened on the other. Yet such savagery had its essential purpose: it scourged the field that had but a few months earlier relinquished its autumn corn in preparation for a new crop cycle and a return to "clean land".

What the grubber tore up was the *growth*, the weeds. The toun's seed ground would be further teased by tine and harrow. It was the harrow, as the old bothy ballad suggests, that was the quintessential tool of seedtime. It was quicker work than the grubber and the walk was livelier: man, harrows and Clydesdales marched and countermarched the landscape in a perpetual swirl of dust, cajoling and cross-hatching, reducing at last what had been earth inert to the friable loam of seedbed. On the old stubble the toothed harrows gave way to the links harrow. After the grubber, its touch was a caress: it rolled the dried *growth* together like a carpet and left it in heaps to be gathered. Above it all, the peewits swooped and birled in a flash of black and white and bottle green, piercing the sky with their shrill cries. Theirs was the music of a northern seedtime.

The gathering of *growth* has now been made unnecessary by the march of weed-killing chemicals and the kind of stage-management far from the routines of the old farmtoun fields. Yet once "gathering *growth*" was a ritual that brought unaccustomed folk to the fields, usually the feeing bailies, most reluctantly, bringing with them their four-pronged forks with a spare for the grieve, who might lend a hand. (When the touns advertised for "working grieves" they meant it.) The *growth*-gathering was a sort of muck-spreading in reverse and brought a similar pattern to the parks: heaps grided across the field (and sometimes burned as they stood) were carted to the *growth* midden, built usually in the middle of the field. Strange and illogical that seemed until you learned that, pushed to the dykeside, it could become a launching pad for an old ewe with an eye on the greener pastures of the adjoining field.

Less smelly than the dung midden, it stood as a monument as the years and the attrition of the elements gradually "moolded it doon", reducing it finally to compost to be spread again through the field before it went under the plough to be the ley corn. Its prominence meantime — its unsightliness where it interrupted the straight run of the drills — was a constant reminder that it, too, was part and parcel of the cycle of fertility and decay and that nothing in that landscape was ever wasted. Where everything, like man himself, had its cycle, what nature gave up she had inviolably returned to her.

And in the days of spring as the *peesies* pirouetted and shrieked the work too had its pattern, equally inviolable. The ploughed ley was traditionally first to be readied as a seedbed. The harrows alone tore down the furrows, passing and repassing across the field. The sequence was as unrelenting as the seasons themselves, the cultivation varying only slightly with the crop to be sown — that is, with the field's place in the rotational calendar. The ley oats took precedence over the clean-land corn (which would have to wait for the last of the turnips to be cleared off the ground) as did the "yavil crop", a second year's sowing of corn, snatched as a kind of fertility bonus in the rotation, that often gave a modest yield though rarely anything like the return of the first. Yet the fact that such a field became known round the ballad touns as the "yavil shift" indicates that the custom was not at all uncommon and something beyond being merely the opportunist whim of an entrepreneurial grieve. Into the clean-land oats, in the cleaned turnip ground, went the undersown grass seed that would be the following year's hay and ultimately the toun's temporary pasture.

With the seed sown, the harrow returned to its work, across and up and down the park. Only the universal acceptance of the corn-drill, which buried the seed in a shallow trench, would make one pass of that hallowed implement suffice to bury the seed corn beyond the beaks of Murray's "wily craws".

Finally with spring well through, and into the middle of May, it was the turn of the turnip ground. Such then was the frenzy, the need to catch nature while the mood was on her, that it was possible to see cameo'd and telescoped in a single field all the elements of seedtime at work simultaneously — a cameo from Stephens' textbook. On the *neep grun* the drill plough worked at the harrow's tail raising that ribbing of ridges into which at the old traditionist touns the dung would be flung. Spreaders teased it along the drill-bottoms and the bone-davie blessed it, the second horseman with his pair "splitting" the foreman's drills again to bury the muck. In the *neep* park, the seed-barrow went on, leaving its "thread" of seed on the flattened top of the drill. Potato crops in their turn got a similar preparation, with the seed tubers, about the old-fashioned touns, often being cosily nestled in the dung before the drill was "split" to cover them.

Yet the years would change the old springtime rituals: the touns would put away the grubber and the spring-tines with the Clydesdale pairs and into their place would come the steely efficiency of the disc harrows, a fearsome tool more like a weapon of war. The clods trembled before it. It went through them like the knife through a croft-wife's butter. The tide was already beginning to turn; the time coming when man would no longer merely be nature's hand-servant. But the "spirit" of seedtime remained, as all-pervading as it had been in the landscape of Edwin Muir's childhood. The ritual in its essence was unchanged though the powerful image of the sower — that solitary figure, flinging from the waist-level hopper — had faded before the greater precisions of the corndrill and the "broadcast", which was particularly favoured by the touns. Its long seed-kist (dividing to fold parallel with the shafts to pass through the field-gate) slung above equally slim wheels made the corndrill look cumbersome in comparison. Today it would get a design prize for functional elegance. It was, however, but a mechanical nod to the hopper and the quaint and unmusical seed-fiddle, an American invention of the late 1800s, whose bow scattered seed with the same rhythmic insistence.

In the turnip-field too innovation had been similarly slow-footed since the early days of indiscriminate broadcast-sowing. In the early drill husbandry of the crop, before the *neep* barrow with its variable sowing rate had broken upon the scene, a boon in a region so devoted to the turnip, there had evolved the bobbin' john, a device of such devastating simplicity that folk wondered why it had not been thought of two centuries earlier. It was basically a canister on a stick that came unaccountably but not altogether illogically to bear the name of a tepid revolutionary, the Jacobite Earl of Mar. The bobbin' john — gone somewhat from the land of late though it surfaced regularly not so many years ago with the old sheep hand-clippers and the plump churn at old crofters' roups — was the brainchild of Mr Udny, of Udny, that Aberdeenshire parish so much esteemed for the quality of the dairying wives it produced. Again William Alexander, in *Northern Rural Life*, speaking of change:

Dr James Anderson who was a keen improver and reformer of old things generally credits his patron, Mr Udny of Udny, with a useful invention in implements. That gentleman, who filled

the office of a commissioner of excise, was an earnest agricultural improver. He was an early and successful cultivator of the
turnip, and his invention was an improved sower — cost
eightpence to a shilling. It was a perforated tin box with a
wooden handle — neither more nor less than a "Bobbin' John",
which was carried along in the hand over the drill top and shaken
to throw out the seed. Its capabilities as a sower are strongly
lauded by Dr Anderson, by whom it is averred that many
hundreds of persons who could neither have purchased nor used
a fine apparatus had, by the possession of it, been induced to
enter keenly into the cultivation of turnips.

Traditionally it was the horse-roller that put the finishing seal to
the sown and harrowed corn parks, compacting the soil, pressing
down the small stones. In doing so it looked forward to harvest and
the unimpeded progress of the binder, for such obstructions might
foul its cutter-bar. The old five-foot-wide stone roller lingered still
around the touns of the 1930s, invariably red-painted, but the
main roller in the farmtoun fields by then was one machined in the
factory, hollow-cylindered and split in the middle to give ease of
turning on the endrig.

Its passage signalled the end of the corn-sowing. With the *neeps*
sown too the fields lay tidy and transformed. The pace slackened
and the harrow went to the *smiddy* to have its iron teeth sharpened
for another spring. It was time for the farmtoun men to think of a
new *fee* and another toun. It was seldom indeed that the footloose
lads of the bothies who put in a toun's seed stayed on to reap its
harvest.

VII

The Ballet of the Hay

HAYMAKING, IN ANY meaningful way, came late into the northern landscape of the ballad touns. Neglected as a serious art until into the 1800s, with the spread of cultivated hay, it had earlier had a very poor standing in the priority of farmtoun tasks, taking a poor third place at times to both the grain and potato harvests. Cut from the midge-ridden water meadows, it had always been something of a snatched crop anyway. The Scottish minister-novelist S. R. Crockett, the son of a tenant farmer and king among the so-called Kailyarders of his craft, claimed (and one assumes truthfully) to have been making *hairst* bands for the wheat by the age of five and, recalling the days of his Galloway childhood in the farm of Little Duchrae, remembered being summoned from his young bed in the middle of the night to save the meadow hay as the region's River Dee burst its banks:

> . . . in the hastiest attire we rushed out into the night under the light of the stars, or by flickering torches, the older men, the women, the males and even such children as I was, each to wrest from the waters some portion of the spoils; for our hay meant the rent for the farm, the bread for the winter, the daily loaf-mass for many days to come. And into the water we went and snatched all the hay that could be saved, and plunged and groaned and struggled in our fight for our bread against the disastrous waters. I can still see my uncles breast-high in the black flood.

Making due allowance for the minister's trade of letters, there is no doubting that the loss of hay to a toun was something of a setback — though meadow hay was less a factor in northern farmtoun life, where the folk took a bit of bog grass where they could and were duly thankful. It was not, by later standards, great fodder, simply the natural grasses that grew with the *sproats*, the rushes, on the damp, low-lying ground where the dew gathered.

At the start of the 1700s, the hayfield did not exist. It was that indefatigable improver Sir Archibald Grant of Monymusk, never a man to take a back seat, who claimed to have been the first to make cultivated hay north of the Tay. He may have been right, though Mackintosh of Borlum, languishing in his Edinburgh dungeon, gave some credit elsewhere. Haymaking, he said, came north to Moray, northernmost of the ballad counties, in 1706, with an Englishwoman, Lady Elisabeth Mordaunt of Peterborough, when she married the eldest son of the Duke of Gordon. The old Jacobite said of Lady Huntly — most chivalrously considering his situation — that she put "her neighbourhood in the right way of making their Hay, which before they mightily wanted; and in many parts of Scotland still do . . .".

In the Mearns, according to William Alexander in his *Northern Rural Life* ·

Sir William Nicolson of Glenbervie was the first person . . . who raised hay from sown grass, about the year 1730, the seeds he used being the best he could select amongst the natural meadow hay. These he sowed amongst oats of the third or fourth crop from ley; and the result was so superior to the ordinary mode of allowing the soil to replenish itself with wild herbage as to excite the astonishment of his neighbours.

One of them was probably Mr Graham of Morphie, who was the first to introduce to the area "broad clover", the result, it is said, being "a vast acquisition to the night food of the horses, in a country where they had been accustomed to be fed with thistles only, from the corn fields, or with the coarsest of aquatic herbage from the different swamps". Mr Graham, not at all surprisingly, was said to be a man with "very superior cattle and horses".

Still and all, it would be at least 1770 before sown grasses got anything like a general following and became widely cultivated. With them, thanks probably to Lady Huntly, would come one of the most pleasing patterns of yesterday's summers: the disciplined, formal ballet of the hayfield.

It was a pattern well-established in the lush green meadows of the English shires and its methods in the early 1700s have been remarkably well documented by a recently-discovered but unknown artist

whose brush depicted the hay scene of his time at Gloucester-
shire's Dixton Manor in the Severn Valley.

His work shows in the panoramic spread of one large canvas —
in a "set" that could be straight from the stage of Sadler's Wells —
the whole sequence of the manor's haymaking. It shows a large
field with 120 figures, not all of them working. Scythers move
across the field, 23 of them in echelon, a curving line of advance. A
piper plays at their head, emphasising the almost martial patterns
to right and left of them. The hay is seen, fresh-mown, in the
swath, then in small haycocks, and going from small to larger
haycocks. English wagons — graceful almost against the crude
utility of the Scottish farmtoun carts — their four-horse teams
harnessed in-line in traces, traverse the field loaded and unloaded;
a line of celebrating Morris dancers plunge through the hedge into
the darkened foreground. It is possible that the artist may have
seen it so, but more likely that his fascination initially was for the
ritual and pattern of the English haysel or hay harvest that became
lost to us with the coming of the baler, whose own art is a practical
but unromantic cubism. What he has done is to telescope the
pattern and movement into one exquisitely ordered scene.

Yet it is unlikely that its sequences are far agley. Women rake
the swaths; men form the haycocks. It is a scene picked up in in
in somewhat better detail well over a hundred years later in
Stephens' *Book of the Farm*, whose illustrations show near-identical
methods.

This then was the ritual that Grant and his co-improvers
absorbed when they put cultivated hay into their crop rotations.
The haymaking of the ballad touns, however, was a far cry from
the rustic idyllicism of the Cotswold country. Theirs was a dance
mostly to the measure of the slow waltz rather than the birl of
dashing reel: the precise orchestration, as always, depended on the
weather. But of all the patterns that summer imposed on that
cloud-grey landscape, those of the old hay park were by far the
most pleasing.

The hay crop of the old touns was taken in the hallowed cycle
between the clean-land corn and the lying in ley, the arable
grazing. It was undersown in the previous year's grain, its "nurse
crop" — so that a man in the hurry of *hairst* could find himself
suddenly castigated by the grieve for recklessly lowering the
binder's cutter bar to the danger of shooting grass-heads.

The practice of making that first year's grass into hay was not entirely new: those earliest of farming improvers, the monks, had done it. At Coupar Abbey, early fenced fields of sown grass had alternated with corn crops and it had long been the custom by 1463, when we first come to hear of it, to make hay on the first year's ley. It was an example that remarkably foreshadowed the cropping ritual of the farmtouns, and a kind of grass husbandry the touns would eventually revive and bring to a high perfection.

With the hay off the ground the field became grass for years to come, about the only variable in the then almost inviolable cycle and, as we have seen, at once an indicator to the countryside's prosperity: if times were good its acreage diminished; as ill-times loomed the pasture increased in order to save labour and fertilisers as the touns rode out the storm.

The haymaking fell into the farmtoun calendar about mid-July or early August. It was in a way a prelude to *hairst* for long before it was the hand-maiden of the corn-harvest, the hayfield was the scythe's arena. Everybody, including the old crofter men, made "a pickle hay" and in the sweep of the scythe there lingered still the dream of Arcady. The men, grizzled and callow, who went out to mow their meadows, moved down the field in that traditional order so vividly captured by an English brush in a far landscape, the foreman as always in the lead and setting the fastest pace he could.

In the hay-cutting of the mid-1800s and on the later touns of the 1920s and 1930s, the men wore only their shirts and their trousers. It was hot work under a summer sun and the home-brewed ale went out to the field with them in that earlier time if not in the latter years of the era. And if the scene by then lacked a piper, the scythe made its own sweet music. There were old farmtoun men — and there are still a few, virtuosos of the rural blade — whose mastery of it made it all seem effortless and who turned its action, its sweep and curve, into a thing of grace.

In the English shires they liked, ideally, to cut their hay when it was in full flower; the men of the ballad touns took it, as often they took their women, a little past its bloom — in the speak of the old touns, just as it was *gaun owre* and the flower starting to wilt. As the swaths fell neatly from the scythe blade they set the old pattern that would continue up to World War Two and a little beyond it. Even the horse-drawn machine-mower, developed to its full

potential by the last quarter of the 1800s, did not alter the methods
of handling hay; it merely hastened the cutting, heavily reducing
the man-hours and (of course) phasing out that rustic figure
beloved of calendar artists, the scytheman.

The mower now was a new kind of man: he rode his reaping
machine on an iron leaf-sprung seat that dangled him in space well
to the rear of all the machine's mechanisms and the pair of
Clydesdales drawing it. Mostly the machine-mowers had their
cutter-bars to the right so that progress round the standing crop
would be in a clockwise direction, though Continental countries,
with typical contrariness, largely favoured the contra rotation. A
staunchly favoured machine was the Albion made by the firm of
Harrison, MacGregor (alas, in Greater Manchester), though it
was not misplaced patriotism alone that gave it a good name in the
bothies of the time but its record for reliability.

Most mowing machines, like the early binders, had a bout width
of five feet that matched more than favourably with the scyther's cut
of no more than four feet. For the man on its seat the job was an easier
one than driving the binder for if it called for slickness of action it
was usually only with the oilcan. (The liberality of oil about a
farmtoun was prodigious.) It was practically impossible for a man to
make himself the laughing-stock of the parish on the mower, which
he could so easily do on the binder. Again, in the hayfield there was
rarely a procession of machines, close-marshalled, that could be
infuriatingly delayed. Most touns made do with one, a fact not
unconnected with the capital outlay that machine-farming involved.

Beyond its speed, the machine-mower altered little. It left the
hay in the swath as the old scyther had done, ribbing the field like
the stripes on a herringboned tweed. And in the swaths the hay
remained for a day or two, less only if the weather were
exceptionally kind. The handtool of the hay park was the two-
pronged fork bought of the general merchant or more probably the
blacksmith, who was the ironmonger of the old countryside and
stocked such things in his loft. The word on its shaft sounded like
the motto of a Scottish regiment and proclaimed its worth,
promising dowty work with such brand-names as "Standfast" and
"Neverbend". Yet in the end it was the weather that made hay, not
men. A wet summer could be disastrous and men stood helplessly
by as their hopes dwindled.

In the swath, the hay was tossed like candy floss to let the air into it and turned (on to fresh ground) to allow it to wilt and dry and to lose its moisture content. Sun and wind conditioned it; the skill was to preserve its nutrient value as much as possible, though even in ideal weather the process itself led to loss. Late-cut, the hay would become indigestible, in a really bad year, worthless.

The hay was "made" when it was *wun*, fairly dry. The term, peculiar to that countryside, was one that applied its judgement of optimum condition to many commodities of the region, including the brushwood surreptitiously gathered in the laird's wood and brought home to lie by the house-gable till it had mellowed enough to be suitable fire-kindling. The hay in the swath, however, was not turned by the pronged end of the fork but by reversing it, to use the well-polished shaft. The crop might have to be turned several times before it was considered suitably *wun*. With that came the time for closing ranks: working across the swaths with the horse-rake, tumbling them together into bulkier windrows. Four or five rows merged into one, the ratio depending on the weight of the crop, to begin the ever-telescoping patterns that would slowly win the crop and, increasingly with each stage, protect it, in a climate never notably kind to the making of hay, from the effect of bad weather.

Again the line of the mowing and the swath-turning was re-established as the farmtoun men worked down the length of the field, each to his own windrow, pushing the hay in front of his fork to make small *coles* (haycocks) at regular intervals. Each *cole* was about three feet high, no more, and three feet wide at its base. And so it went on . . . up and down the windrows they went until the conical mounds of the small *coles* grided the field in perfect formation.

Nor did the ballet end there. In a day or two, the pattern would be perpetuated more pronouncedly as the small *coles* were knocked into big *coles*, twice the height and similarly girthed, in a ratio usually of three-to-one. In all this, as the men worked down the rows, hardly a step was wasted: nobody about a farmtoun ever walked a step farther than he had to (unless it was to meet the kitchen lass) and the farmer never wanted him to. Economy of movement was the hallmark of a well-managed toun.

Wind-battered and lashed by rain, the big *coles* in a year of "late wark" could stand there nearly for ever, and if need be till after the corn harvest was put past, before being ricked. By then, the field's "second crap" of grass could well be threatening to engulf them. In an intermediary operation, however, the *coles* might be gathered into *trump coles*, built perhaps in a corner of the field, their name indicating the intervention of the heavy farmtoun foot and their compaction under the tackety boots of the man who *trumpit* them as they were built.

Yet occasionally, and almost unbelievably, there were summers when the extended ballet of the hay park could be dramatically foreshortened. Then the weather smiled on the touns and their hay could be ricked straight from the small *coles*. It came home to the toun on the carts with their *hairst* frames fitted, the loads built to a height of three feet or so above them, the horseman, as in *hairst*, sliding off the back of his load to lead his pair home.

The stacks were built in a corner of the cornyard and the hay was never ricked wet, in case it "heated" and caught fire. The ricks, though they too had to keep the rain out, demanded less finesse of the builder than the corn stacks, and often stood a little taller in the yard. The size, with that faultless logic, would depend on the size of the hayloft; good touns worked on an honoured equation: that the volume of one should match the capacity of the other. The idea had its aesthetic as well as its practical appeal: it avoided that eyesore of a cornyard, the tattered stump of a rick sprawled over its *foon* and the need to protect it meantime by drawing an old tarpaulin over it.

But just as frequently the ricks might be built in a corner of the hayfield and fenced off to foil the beasts that would later graze it. For that, it was simply a matter of "dragging the *coles*" to the side of the field, a task that needed only a docile horse and the chain or rope to loop round the base of the haycock. The chain was attached to the *theets* or to the swingletree and the horseman took a *hurl* on the *cole*, ostensibly to make it sit better on the rope or chain and glide more smoothly over the shorn field. It was a fine excuse for laziness and gave him the chance to fill his pipe since the Clydesdale knew the way to the rick as well as he did. Not a few of the touns hoarded their bits of *cairt girdin*, parts of old iron wheel-rims, to make a loop for "dragging the *coles*".

There were places where they built *soos* (sows) rather than ricks; it was the nearest a poor beleaguered countryside came to recognising the function of the Dutch barn. Like the *strae soo* built during the visits of the threshing-mill, these were rectangular in shape, twelve feet at least (and often a bit more) in height before being *heided oot* to an over-all eighteen to twenty feet. About a modest toun the hay *soo* would be perhaps 25 feet long, although there was no limit except the boundary ditch of the stackyard. *Trumpin* it (compacting the hay) was the only building problem; as with the *strae soo*, horses were sometimes used, later being lowered to terra firma in a sling. It always helped, of course, if you had a Clydesdale with a head for heights — or failing that, an *orra loon*, leading it round, who liked to live dangerously.

Stephens called haymaking the "handmaid of stock-rearing" and, unaware of the mechanical revolution soon to come, somewhat rashly predicted: "As stock-rearing increases or diminishes so in all probability will haymaking." His words, all the same, underline how closely the task once stood to the core of farmtoun activity. If your toun went short of hay you went cap in hand to your neighbour to see if he had some to sell, a second-year rick perhaps, inconveniently still occupying a corner of his cornyard. He might sell it to you with great glee, having long convinced himself that he would never get rid of it. High loads travelled between one toun and the next, roped securely against a wind that was always a-blow and sometimes strong enough to take your bonnet into the next county. For it was not cheap: £4 to £5 a ton in 1891 when the foreman's weekly wage was less than a quarter of that figure. Crofter folk, always with less *siller* and fewer friends, turned the clock back when all else failed and went to the hill to harvest the whins and broom that grew there to feed to their stock.

For all its importance, there seems to have been no great rush into the early machinery of haymaking. *Tummlin tams* were a feature of farming life, yet a great many touns managed to live without them, and so long as labour was cheap and freely available tedders and swath-turners were not widely sought to do the job that teams of bothymen could do with their pitchfork handles. Most touns, it would seem, took the view that if you had the one, what possible use could you have for the other.

Even as the first fever for silage took hold in the 1930s and the forward-looking dairytouns turned their attention to the alternatives, cutting tares for their tower silos before *hairst* and pitting draff bought cheap from the surrounding distilleries, the reliance on hay hardly slackened. In 1934, Aberdeenshire alone, heartland of the ballad touns, took 81,000 tons of sweet-smelling hay off 55,000 acres at an average weight of 30 hundredweight per acre, with a further 3,640 tons off 3,250 acres of permanent grass — by far the biggest tonnage that year to go into the haylofts of any county in Scotland.

Hay in fact would continue to be made round the northern touns for as long as their stables housed Clydesdale pairs. Waistcoated men on the mower-seat (for it was not the hot work of the scythe) would take round the clover parks on an easy rein to initiate the old sacrosanct patterns that had once long ago percolated north, part of another age and a merrier England.

In time the crop would come in from the cornyard to fill the hayloft above the stable. It was a comfortable place the hayloft, a sanctuary for northern convicts on the run, for wandering tramps and circumspect lovers. For a toun's bairns it was a place to tumble boisterously in the hours after school was out, occasionally for the lonely child a place of solitude and secret enchantment, as John R. Allan, in his evocative *Farmer's Boy*, remembers:

The hayloft above the stable always fascinated me with its floor polished smooth as a mirror by a hundred hay harvests. It had a door in the gable end through which the hay was forked from a long cart and packed in tightly to the roof. . . . Once deep in the hay, you felt secure from the world. . . .

With the hay off it, a field slid into its years of lying in ley, the temporary grass on which the touns grazed their black *stirks*, their dairy cows and their Clydesdale pairs. It was a time that took the field out of the yearly cropping cycle yet it was by no means neglected. There were old farmer men with bad breaths and inescapable debts who had as high a fetish about their grass and as unshakeable a belief in it as they had in their turnips. They saw it as the great succourer of stock.

Going through their byres as spring wore on, they might pause by a beast that was thriving indifferently on a diet of straw and turnips and nod understandingly as they put a kindly hand on its rump: "Nivver ye min', man. Ye'll be fine aince ye wir oot tae the girss. That'll pit claes on ye" — meaning that the pasture would fill out the beast's frame and put a gloss on its coat.

Most of those grizzled old diehards, men with an earthy wit and drooping Kitcheners, liked to see "a guid pluck" of grass before they put out their *nowt* after their winter confinement. But grass-conscious though they were, few touns pushed their preoccupation with it as far as Collynie, the stronghold of William Duthie, Shorthorn king. There, in the 1920s, when the thistle-cutting time came round, just after the turnip-hoeing, the task took most of the week. Horsemen, divorced from their pairs, patrolled the toun's parks not only with scythes sharpened and at the ready but also with knapsacks on their backs and small spades slung over their shoulders so that they could at the same time take out any docken plants that were clouding the sward.

Not many touns were as fussy about dockens, and you could not live long about a farmtoun before becoming grateful for them, especially when you were taken a bit short in the cornyard. Kleeney did not have a big following in the old countryside. Most touns, however, liked to keep the thistles down and at least sent the bailie out with the scythe occasionally in the hope that he would do more damage to the plants than to himself. About small places, the task fell to the farmer himself: with his supper taken and his pipe lit in the long summer evenings, he took his scythe down and went out to wander the parks.

VIII

The Rituals of Harvest

THERE IS SOME uncertainty now about who first put the scythe among the northern corn, though, significantly, the two principal claimants were men of the Aberdeenshire countryside. The Rev. J. B. Pratt, historian of the flat Buchan plain, would hear of no other than a Mr Gordon of Cairnbulg, in 1808. Mr Gordon had been in faraway Devon and there seen the scythe used to reap the grain crops. Returning to his toun, the Home Farm of Cortes, with all the passion of a committed convert, he ordered the scythers into the oats — only to make himself, poor man, the speak and laughing-stock of the immediate district. But whether he was first or not, Mr Gordon was not alone for very long. Says John Ord, the Glasgow police chief who collected the old bothy songs with such diligence and published his *Bothy Songs and Ballads* about 1930:

> The reaping scythe was introduced into the North of Scotland by William Anderson, farmer, Hatton of Fintray, Aberdeen-shire, in 1810, but the old shearing hook was not quite superseded by the scythe for many years afterwards. The shearing was mostly done by women. The value of a day's work was calculated by the number of thraves cut. . . .
>
> After the introduction of the scythe, the best men cut the corn, the women gathered it into sheaves, and made the bands, while the younger men, as a rule, bound and stooked the sheaves.

There was competition amid the corn-rigs, as there had always been, though now it got a macho element. Thus the opening lines of the bothy ballad, "The Kiethen Hairst":

> The hairst began on Kiethen land
> The seventeenth of September,
> In the year of eighteen seventy-two,
> As we may well remember.

When Willie Moir with scythe in hand,
    He quickly led the van,
Says, "Now, my lads, it's rig and rig,
    We will see wha's the man."

It was a challenge, directly laid, as contentious as prize-fighting. But let Helen Beaton, in her book *At the Back o' Benachie*, set the scene as a modest uplands toun takes up the song of *hairst*:

Let us bring before our mind's eye a ripe field of yellow corn. Three strong men have got their scythe blades . . . into grand "fettle" and denuding themselves of all clothing except their shirts and trousers, the latter garment being suspended only by one brace, and carefully lifting their scythes to the other side of the dyke, they vault over and stand with the corn nearly reaching their shoulders.

Thus was the entry of the gladiators into the field of contest:

When extra hands were required for the harvest there was often an "ill-will" at the foreman, or probably some old strife might rankle in the mind of one of the "cutters", when it would be determined that the foreman should have a hot time by "cutting him oot". This meant keeping so close behind him on the harvest field that he would find it impossible to take on so much as he would like on his scythe. When this occurred the tempers of all the workers were ruffled more or less, and as the women would take no time to make correct bands, and would substitute "wisps" the bandsters would give utterance to words not to be found in the dictionary, as they ran between the sheaves, with the perspiration flowing down their faces.

Yet, where the pattern of work was more orderly, the scene could almost have an idyllic quality as the old rhythms of *hairst* transcended the years and lit delight in the country heart.

It was a fine spectacle to watch three or more scythes "swish, swishing" through the corn, and the rhythm of them as they swung on and on, while the men's feet moved forward in unison, and all were joyous and happy.

But if there were sweet *hairsts* that stayed long in the mind, there
were heavy ones whose memory lingered even longer:

> Sometimes . . . the corn crop was a heavy one and the gatherers
> would be hard-pressed. . . . The bandsters had comparatively
> easy work and frequently stooked also unless they were very
> young lads. Tailors, joiners and smiths often engaged themselves
> to the farmer for the harvest season. The tailor's hands were soft,
> and the knuckles of the right hand got scratched and sore by
> putting in the band knot. In those days the raker was least to be
> envied on the harvest field. With a belt across his shoulders and
> breast and with a hand on the handle of the rake, he would pull
> along until his knees were almost bent to the ground, and if the
> grass was thick and the stubble long, he deserved all pity.

The observer again is Helen Beaton, and her words catch the tenor
of the old *hairsts*, the trials and the rituals, the old pattern of work
familiar in the fields of the ballad touns until 1870 or so.

If it had its own strict customs, those that the scythe usurped had
been part of an even more complex organisation and the days of the
sickle or *heuk*. Then, as Ord says, the shearing was done mainly by
the women of the countryside. In the Highlands and even in the
Lowlands — one Mearns piper at least got his *hairst fee* with the rest
of the shearing gang — the work had an almost martial flavour, as the
roving Dr Johnson, during his celebrated tour, noted in Raasay:

> I saw the harvest of a small field. The women reaped the corn and
> the men bound up the sheaves. The strokes of the sickle were
> timed by the modulation of the harvest song, in which all their
> voices were united. They accompany, in the Highlands, every
> action which can be done in equal time, with an appropriate strain
> which has, they say, not much meaning; but its effects are
> regularity and cheerfulness.

Edward Burt, in the Highlands earlier in the 1700s, with his army
connection, drew an even closer analogy with the military:

> In the larger farms, belonging to the gentlemen of the clan, where
> there are a number of women employed in the harvest-work, they
> all keep time together, by several tones of the voice; and stoop and

rise together, as regularly as a rank of soldiers, when they ground their arms. Sometimes they are incited to their work by the sound of a bagpipe; and by either of these, they proceed with great alacrity, it being disgraceful for any one to be out of time with the sickle.

In later time, when the old clan system had been smashed for ever, the piper would remain at times a part of the *hairst* scene, hired as always in the hope of heating the harvesters' blood and getting faster results. Still, it may have kept a piper or two in work at a time when they were facing a high rate of redundancy.

That old handtool, the *heuk*, linked the *hairst* with the feudal past and a time when the laird had taken his dues as a matter of right: in the early 1800s a Haddo House tenant would still be giving a day's shearing at harvest to the reckoning of sixpence a day, for the laird's rent-roll about then brought him 462 estate *heuks* (or days). The *heuk* existed in two forms: the toothed sickle and as a smooth-edged blade. Henry Stephens, that expert on mid-1800s' farmtoun affairs, is precise and illuminating:

The toothed sickle . . . has a blade of iron, with an edging of steel. The teeth are formed by striking with a chisel and hammer, in the manner of file-cutting, the cutting being only on the lower side; but when the blade has been bent to the proper form, tempered, and ground on the smooth side, the serratures are brought prominently out on the edge of the blade; and as the striking of the teeth is performed in a position oblique to the edge of the blade, at an angle of about 70°, the serratures on the edge acquire what is called a *hook* towards the helve, thus causing the implement to cut keenly in that direction when drawn through the standing corn. When the blade has been thus finished, a wooden helve of the simplest form is fitted upon the pointed tine at its root.

Of the larger, smooth-edged version, he says it

has a curvature approaching very near to that which, in this implement, may be termed the curve of least exertion; and throughout that portion of the sickle which performs the cutting process, it possesses this peculiar property from the following circumstances, that lines diverging from the centre of the handle of the sickle and intersecting the curve of the cutting edge, all the diverging lines will form equal angles with the tangents to the curve at the points of intersection. This property gives to the cutting edge a uniform tendency to cut at every point in its length without any other exertion than a direct pull upon the helve.

Stephens' conclusion was that the smooth-edged blade was much easier to use, though he concedes that "the dexterous use of either depends altogether on habit and practice".

For *hairst*, the smooth-bladed tool, which could be sharpened by *straiking* with a stone, ousted its toothed variant (which had to go to the blacksmith's to have its teeth renewed) by about 1800. The term *heuk*, it seems, passed down to popularly embrace it.

The work-unit for the *heuk* was the bandwin, a team whose reaping output was within the capacity of one bandster. The term was common in the ballad counties of the North-east Lowlands by the mid-1600s. It was a unit of seven, sometimes nine, normally working two rig-widths of fifteen to eighteen feet each simultaneously, three (or four) shearers to each ridge, with the spare hand binding and stooking. With the toothed *heuk*, the shearers moved along the rig; with the smoothed-edge blade they worked across it. A bandwin's output was reckoned at two to two and a half acres a day and it was paid as a unit.

The other method of piece-work harvesting by the *heuk*, continued longest nearer the larger towns with their reservoirs of seasonal labour readily available, was known as threaving. A threave, the unit for payment, was 24 sheaves (or two stooks) of oats or barley, 28 sheaves of wheat. In such circumstances, human nature being the way it is, sheaf size became a matter of some concern, and the diameters were checked by means of a sheaf-gauge. To see fair play in this, and to avoid conflict at the end of the day, the bandster and stooker in this case was more likely to be the farmtoun's man, the checker at night the toun grieve, who then took the day's tally of sheaves cut by each reaper or gang. Sheaf diameters varied through Scotland (as must have the rates), the largest sheaves of the Lothians being twelve inches (30 cm) while those of the North-east diminished to ten inches (25 cm) or even less. But then, in its scale, the northern farming was always smaller.

Though it was not only about the southern touns that a host of bandwins and shearers crowded the old fields of harvest, there, certainly, the onset of *hairst* brought with it a vast arrival of folk. It was nothing for a man, in the hiring fair, to *fee* 50 girl shearers in a single day; as many as three dozen rigs of shearers might be at work together, a small army working its way slowly across the landscape.

As the old *hairst* came on shearers with their *heuks* passed south on the old roads bound for the hiring fairs: most of them Highland lasses with their bundles of small clothes and each with the poke of meal that sustained her on the journey. If the influx of Highland labour came to its head in the early 1800s, it was nothing terribly new, for the yearly migration, it is thought, dated from the 1600s. There was a shearers' market in Airdrie by 1700, and soon after that, in East Lothian — the country's prime grain-growing region — there were weekly markets for shearers. The idea spread ever wider to gathering points such as Edinburgh's West Port and, on the other side of the country, Glasgow Cross, till Highland lasses were being *fee'd* by the thousand.

Nor did they travel only to the southern counties; in the central region they came over the Mounth of the Grampians that separated Gaeldom from the Lowlands in droves to the shearing of the Angus farms, where they were called threavers, from their piece-work method of employment there. Yet that was by no means the only system in use by then. Says Ord:

. . . it was usual for harvest contractors to . . . undertake to cut, gather, and stook grain crops at an arranged price per acre. The contractor, or master as he was called by the workers, engaged a foreman, who was held responsible by the contractor for carrying out the various contracts.

By then the work had brought a closer partnership to the harvest field: the pairing of a man and a woman, the latter to cut, the man to bind. It was the kind of pairing often highly agreeable to both and it led on to other things, for *hairst* had its own heightened atmosphere of love and sometimes even a heated carnality that shocked the genteel. Yet the songs of the *hairst* rig were also spiritually joyous. Christian Watt, the Broadsea fishertoun lass who wrote her memoirs in the tragic seclusion of Aberdeen's Cornhill institution, remembered the *hairst fees* of her more carefree youth:

It was a moving thing to hear a whole park of reapers sing "The Lord is My Shepherd" with everybody joining in, or maybe the "Old Rugged Cross" and all the old hymns. The melody and the tune carried for miles in the hot sun, we were as brown as a berry by the time we finished hairsting, it was so healthy. There were eight Broadsea girls in the hayloft with me, there must have been the best part of 100 folk hairsting.

She would recall, most poignantly in the circumstances, the "great healing of the mind" found in the harvest field.

For all that, not all was sweetness and holy light. In this festival of hard work and so much jollity, there could be uncompromising labour militancy. Those Highland lasses of so much guile who spoke in the gentle Gaelic and won the southern crops expected to earn half-a-crown a day in the mid-1800s. It seems to have been about the going rate for the time and area and they were keen to keep it so by unseemly threats of vengeance against girl shearers who worked for less.

Such problems passed though in another decade or so as the shearing gangs faded from the Lothian scene, though the sickle was not entirely put away: it remained, says Stephens, until near the end of the century in that area as the conqueror of the laid and twisted crop.

The scythe changed the pace of harvest, and in that its impact in the North-east was considerable. Gordon of Cairnbulg, ridiculed at first, finally had the last laugh on his sceptical neighbours when they too reluctantly surrendered to his example. With his *hairst* of 1810, that other pioneer, William Anderson of Fintray, was delighted to find that with the use of the scythe fifteen people would harvest six acres a day. It was a speed that made the *heuk*'s progress seem primitive. Yet the *heuk*, even in the north, was not immediately superseded: in the parish of Methlick, for instance, in the heart of the ballad country, the bere (the barley) was won by the sickle for a long time afterwards, and in upcountry Alford, even as the mid-century approached, there were dour and stubborn hill folk who could not be persuaded to forsake it.

In the south there would be areas where the scythe's adoption would be so long delayed that it would be used only to *redd* roads (clear a path round the perimeter of the crop) for the mechanical reaper — a parallel almost with the later case of the caschrom of the

Hebridean landscape, where primitive cultivation leapt through the aeons of agricultural time to embrace at once the tractor and the machine-drawn plough.

Elsewhere, however, the scythes of summer left the hayfield, where they had long reigned, for the corn rigs, irrevocably altering the old social patterns of harvest and the old work methods that had been part of them. By 1831, in ·Kennethmont, another upcountry Aberdeenshire parish, sandwiched between the somewhat greater farming might of the Garioch and the realms of Strathbogie with its famous touns, it had ousted the *heuk* and understandably found champions. Its swath-width or bout was up to four and a half feet and there was a neatness to it, in the way the crop came off the blade.

The North-east led the revolution. There had, before Gordon's and Anderson's time, in the south been something of a false dawn for the scythe as the implement of *hairst*. That unquenchable pioneer Lord Kames had supported it; most of his contemporaries, however, would have nothing to do with it, declaring that it "shook the corn". The ballad touns, once smitten by its speed, had no such reservation and its reign there would continue uninterrupted until about the 1880s.

There was, briefly and between-times, a flirtation with the Flemish scythe, a handtool that was neither one thing nor the other. Its blade was a little over two feet in length and there was some fairly determined effort to introduce it, particularly under the sponsorship of the then Highland and Agricultural Society. Henry Stephens, in 1825, accompanied two Flemish reapers through the Forfarshire countryside to report on their pioneering impact. The farmtouns he found were less than impressed.

In his meticulous way, Stephens described the implement that by then was outstripping all competition in the Lowlands, emphasising in particular the use of the scythe's cradle attachment, which faded from use with the later, stronger-growing crop varieties and lingered on only where some old crofter man was a sworn advocate of it for laying the grain more neatly into the swath. The cradle-scythe, Stephens says, was

. . . once very common in the North-east of Scotland. . . . In this form the scythe-blade is 3 feet–4 inches to 3 feet–6 inches long. The principal helve handle is 4 feet in length, to which the blade is attached in the usual way, the hook of the tine being sunk into the wood, and an iron ferrule brought down over the tine, binding it firmly to the wood, the blade being further supported by the addition of a light stay, the *grass-nail*. The minor helve, 3 feet in length, often much shorter, is tenoned into the principal, and the two handles are adjusted by wedges in the usual way to the height and mode of working of the mower, the distance between the helves at the handles being about 24 inches.

The cradle or rake consists of a little wooden standard, about 8 inches high, jointed to the heel of the blade, so as to fold a little up or down across the blade. Into this are inserted three or four slender teeth, following the direction of the blade, and from 6 to 15 inches long: the head of the standard is supported by a slender rod of iron, which stretches about 18 inches up the handle, where it is secured by a small screw-nut capable of being shifted up or down to alter the position of the standard and its teeth to suit the lay of the corn.

The function of the cradle was to carry the cut corn round with the sweep of the scythe. Except for a very short crop, however, the cradle is really not necessary, and was latterly to a large extent dispensed with.

Thus Henry Stephens on the mechanics of the scythe, whose handles in the harvester's hands took the shape of a slanting "Y" and whose use was so natural once to countrymen that it seemed but an extension of their own limbs. A good scytheman accounted for one and a half to two acres of oats or barley a day against the *heuk*'s maximum of one-third of an acre. And the scythe also had another dramatic effect: harvesting costs were cut almost by half. Stephens' estimate by the acre was: for the bandwin team (food and wages), 9s 5¾d; the scythe team, 5s 2½d. And it banished a large number of lasses from the *hairst* park for ever.

The scythe team numbered three: two men and one girl. Some of the old bothy ballads written to celebrate the harvest and the goodwill of men, generally, one to another (something else the world has grown damnably short of) survive to remind us of how the unit functioned. Among them is "The Boghead Crew":

John MacNab our foremost man
Was sturdy, brave and strong.
Sae canny he pits in his scythe
And carries on the thrang.

His gatherer she cam' frae Greenbank
Maclennan was her name.
She was the flo'er o' a' oor flock.
A handsome clever dame.

And Esslemont he ban' to her
He was a sturdy cheil.
Ye wadna seen a jollier crew
Upon a harvest field.

The scytheman cut the grain, the girl gathered it into sheaf-size bundles, and the third member of the team, the bandster, bound the sheaves and stooked them. What the girl of the team also did was to make the bands for tying the sheaves and, traditionally, the bandster could claim a kiss if a band broke or slipped. How hard the lass worked to avoid that penalty depended on the bandster and doubtless any good-looking *loon* could end up doing a lot more than he had bargained for. There would likely be circumstances, too, when a girl would work hard, anxious to make her bands secure, a job less easy than it sometimes seemed. Stephens, that master of method, again:

The cornband is made by taking a handful of corn, dividing it into two parts, laying the corn ends of the straw across each other, and twisting them round so that the ears shall lie above the twist—the twist acting as a knot, making the band firm. The reaper then lays the band stretched at length upon the ground to receive the corn with the ears of the band and of the sheaf away from him.

When the band has been laid on the ground, the stubble ends of the straw in the sheaf should be quickly squared by pushing up any straws that are too far down. The sheaf should then be rolled together from the side next the standing grain, caught firmly in the arms, laid on the band and bound, any loose straws at the cut end being pulled off as the sheaf is thrown to one side.

Stephens' gaze now moves to the bandster:

Going to the stubble end of the sheaf, with his face to the corn-end, the binder gathers the spread corn on either side into the middle of the band with both hands, and, taking a hold of the band in each hand, near the ends, he turns the sheaf as much round as to place the corn-ends beyond his left elbow; then, crossing the ends of the band, pulls forcibly with the right hand close to the sheaf, and keeps the purchase thus obtained with the underside of the left hand, while he carries the end in the right hand, below and behind his left hand; and then, taking both ends in both hands, twists them firmly and thrusts the twist under the band with the right hand, as far as to keep a firm hold. In the bound sheaf, the corn-knot in the middle of the band is held firm by the pressure of the sheaf against the ears of corn and the twisted part of the band.

It will be possible a thousand years from now to recreate the old farming of the 1800s solely from the instructions in Stephens' manual and here, though he makes fairly heavy weather of it, his method is an accurate description of a task almost every Scottish farmtoun child was once proficient at. It was a job with its own painful legacy:

> O busy's the banster at e'en.
> Till bedtime he sits an' he glooms,
> An' aye he cries "Lassie, a preen"
> An' worries the stobs in his thooms.

The squad that took the harvest field while the scythe reigned were, as Helen Beaton suggests, a motley crew, actors from every walk of country life: tailor, molecatcher, roadmender, carpenters and tradesmen of all persuasions. And though the scythe had diminished their number some women still "took a *hairst*": cottar-wives supplemented their men's meagre wages and croft wives gathered at surrounding touns to make economic ends meet on their own small holdings, gathering in their own *hairsts* when they could. Old crones, new brides and young lasses as yet in no way compromised took to the corn rigs, the latter sometimes with the light of love in their eyes if their scyther was also a fine macaroni:

It's braw wi' the tweezlelock to twine
Lang rapes in the barn sae lythe.
Yet better by far when it's fine
An' I gaither after his scythe.

The poet again is Charles Murray and so that there need be no misunderstanding in southern minds one should say at once that "rapes" is the dialect for the ropes made by twining straw together.

Well before the month of September farmers would be seeking such folk in the old country fairs of the region, such occasions as Lowrin (St Lawrence) and St Sairs in the shadow of Bennachie; at St Paldie's farther south, near Lord Gardenstone's little town of Laurencekirk in the last days of July. Those for hire, the folk looking for a *hairst fee*, announced it by sporting an appropriate emblem: say a shoot of green-speared corn worn in the bonnet or lapel, an indication of their willingness to "bargain".

Once, as the days of harvest drew close, such a token would have appeared mysteriously on the dominie's desk as a reminder to him that the time was coming when some of his scholars would be needed elsewhere.

Where there was no hiring fair there was always the mart, the livestock auction sale, held frequently in the country's market towns. Here too a man might seek a *hairst fee* and many an old horseman recalls yet the day he went to "seek a *hairst*".

So I gangs doon tae Ellon. . . . I thocht I'd seek a hairst maybe, see what was gaun. Doon I goes. . . . I'd be comin' on saxteen by then. The mart wis gey busy, a great steer o' folk. . . . An' I'm jist standin' there when my uncle comes up on me. "Michty, loon, fit're ye daein' here the day?" says he. "Dyod," I says tae him, "I some thocht I'd hae a hairst fee." He jist laucht, ye ken, nae sayin' muckle aboot it. "Likely than," he says, "you an' a gey puckle mair. . . ."

So awa' he goes again — he hid a sma' tounie an' a dairy in Aiberdeen's John Street — an' I'm jist left stannin'. But oh-ho, back he comes syne afore lang, anither fairmer lad wi' him. "Yer lookin' for a fee?" the fairmer says. "Aye fairly," I says. The auld fairmer looks at me a meenit or twa, sizes me up. "I'm needin' a hairster," he says, "wid ye be interested?" "Oh, mebbe," I says. "Can ye stook?" he says tae me. "Losh, I can stook," I says. "Ca' horse?" he speirs. I couldnae say muckle tae that but "Well," he says, "I'm payin' twa-poun'-ten i' the week. That suit ye?" "Oh, fine," I says.

So the grieve's son, the Big Hoose's bailie *loon* who had left school at thirteen and a half and been "sorting" twelve milk cows daily before his fourteenth birthday and milking them (with help from the manager's wife and daughter) each morning before walking the long avenue with the milk that would cool the laird's porridge, went home to a new toun.

So I gangs hame tae Chapelhall. There wis twa lads i' the bothy already: the third horseman and anither hairster. I got on jist fine. . . . The hairst cam' tae an eyn an' jist aboot then the third horseman tak's tonsilitis an' finally gangs hame tae his folk. So . . . I wis rale keen on the horse, ye ken, and since the lad wisnae weel, I hid been rising early tae sort his beasts for him. An' that's jist fit I'm at ae mornin' fin in comes the grieve intae the stable — tae dae it himsel'. An' he jist looks at me. . . . "Weel, weel," he says, "gin yer that keen jist cairry on." An' syne, later on, the grieve comes tae me and he speirs, "Can ye ploo?" "Dyod, I widnae winnir," I says. The grieve jist laucht. . . .

So the *hairster*, in the speak of the old touns, was "speired tae bide". Under the strict eye of the toun's second horseman he took hold of the plough-stilts for the first time and began his horseman's days and the peripatetic round of the North-east Lowlands touns first as bothy lad and then as a cottar.

His story is typical, for many another began his bothy days in the same way. For the young lad though, there was a sad come-down in his new position: as third horseman in the toun's regular crew he got a wage of only £1 a week. But then, *hairst fees* had always come high, a sign of the job's crucial importance to the toun's economy.

By then, the touns were into their binder days. Between times the mechanical reaper had usurped the scythe; though it had little altered the pattern of harvest it had nudged the touns nearer to the days of full mechanisation and again cut labour needs — at the expense of higher capital investment. Even so, there were, at first, folk — in the fields of Flora Thompson's *Lark Rise* Oxfordshire as well as in Scotland's Lowlands — who considered it only as a useful auxiliary to the scythe.

Its acceptance was somehow grudgingly delayed even round the forward-looking ballad touns, though several Bell machines, manufactured in Dundee, were working in Forfarshire by 1834, some seven years after the machine's invention. Among those who watched it at work (you've guessed it) was Henry Stephens. It was the countryside in which he had seen the Flemish scythe fail so miserably. The reaper, he concluded, cut the cost of harvesting by scythe by nearly half. Output, based on the ten- to twelve-hour day, was fourteen acres.

The machine cut the corn, closing to the centre of the field. And though the crop was left in sheaf-sized bundles, it had not overcome the need for gatherers or the bandster's skill to form a satisfactory sheaf. Those women who had followed the scythe were still needed on the same old seasonal basis. But some of the banter had gone out of the task, the teasing and the tantrums and the devious ploys of the scythemen with whom they had once been so closely partnered. Now they were located at the periphery of the cutting, each with her own area of operation sharply demarcated. The stooking, and often the binding, was still done by the men.

In Scotland's central counties it was the back-delivery machine that was most widely used. This meant that the woman gatherer had to have her pitch cleared before the reaper came round again. The side-delivery reaper soon followed. A more sociable machine, it threw its sheaf-bundle obligingly to the side, the way the binder would do.

Now, the reaper may not be seen as so wildly revolutionary. Nevertheless, it was the first surge in a tide of progress that would eventually sweep away a whole area of community involvement in the harvest field. And it deeply moved the dour, pragmatic Stephens. With an unaccustomed touch of poetry, he announced: "The merry whir of the modern reaper has drowned the dull hum of the primitive shearing of ancient time."

So it had. The farmtouns were finally turning their backs on the past.

IX

Binder Days

IF THERE WAS a thread at all that ran through the endless days of the old farmtoun *hairst* it was the substantial yet sometimes unreliable "thread" of the binder twine itself. It came home to the toun in reels sewn into jute bags, and sat for weeks beforehand in the corner dark of the implement shed, as secret as the dice in a gambler's fist. Not until it was relentlessly unfurling from the binder canister could you say what kind of *hairst* it would be.

There were times when the thread of harvest ran smooth and fine and unhindered, binding sheaf upon perfect sheaf with an effortless ease that made the heart sing. There were other *hairsts* too that left a mark in the mind, when nothing went right. All the same, the binder twine took the blame for things away and beyond its fault. There were rogue binders that put savage and unaccountable strain upon it so that it snapped before it had time to secure the sheaf, and there were yet others with sheaf-tying mechanisms that could, so to speak, neither "haud nor bin' " and would abort before the twine had a chance. The work of the *hairst* field came to an anguished halt then while the red-faced grieve and any farmtoun lad with mechanical leanings *fichered* and spat and considered and took turns to tinker with the Albion or Massey-Harris.

Some were men with vastly more thumbs than fingers in which all sensitivity had long been numbed and they would have done better to keep their hands in their *pooches*. But again, there were others with a knack, a touch so delicate — a gift beyond all farmtoun understanding — that they made the whole thing seem as easy as threading a needle and became men to be deferred to, at least during harvest-time.

It was all a tense time for the horseman on the binder seat. Whatever went wrong he bore the burden of guilt. He got more advice always than he got breakdowns, not all of it confined to the workings of the binder. For his was the lynchpin role in the whole operation and if there was a sin more grievous than letting the machine break down it was to run out of binder twine in mid-*yoking*: that was unforgivable and come the November Term, the horseman knew, he would be looking for a new toun. For all that though, the man on the binder was a king:

Ye thocht yersel' a gey lad when ye got tae drive the binder. . . . A fine job? Ah, well . . . ye see, it a' depended on yer crop again . . . for yer shaeffin' gear. That wis the main bit o't . . . o' drivin' the binder. The first fyow bouts o' a crop were the warst, needin' adjustment o' the binder. Then ye micht come up against a short bittie o' crop maybe. Then ye hid tae watch yer flashes — the flaughts we aye ca'd them — that took yer crop on tae the platform o' yer binder. Oh, aye, ye hid tae watch yer shaeffin' gear. When ye hid a short bittie o' crop ye hid tae lower the reel. . . . Oh, there wis fairly something til't fan ye cam' tae drive the binder.

The horseman in fact had also to watch the canvas, the webbing that carried the cut corn, conveyor-style, to the sheafing mechanism. It had to be slackened for a shower or a heavy dew, gradually tightened as conditions became drier.

On most touns the foreman and the second horseman drove the binders. At some, just a few where democracy had an unaccustomed stronghold, the horsemen took it in turns. Thus was bothy friction avoided. The foreman drove the lead binder, with the "second" (and maybe the "third" about large touns) following in order. There was great jealousy about the job and to be passed over when it fell to your stable ranking was deadly insult. Men packed their kists and left the parish for less.

Yet it was not merely a matter of follow-my-leader. Far from it. The space between the machines when they were in work had to be such as to allow one machine to negotiate the corner of the crop without halting the machine coming behind — an interval very conveniently shortened when the sheaf-catcher fitment came on the scene. This enabled a machine to retain its bound sheaves, removing all hindrance, while it executed the turn out at the end of one bout and into the start of the next, something that had previously been an awkward, delaying manoeuvre.

That was generally the kind of fairly close formation worked. Yet there were grieves with such a profound distrust of anything

mechanical, and the binder especially, men who trusted only the
scythe of their youth and were so fearful of breakdowns that they
would not let the second machine into the bout until the first one had
cleared it. This applied particularly when laid crops were being
harvested. Then cutting was frequently down only one side of the
crop and into the face of the lying grain. Their caution was evoked
because of the danger of a machine becoming choked or completely
bogged down in the unfavourable harvesting conditions.

Hairst then, as in the earlier days of the scythe, was still the
highpoint of the country year and it brought extra duties to every
able body about a toun and more than most to the kitchen maid, that
queen of the baking griddle and churn whose daily norm anyway
was about eighteen hours of unremitting slavery. To her usual
work, about the smaller touns—making meals, washing, scrubbing
floors, polishing the fire-range and milking the cows —there would
be added the "sorting of the nowt", the tending of the cattle-beasts,
so that the *orra loon* could be freed for the onslaught in the harvest
field. Likely, in the end of the day, it was she who got the least
thanks.

That busy time came in September running into October,
though earlier *hairsts* were not unknown and there were, equally,
times when they dragged into November and cast a gloom on the
land. Those times were hard on men far in at the bank, for as the days
slipped by their chances of salvation went with them. Maybe that
was why, when it came, *hairst* so heated the blood and added an
edginess even to the humour of men who had years of putting *hairsts*
both haggard and glorious behind them.

They waited patiently enough, hardly believing their luck if the
weather held, cursing quietly below the breath when it betrayed
them and deluging rain battered their grain and their hopes into the
ground. For as long as they could mind that had been the way of it.
Worst-hit were the small touns and the crofter folk whose fields were
usually wettest due to bad drainage and whose sowing, and
therefore harvests, were late because of it. Such parks at times were
barely able to support the weight of a machine. It was always the
plight of the small men, and the harder the times, the greater the
difficulty in getting the laird's ear.

But *hairst* was never easy. It meant long days in the fields. John R.
Allan, in his *Farmer's Boy*, recalls the horseman's long hours:
"In harvest they might work on till ten or eleven, if the dew did not

fall heavily, and I remember two autumns at least when the binder worked till midnight under the great red harvest moon."

The binder was a fine machine: it could do all the reaper did with more technological panache and added to that the splendid sophistication of automatically tying the sheaves before ejecting them on to the stubble. That superior technology bowed to the past only in the "roads" that had to be *redd* round the periphery of the crop initially, to let the machine make its first circuit — a track that only two Clydesdales could tread, dragging its flashing blades behind them. Thereafter, the third horse would join the team.

In the sweetness of its action the binder drove men almost to ecstasy in their appreciation. The sober Stephens called it "one of the most useful agricultural inventions of the nineteenth century". That it certainly was. More recently, writer David Toulmin, whose time round the farmtouns has given him a deep knowledge of the life, in *Harvest Home* graphically describes the binder's conquering progress and the urgency it brought into the harvest field, with its

> . . . corn reels striding into the standing grain, swathing it on to the cutter bar, the blade in lightning motion, slashing the feet from the ripened corn as it falls on the platform canvas, to be hustled into the guts of the machine, the packer arms grabbing furtively at the corn stalks, getting them into bundles with the ears to the tail of the binder, the wooden butter tidying the shear of the sheaf, the long steel needle curving up through to put a string round it from the canister under the driver's seat, the knotter tying it, the knife cutting the string, the delivery arms tossing the bound sheaves on to the shorn stubble at regular intervals, all as quick as the eye can follow, faster than human being could ever perform it.

Cleverly, the binder gave a choice of sheaf sizes and, predictably, that size diminished as it had always done as one moved north. The size determined the rate of drying and in a wet countryside where the morning dew was sometimes slow to lift, that was still important. Not that all the touns were fussy about waiting for the dew to lift, any more than they were about waiting for the corn to ripen; there was a belief that cutting the oats a little green improved the quality of the subsequent straw. Barley, however, *had* to be ripe and "drappin' in the heid" (and hard to the teeth) before they dared to put the binder into it.

Yet, above all, in the frenzy of *hairst* it was the nightmare of breakdowns that haunted the grieve's sleep — and even his waking hours as he stood by the park gate at his trestle, sharpening the binders' blades and keeping a wary eye on the scene before him. Each blade did a *yoking*'s work; each binder had two blades. Most of the farmtoun binders had a left-hand cut — that is, the cutter bar extended to the left of the machine, so that progress round the crop, for once, was in an anti-clockwise direction. The machines worked in diminishing circuits towards the centre of the field.

While blade and binder twine held out, the old grieve at the gate soughed a tune under his breath, giving way at times to good humour. But stoppage brought him running and the sight of, say, three machines frozen in mid-bout could endow even the kirk-going man with a fine choice of language at the expense of machine or the unfortunate man aloft on it — a man caught unawares perhaps by a sudden and unexpected patch of boggy ground. If there was one thing a grieve needed even less than a binder with a tetchy knotter it was one bogged down to its platform and choked with corn.

That caused chaos, the machines in the following bouts being stuck behind it until it could be made operational again. There was a reluctance simply to take them out of work in mid-bout — that ruined the whole symmetry of *hairst* and the operational pattern of the work. Whenever trouble threatened a machine the man on its seat would be incited to "Get oot at the eyn, man. Oot at the eyn!" There his machine could be *lowsed* out of all contention without leaving a haggard design on the field.

The binders of the old touns that took them from the days of the reaper to the technology of the combine-harvester — through the first 50 years of the century, for a binder was a rarity still in 1890 in John Strachan's countryside — were mainly five-foot-cut machines, though latterly binders that cut a six-foot bout were around in some numbers. There were exceptions, of course: Ellon's Mains of Rannieston in 1917, doubtless pressured by war want, found a small niche in local history by having not only one of the first tractors in the region, an aptly-named Overtime, but a new Massey-Harris binder, cutting a seven-foot width, to hitch to it. The binder, incidentally, was one of the first to be fitted with a

sheaf-carrier, that useful innovation that "collected" four or five
sheaves at the bout corners, and doubtless lined the curious of its
time along the dykeside. But there were other makes too whose
names drifted through the Bogie-reek and the bothy talk in the
1920s and 1930s, among them the Deering, the Hornsby and not
least the McCormick, a mechanical memorial to the man whose
early persistence had so dramatically altered the harvest scene
from the days of the sickle and the scythe.

Mostly though, it was the Clydesdales' pace that governed the
speed of the cutting. Commentators of the late 1800s, perhaps
ambitious for the machine, reckoned its work-rate at one and a half
acres per hour. The farmtouns of the later 1920s and 1930s were
more realistic and, wary of such projections, relied on the old
formula of an acre per foot per *yoking*, or an acre an hour. To
better that, it is said, there were touns where they used the special
binder whip to spur the Clydes. Such touns, however, would seem
to have been an insignificant minority.

If there was protocol in the *hairst* park, there was also guile. As
the end of the *yoking* came round, the man on the second or third
machine (his commitment always somewhat less than the foreman's) might be tempted to sneak a glance at the time, his big
double-cased watch leaping from his breeks' pocket into the
hooded palm of his hand with a conjurer's skill when everybody's
back was turned. If it told him it was getting close to *lowsing*-time,
he might quietly slow his team so that on their arrival at the gate
the grieve might feel it hardly worth his while to embark on a
further circuit. Bolder men were known to improvise breakdowns
or a pause for "adjustments" for the same reason. But the grieves of
the old touns were wily birds, far too wise to fall for such tricks.
Many justified their extra few pounds a year by their awareness of
such dodges — and the horseman, as he came round, would be
quietly advised: "Jist keep ye gaun, laddie. I'll lat ye ken fin it's
suppertime." In the hurry of harvest leniency was something a
grieve could not afford.

Few touns were unaware of the benefits the binder had brought
them. Where they did not run to the expense of an implement shed
they recognised its superior sophistication by running it into the
cornyard at the end of cutting and later building a rick over it to
protect it. More often it was a rick of straw that cocooned it, after
the first threshing. Or it might be just a cover of thatch. Alas, there

were sad and forlorn touns with too few outbuildings and too few folk, where the machine sat the year round in the close or in the corner of the field it had harvested last, and where it steadily rusted in the smirr rain. In places of such dismal comfort the hens at least were glad of it as a place to roost, and scattered their droppings liberally over its once-shiny paint.

Yet, superb innovation though it was, the binder did not quite carry all before it. In the uplands of the ballad country, round the lonely hill of Bennachie, as late as the 1930s there were small touns where the old reaping machine prevailed, not just for reasons of poverty but because the third beast needed for the binder could neither be afforded nor borrowed at that particularly busy time of the year. The sheaf-binders then were the toun's womenfolk. They were less subject to breakdown.

By then—in 1932—the combine-harvester had its first tentative toehold in Scotland, when a Clayton machine took to the fields of Lord Balfour's Whittinghame Mains in the great grain region of East Lothian. But the binder would remain to take the farmtouns through the vital *hairsts* of World War Two. It even had advantages over the "combine" in allowing the oats to be cut a little green to let the crop ripen in the stook. The old touns were always thankful for that.

They finally parted with their old Hornsbys and Albions a bit reluctantly; for all their breakdowns, they had with the years grown rather fond of them. You will hardly see one now in the whole wide sweep of that northern countryside, except as a protected species in the sanctuary of a farm museum.

Yet there are small places still where the old *hairst* lingers: small crofts in the outposts of Buchan . . . in uplands Keig, where the binder returns briefly to the September fields. Things were always a little backward there. Its minister of the mid-1790s stated then that the infield and outfield system continued there, that the parish's 47 ploughs were drawn by a variety of animals—88 horses, 87 cows and 153 oxen—and that the cart was a stranger, with dung going to the field still on creels straddling the horse's back. Besides which, "there are neither green crops, hay enclosures nor winter herding". Keig it seems was always a place to cling to old loyalties: one of its earlier ministers had to be deposed for supporting the Old Pretender—long after he should have known what was good for him.

X

Old Alignments

THE COMBINE-HARVESTER has destroyed the old harmonies of harvest, dramatically altering the hallowed relationship of men to that time of farming fulfilment. It has swept away the ancient architecture and the old symmetry of the farmtoun *hairsts*, for it leaves no traditional pattern in the field, no gleam of gold in the stooks nor in the bonnie stacks of the cornyard, no grace to lighten the days of autumn — only, remorselessly, an endless "ribbing" of straw on the stubble to be balered quick or sold in the swath or, increasingly and controversially, burned where it lies. For straw, once so valuable about a farmtoun that even the staidest of grieves would incite reckless young horsemen on the binder to "Lower yer cutter bar, laddie. Lower yer cutter bar . . ." to get every available inch for feeding and bedding, is now but an embarrassment. The "combine", irrevocably, has taken much of the triumph out of winning the harvest.

While the binder remained, the men of the old North-east Lowlands landscape, pressing hard on its heels as they stooked the corn to ripen in its wake, united themselves with long-forgotten generations of farming men. In the height of *hairst*, in field after field, toun after toun all round the countryside the pattern of the stooks — the shocks of the English landscape — was repeated for as far as the eye could see, until it lost vision in the haze of the horizon. The stooks stood at the centre of harvest, tokens of hope but with a long way still to go.

As the cutting went on, the stookers strode the fields, many of them, even in the binder days, men who had come far to take a *hairst fee*. There was a rhythm to their work, an even momentum between prostrate sheaf and the forming stook, their timing such that one man never impeded or baulked the step of another. Sheaves were firmly seized, just below the corn ears and as though they might yet escape, and tucked deftly in one swift swoop of the body into the lock of an armpit while a further two — in the case of a light crop — might also be snatched and pinioned to the rib-cage and the close embrace of a dungaree jacket. It was not easy work, though the knack, after years of enforced practice, some-times made it seem so and certainly made it less arduous. It was an art that came as second-nature to the men of the touns: just how to pick up a sheaf and where to plonk it down, all of it so natural that it didn't need thinking about. And Stephens, naturally, had studied it: his instructions as always are precise, though to any old farming man, had he heard them, they would have seemed a blinding glimpse of the obvious:

> In building a stook, the centre pair of sheaves should always be set up first. Each sheaf should get a good solid dump on its butt end, so as to give it a firm foundation; and the two sheaves should be firmly pressed together at the top, by putting a hand on the outside of each a little above the bands, and exerting considerable pressure on these parts. Each following pair of sheaves should be put at opposite ends of the stook, in such a position that they only very slightly incline their heads towards the centre of the stook.

Stephens, by the way, was not joking about the "butt end" of the sheaf; it is the correct term. In fact, if there is a fault at all in his excellent manuals it is, as Neill, that radical educator and Scot from the same region, said of the Bible, that he has no jokes.

Stooking was man's work and it always had been — which is not to say that there were not sonsie cottar wives who could stook with the best of them, taking great armfuls of sheaves so purposefully into their oxters, their armpits, that one was tempted to speculate about their private lives. About the bigger touns they were called upon only in the bitterest thraw of a bad *hairst*. The crofter's wife was less fortunate; hers was a necessary assistance. Many, from both classes, could fork as easily to the *hairst* carts and frequently did so, their amazonian arms browning in the harvest sun.

The stooks of the old Scottish countryside differed widely in their stature, from the crofter's pitiful prop of sheaves (as few as four perhaps on the Highland fringe) to the grandiose gesture of sixteen, though the latter diminished with the years and the farmtouns, with the coming of the binder, settled on a middle course with ten, or even eight, sheaves to the stook. Stephens in his

Book of the Farm explains the traditional alignments and why the Howe of the Mearns and the uplands of Strathbogie could seem as though they had been stooked by the same hand:

> When finished, the stooks should always point as nearly as possible between south and south-west — to the one o'clock sun — as the prevailing winds then strike them on the end and blow right through the stook. In this direction the sun dries each side of the stook about equally, which, in a wet or late harvest, is a matter of considerable importance.

The ballad touns held to that rule, more or less, setting their stooks north/south to catch the noon sun. And the stookers' ritual round the big farmtouns, if not on the crofts and small places, was hallowed and time-worn. Round and round they went, in their diminishing circuits, beginning from one corner of the field and working contra to the machine's circuit. They worked in teams of three (two such teams perhaps beginning from diagonally opposite corners of the park). There were subtleties to their pattern of work, to the pacing and counter-pacing, that eluded all but the knowledgeable eye.

The team of three took in six binder bouts, six rows of sheaves still prostrate on the stubble, the first man taking rows one and two, the second man rows three and four, and the third, bouts five and six. Traditionally the stooker working the central rows (three and four) would work a little ahead of his flanking companions. The stook would be set up in the wake of his rows and it was his task to mark its location by placing the first sheaves while his colleagues, with farther to walk, gathered in to it.

Where only two stookers worked as a team, usually only five rows of sheaves were collected: two rows each, with the sheaves of the centre bout being collected alternately by the men, the stook forming itself on the line of the centre row, so that each stooker gathered three then two, three then two rows as they moved round the field. Each in turn had the honour of deciding where the stook should stand. It was a system that covered the ground and again, with an unrustic shrewdness, had great economy of movement. Its high efficiency could send hard-to-please grieves home to their suppers purring with delight and determined to speak kindly to their wives. Two stookers at least were considered necessary for each binder working in order to keep up with the work and push forward the momentum of *hairst*.

For all that, with the stooking ended, the touns had to wait — though it was a pause nobody wanted — for the crop to *wun*, for the wind blowing through the heart of the stooks to take the sap out of the straw, and for the sun to dry the grain heads. How long that took depended only on the weather and not even a grieve could hurry that. He could, however, ensure that the *hairst* hands he had about the place were far from idle: they put past the intervening days and subsequent wet mornings ensconced in the long byre, cleared for the summer of its beef beasts, making ropes or, on dry mornings, *foon*-clearing in the cornyard.

The straw ropes that would later lash down the rick thatch against the tearing fury of the northern wind were made yearly, from the straw of the previous year's crop. The handtool that fashioned them was the thraw-crook, a brace-like gadget of some ingenuity and eccentric in its variety of design. It was "cranked" by one man, twisting the rope, while his partner "fed in" the straw that continuously extended the rope as the winder retreated backwards down the length of the byre. The "feeding in" of the straw was the difficult part of the operation and tried the patience, and though the art would continue down to our own time in the Highland and Hebridean landscape, it was a skill that faded from the old touns of the 1920s, without a *stoon* of regret, as the last of its old exponents finally laid past their cords and their nicky-tams.

Accidental release, for instance, allowed the rope, the *raip*, immediately to fly asunder, making it fit only for the muck midden, where it would be promptly thrown and a fresh start made. But there were further elements that interrupted and seriously hindered the work of rope-making: that competitive edge that developed wherever two or three pairs were employed together at the task — a quality fostered always by cunning grieves — and the incitement to sheer devilment that such a situation engendered. Few of the young horsemen could resist the mischief that discomfited the too-worthy contender and it may be that more ropes were ruined by horse-play than were ever *connached* by incompetence. In the circumstances, few of the young horsemen of the later farmtoun era ever really mastered the skill or showed any desire to do so in the years that ushered in the coir-yarn rope that came hairy and in clews from the merchant and could last from one *hairst* to the next.

The cornyard *foon*-clearing, the weeding between the stones of the circular foundations on which the ricks would be raised, was as much a part of the harvest. It took more brawn and less skill but it too followed a well-tried method. The stones of one semi-circle of the *foon* would be thrown on top of those of the other half-circle while the earth underneath them was freed of weeds. Then the process would be reversed. Most of the big touns marked the circular outline of the *foons* with large stones, containing within them the smaller field gatherings that would keep the sheaves off the ground.

Yet both were ancillary tasks, an interlude that never for a moment disguised the real anxiety of *hairst* or the days of hazard as the crop sat vulnerably in the stook. As time wore on wizened old farmer men took to wandering their parks early and late, seizing hold of a sheaf from a stook here, a stook there, gauging its weight in the hand, shaking its head to hear the sound of the grain. When the *reeshle* of the cornheads was right, only then was it time to bring the harvest home. To the old farmer men that sound was the music of *hairst*.

The "leading", when it began, had its own pattern as inviolably imprinted on those old farmtoun days. Implicit in it was the contest against time: a race that continued at times by moonlight. That element of haste was nothing new. John Ramsay, that great social commentator and author of *Scotland and Scotsmen in the Eighteenth Century*, recalled that in the harvest of 1782, in the first fever of improvement, he "began to lead about midnight between 24th and 25th October in clear moonshine . . .". That harvest was an execrable one, dogged by foul weather and made more crucial by the needs of a time of much deprivation. About any toun of the depressed time between this century's two World Wars, the outcome might have been almost as critical for the farmtoun if not for the nation.

Later and nearer to our own time, and from the upcountry region of the ballad touns, comes confirmation that leading by moonlight was in no way unusual. Folklorist Helen Beaton, speaking of the late 1800s, remembered: "When weather permitted, 'an' the stuff was in order', the leading of the crop was continued till late and sometimes, when it was 'a leading mornin' ' a start would be made at two or three o'clock and would go on until stopped by a shower or by damp sheaves."

In the lush Lothians where the crops were early and often bountiful, the graceful longcarts brought home the *hairst*; in the bleaker North-east Lowlands it was the clumsy, square boxcarts girdled by their harvest frames that became the winged chariots that bore home the golden sheaves. The wooden frames, painted a primal red like the carts' wheels, measured about ten feet by seven feet and were made locally by the joiner. They widened considerably the load parameters of the deep, squat carts.

Leading began from the outside of the stooked field and moved clockwise as the stookers had done. About any sizeable toun it brought again into play a grand orchestration of labour. Its choreography was the grieve's but its rhythms were those rehearsed in *hairsts* long past. In the hurry, every Clydesdale pair that could be kept occupied was yoked into its carts.

In the field, the horseman built his first cart's load while a "spare man" built the second. Loads flowed to the cornyard in an uninterrupted sequence. In the park forkers finished with one pair of carts found another already in at the gate.

In the cornyard the horseman forked off the load he had *biggit* while another "spare man" forked off the second. Thus, with a speed and interlocking of effort, two ricks rose simultaneously cheek by jowl. It all slid together with the cunning of a Chinese puzzle.

The *bigging* of the carts followed an established pattern. It was not a difficult task but given the nature of old farmtoun roads, so rutted and potholed, and the lurching gait of the Clydesdale, it behoved a horseman to build well and so avoid if he could the fearful disgrace of having his load slide off just as it came in sight of the cornyard — and within distance of the grieve's scarifying tongue.

First the well of the cart was filled with sheaves and *weel trumpit* — well trampled down — and then the sheaves were built round the harvest frames, butt ends outwards, beginning from the rear left-hand corner and working clockwise. In the old touns' terminology each level of sheaves was a *gang* and *bigging* stopped usually about four-*gang* level, particularly on the clean-land crop, though it was not the fear of heights that deterred them but fear of what damage the iron-runged wheels of too-heavy a load might do to the young grass in the stubble.

His load built, the horseman slid off the back of his cart. That was an option the horse-lorry builder did not take, for it was not only the boxcarts that brought in the sheaves. Horse lorries kept for ferrying corn to the railhead or just to convey milk churns to the road end, were yoked for the fray of harvest, far too useful to lie idle.

With *hairst*-frames fitted, the sheaves would again be built in *gangs*, possibly to a greater level, and the horseman, when he had finished *bigging*, gathered the reins from the high pole at the front of his lorry where they had been tied and stayed with his load as it jolted all the way home. Understandably, lorry-driving horsemen built with some care and were never sorry to see the cornyard ahead of them.

In the field, the Clydesdales were left to their own devices, docile as they waited the forker's "Hup" and "Whoa" that advanced them from one stook to the next — though there were, to be sure, old beasts among them that knew well enough when it was time to move on and had likely seen a lot more *hairsts* than their horseman had done.

But it was the stackyard that was the focus of the day. Here the rick-builder rose with his work to the bitter end and to an altitude that gave him a fine view over the steading's slates and the countryside beyond, which was always useful if he were the grieve and wanted to keep an eye as well on the folk in the harvest field. He was up there until they brought a ladder to let him down. His was the single most important task of the *hairst* for, finally, it was the stackyard that was important if the wealth of a good harvest was not to be lost. That importance is commemorated still in the names of some of the ballad touns; the look of its stackyard could tell you even more about the state of a place — the quality of its crops and maybe the worth of its tenant, for instance — than the look of its ploughing. It was the place, above all, where reputations were won or irretrievably lost, where the lesser-gifted might go down in parish history as "the man who let the weet into Hilly's cornyard".

Not all the farmtoun men were good rick-builders. Far from it. For all that, there was jealousy about a toun when it came to considering who was competent to *bigg* — more so perhaps than about who was entitled to drive the binder. Grieves, more distrustful than usual, tended to take on the job themselves, such was its importance and their conviction that no one else could do it. They persisted some of them till they were long past it and until they became a cause of concern.

It was a time in the farmtoun year when the expert might be paid a bonus for his talent, and while the job might also fall to the *orra man* (a senior member of the farmtoun crew, however much his title belied it), a gifted bailie could also be brought out of hiding for a week or two to become the "man of the toun".

But whoever he was, the stack-builder was never short of advice, much of it given in the safe knowledge that the recipient was beyond physical dissent. Grounded grieves were the worst: their raw, raucous voices sang a litany through the long *hairst* day.

"Come in, man. Come in, damn ye noo. . . ."

"Haud in yer easin's."

Or just as likely since there was no pleasing them:

"Lat oot yer easin's."

Or, initially, as the rick began to take shape:

"Keep up yer hert, noo" — which had not a damned thing to do with the builder's flagging spirits (which were of no concern to the grieve anyway) but an instruction to keep the sheaves and their heads higher at the centre of the rick so that any water penetrating it would run *out*, not *in*. The easings were the tricky point at which the stack began its slow taper into the final conical top. It was strongly held that a well-built rick should sway, six inches or so, at the easings and a critical or ill-humoured grieve would test this — and the builder's workmanship — by plunging his hands, armpit deep, into the rick and grabbing hold of two sheaves in it, to see whether it did so.

There were rick-builders who wore protective pads on their knees, usually folded seed-corn bags lashed in place round their cords with binder twine. Ostensibly the practice was to cushion the knees in a pre-chemical age against thistle-stobs, but in the hard-up days between the wars a man's main concern might be not to wear his *breeks* out before he saw where the next pair were to come from. Some grieves kept an old pair of *breeks* from one *hairst* to the next, especially for the job. Either way, the builder's hands had to take their chance — and the late dusk would find him busy on his doorstep with one of his wife's sewing needles, extracting the painful thistle-pricks from his thumbs.

If there was no end of advice for the novice builder, there was also about many of the North-east Lowlands touns something of more practical assistance: the poles that rose from the centre of the *foons* by courtesy of the Post Office's telegraphic department and (usually) legitimately obtained. Up to eight feet or ten feet in height, they rose from the foundation stones, giving the young builder a chance to keep his bearings and get his rick reasonably straight off the ground.

Like the cart-builders, the rick-builder worked in a clockwise direction, grabbing sheaves with his left hand, placing them, kneeing them down. . . . It was in the cornyard that the whole orchestration of the day melded and coalesced; that one saw, for instance, the reason behind the *gang* uniformity of the harvest carts: it evened out the loading and unloading times, the number of sheaves (more or less) that went into each of the stacks, the journey-times between field and farmtoun. All the horseman did who wanted to demonstrate his skill by building to six or eight *gangs* was to throw the day out of kilter and to ensure from the grieve a brief assessment about his future.

The ricks that rose on the stone *foons* — spread often with brushwood so that the heads of grain would not fall into them — were modest by the grand standards of the Lothians, nodding their heads at little more than twenty feet (and often a bit less) and rarely more than ten feet across. Each absorbed about six shelvinged loads of sheaves, each load taking about ten minutes to unload, though this depended on what stage rick-building had reached, and each rick taking around one hour to complete.

And behind that *hairst* day's pattern lay another, one that looked forward to another time, for each rick was the size, the capacity, of an afternoon's *thrash* with the barn mill: it contained the number of sheaves that could be carted-in and comfortably accommodated in the barn before the *yoking*'s threshing began. Thus there was no awkward rump of a rick left in the cornyard to cover with an old tarpaulin to wait for another day. Nor was there the need to *tirr* another rick in order to fill the straw-shed. On the kind of rough reckoning that was a godsend to grieves who had been slow at their sums, each rick absorbed an acre of crop; thus a hundred acres of oats would raise a hundred ricks in the cornyard.

The considerations, after all, were anything but prosaic.

But if the day was the rick-builder's, the folk on whom it pivoted were the forkers: their knack maintained its momentum, that endless shuttling chain of carts between field and cornyard. Their implement, the handtool of harvest as of the hay park, was the two-tined fork. It tossed sheaves from the stook to the cart and from the cart to the stack.

A good forker worked with the wind, never against it, taking two sheaves at a time — for balance, just below the band or the twine. One sheaf would have been unmanly, three bordering on ex-hibitionism. Now and then, desperate for haste, an old grieve, having delegated his stack-building, might descend in fury on the field to tear a fork from calloused hands and hurl whole stooks (or so it seemed whiles) at the surprised cart-builder. But then, there was always a lot of exhibitionism about a farmtoun.

In a light crop, the forker could take four sheaves at a time and might well do so, since accuracy was never a factor in forking to the cart. It did not matter too much where they fell: "sae lang as ye got them on tae the cairt, the man biggin' it could dae fit he liked wi' them."

Most, in fact, fell on the centre of the cart, where the man *bigging* it simply trampled some into the well with his feet while his hands deftly and simultaneously built the outer sheaves on to the frames.

In the cornyard it was another story. Here the rick-builder wanted his sheaves one at a time and at the pace that suited him. And it was here that the good forker came into his own. His mastery of the knack, that flick of the wrist, could deliver a sheaf exactly where it was wanted. Such men, in the rick's final stages, would balance themselves backwards on ladders thrown precari-ously against the side of the stack, as link-man between the low cart and the high rick-top, and send up sheaves unerringly and seemingly by instinct. Invariably, it seems now, they were tall steely men with horny hands and black moustaches who patently enjoyed the hazard of it.

Like the cutting, the leading brought the young horseman an opportunity he could not resist: the chance, if he could work it, to *lowse* a few minutes early. He contrived to reach the cornyard with time to off-load his sheaves but not to return to the field for another full load. His hope was that instead he would be sent to the stable.

Most grieves in fact had no trouble in dealing with that kind of thing and one at least found a way that quite silenced all dispute. A horseman took his cart back to the harvest field supposing he had time to load only one *gang* of sheaves before returning to the toun, where the cart was then backed into the cartshed and "propped" overnight. Such was the character and the iron will of the old farmtoun boss-men. Most were as strong in the mind as they were in body.

The thatching of the stacks, though it was important, might be left for a time, until the end of *hairst*. A stack well-built was by that fact watertight. And there was just then another anxiety, particularly round those touns where they had begun work at times while there was still dew on the stook: the fear of the stacks heating and destroying the grain. As the leading went on the cornyards became increasingly full of worried men thrusting their arms anxiously, and up to the armpit, into the new-built stacks to test their temperature.

The thatching was done with the previous year's straw or with rushes cut from the burnside, lashed down with ropes in a diamond pattern over the cone of the rick, the so-called lozenge pattern. It was the method that Stephens considered not only the most effective but the best-looking. And he was not an easy man to please. He describes the process of anchoring the thatch ropes, an art made so fast by the old farmtoun hand that its speed quite dazzled the eye: "The ends of the ropes are fastened to the stack by pulling out a little straw from a sheaf, twisting the rope and the straw together, and pushing through the twisted end between the rope and the stack."

There were grieves, for such was the pride of the old touns, who took the scythe to shave the side of their new-built ricks. Theirs was a quest for pure symmetry and perfection. And there were, well into the 1900s, still a few farmer men who put *tappies* (tops) on their stacks, to be tied down with the thatch. If the effect was highly ornamental, and maybe looked back to an ancient time and a darker superstition, the *tappies* were not without their functional purpose: they too were an additional means of keeping the rain out of the crown of the rick.

There was never any doubt about the relief a toun felt when it had all its crop home and into the cornyard, when (in the speak of the farmtoun men) it had "gotten winter" and the stacks stood

stately and proud in their rows as though ranked for inspection.
Their appearance in good order moved the heart and often
delighted the eye, though alas, there were small touns with
hurried cornyards where the ricks lurched like a *fee'd loon* at the
end of a fair day. Their haggard *hairsts* were something else
again, lacking that sweet orchestration and devoid of all grandeur. Their pool of labour ran to one horseman and his pair, an
orra loon and the gudewife who came aproned out from her
chores to fork to her gudeman building the stack. Theirs was
always a dour fight against the odds.

Still and all, even for them — and maybe most of all for them
— it was a landmark in the year when the *hairst* was home.

In the late evening light in the days that followed, when they
had their suppers taken and their Stonehaven pipes lit, old
farmer men took to haunting their cornyards in a deep contentment that only the landsman could know. It was a strange
compact that drew them and held them, a bond that ended only
in the grave. For the farmtoun's bairns the cornyard became a
place for *taakie* and plain malicious mischief as they waited
round the evening steading to collect their cottared fathers'
nightly flagons of warm milk.

It had other uses, too, the farmtoun stackyard, not least as a
refuge for the regular relief of nature in an unsanitary world
(whatever the wind's *airt*, you could squat there, safely out of it)
so that as the year drew on circumnavigation of the ricks became
necessarily more circumspect. And whiles, on mild moonlight
nights when a meal-and-ale or a Hogmanay ball had heightened
the blood, it became suddenly a place of clumsy and fevered
excitement.

The poets sang of the end of a hard-won *hairst*, Burns once
among them:

> That merry night we got the corn in,
> O sweetly, then, thou reems the horn in!

Maybe the later folk of the old northern touns lacked a little of his
exuberance. It is another poet, the homesick Charles Murray,
who superbly captures the feeling of heartfelt satisfaction they
felt as they at last took their breath and watched autumn's days
draw in to winter. "The Hint o' Hairst", however, does some-

thing else: it emphasises that continuity that was the flow of the
seasons, one into the next, that enduring involvement of man with
nature:

> O for a day at the Hint o' Hairst,
>   With the craps weel in an' stackit,
> When the farmer steps thro' the corn-yard,
>   An' counts a' the rucks he's thackit:
>
> When the smith stirs up his fire again,
>   To sharpen the ploughman's coulter;
> When the miller sets a new picked stane,
>   An' dreams o' a muckle moulter:
>
> When cottars' kail get a touch o' frost,
>   'That mak's them but taste the better;
> An' thro' the neeps strides the leggined laird,
>   Wi's gun an' a draggled setter:
>
> When the forester wi' axe an' keel
>   Is markin' the wind-blawn timmer,
> An' there's truffs aneuch at the barn gale
>   To reist a' the fires till simmer.
>
> Syne O for a nicht, ae lang forenicht,
>   Ower the dambrod spent or cairtin',
> Or keepin' tryst wi' a neebour's lass —
>   An' a mou' held up at pairtin'.

The note of melancholy is understandable, for Murray was far
from his Alford home, an exile on the South African veldt, when
he wrote it.

More dour but no less authentic is the mood of fulfilment caught
in the voice of another North-east poet, later in time but quite
poignantly reflecting the emptiness of fields shorn finally of their
harvest architecture:

> An we got her aff the grun', ae mair hairst!
> An noo fae Mormond Hill as far's Bennachie,
> The raikit stibble parks lie teem an quaet,
>   Wytin' for the ploo.

The poet is Flora Garry, the poem "Ae Mair Hairst". Strikingly, her lines reveal that custom of the old farmtoun men to refer to the year and its seasons as well as the land itself in the feminine gender. Thus, thankfully:

"She's been a guid hairst, this year bypast."

Or maybe, as was always more frequent:

"She's been an ill-hairst."

Or, reflecting:

"She was a fine spring thon year."

"She was a dour bitch of a back-end, yon."

Their old slow speak had its own spare elegance.

So the sinews slackened and the Clydesdale's gait, and the horseman's step slowed again.

There were years, indeed, when the *hairst* was a heartbreak, a near-endless onding of rain, when the corn sprouted in the stook. In the brief intervals when the weather faired, yellow-oil-skinned men would be seen in the fields, figures slow-motioned as in a moonscape, re-setting the stooks the winds and the nights of storm had torn down — or maybe themselves tearing down the stooks on the clean-land ground where the grass was already growing up the sheaves, capillarying damp. You marvelled whiles at their persistence, their stoicism. There were few years, in fact, when the farmtoun *hairsts* were not late or wet, or more likely both — a few so late indeed that the bothy lads of one toun might "get winter" a few days before Martinmas, the Term that ended their six-month engagement, and go home to another to begin leading again.

The countryside would be cast down by the tragedy of it all, so that cottars at their Sunday evening doors quizzed home-coming bothymen about the state of the crops in neighbouring parishes. Going by on their bikes, the bothy lads laconically reported:

"Hillheid's fair flat – ivvery park."

Or:

"Stobshill's crap is just fair connached."

Folk felt for Hilly and Stobby, an unspoken grief, sly rascals though they were both of them in the feeing fair.

XI

The Gold of Autumn

A WELL-BUILT CORNYARD was a joyous thing; it gladdened the heart and gleamed in the last glow of the evening sunlight. In its ordered ranks and under its pleasing uniformity — for its stacks were built the same size regardless of crop, barley alongside the ubiquitous oat — lay a pattern that subtly demarcated and graded. Its secrets were noted in blunt pencil (well wetted with spittle) in a distressed notebook that was the farmer's only diary, or locked in the clutter of the grieve's mind. The one was only marginally more reliable than the other.

Such groupings distinguished, on the toun's own estimate, possible milling oats (for oatmeal, that grand staple of northern life) from feeding oats (for livestock consumption) and discreetly cloistered the stacks of good-quality crop that might be threshed-out for seed corn when the New Year was put past and the merchant's price was such that it might bring in a penny or two. Long weeks after the crop had been brought in there had to be found without error the good from the indifferent.

Yet no space was wasted. As the ricks rose on their *foons* the avenues between them had to be wide enough to let the travelling threshing-mill — the drum of the English countryside — pass between them. Too wide, however, and the avenues would make the *thrashing* cumbersome and ungainly, less the compact, tightly-contained operation it should be.

Stephens believed the best place for the cornyard was to the north side of the toun's *biggings*, where it would be exposed to the north-east and west winds. An earlier student of farming affairs, Lord Belhaven, had in 1699 favoured both barn and barnyard on the west side of the toun, preferably on a bit of a knoll where the wind could get to the ricks. Not every toun was so concerned about its setting, which might be a little apart from the main cluster of buildings and the barn. Yet there were few touns not preoccupied with its contents or the bounty it might bring them.

For grain was the gold of the farmtouns, as it had been of old Scotland. It paid ransom and reward; more than his *stirks* it took a man back from the brink. If it no longer paid the tradesman's account directly, as once it had done, or (in part) the tenant's rent, the minister's stipend (collected in his vast girnal at the manse and sold as needs arose) or the hangman's fee (by "lock" or handful taken from each sack on market day), it was still the hardest currency of the old landscape. A sharp dip in its price, as all through history, sent men scurrying from corn and into the new security of cattle beasts, its upsurges as quickly hastening their return to the plough. That was the way of it in the bare-knuckle land of the North-east Lowlands, as elsewhere.

Happy though he would be to get a good price in the mart for his black *stots*, his fattened steers, it was traditionally to his grain crop that a farmer looked to take him out of debt. A man far in at the bank or behindhand in his settlement with his seed merchant, would have the threshing-mill about his toun almost in the middle of *hairst* — set up in a corner of the harvest field to thresh straight out of the stook. In such haste, that told its own story to a knowledgeable countryside, the sheaves went straight off the "leading" carts on to the drum's shelving. The price per quarter would not be what he wanted, to be sure, but then again the handling circumvented the long labour of stack-building in the cornyard and even the *strae soo* that resulted would probably be built in the same corner of the field. If it was a little unseemly, it was also the kind of agriculture that let a man live to farm another day.

But if corn was the hard currency of the land, it was also a part of its deep-rooted history, a factor in some of its bitterest chapters. The touns of the old landscape looked back on a past that had seen famine, riot and strife, with the laird himself hardly immune: his "rents in kind" gave him the wide circle of friends needed to empty his girnals and the backlog to stave off starvation but not the kind of *siller* to lock into his London bank or that enabled him to cut a figure in its society. There had been times when tempers ran dangerously high, with the precious grain locked for export into shore-side granaries when it was more needed in the countryside that had produced it. Out of the gaunt granaries of the region's coastal ports — some still to be seen, severe and prison-like in their dour vernacular architecture — and on to waiting vessels to line

the speculator's pocket went grain needed to feed hungry Scottish
mouths. In the black thraw of the late 1700s, when the crops failed
widely, merchants unscrupulously bought up oatmeal for ship-
ment abroad at a handsome profit, and brought trouble to
quaysides round the north-east coast, that of the oil-town of
Peterhead among them. The authorities there, not new to strife,
were driven to issue a stern warning in the May of 1793:

> Whereas it appears that several of the inhabitants of this place
> are apprehensive that there will be a scarcity of meal here this
> summer, owing to the greatest part of the farm meal in the
> neighbourhood being sold for exportation, and also to the great
> quantities of meal which have been monopolised and bought up
> by meal dealers, and whereas it further appears from an
> advertisement or handbill put up on the warehouse, that some of
> the inhabitants are disposed to mob and prevent by force any
> meal from being shipped from this port, which might be
> attended by very serious consequences, not only to themselves
> but to the publick at large. Therefore, in order to quiet the
> minds of the people and to prevent their having recourse to any
> improper measures, it is requested that all inhabitants who are
> not already supplied, or who have not sufficient stock in hand,
> will give note of the quantities required by them for the support
> of themselves and their families for six months to William Jack,
> mealseller in Peterhead . . . that it may be known what quantity
> will be necessary for the supply of the town till the new crops can
> be ready, and that proper steps can be taken to purchase and
> secure this quantity so as to prevent any dread of scarcity. And,
> in the meantime, it is earnestly recommended to all the
> inhabitants not to proceed to any acts of outrage, as mobs and
> unlawful combinations are, at all times, improper and highly
> punishable, and particularly so at this time as being destructive
> of the peace, order and welfare of society.

In such times of crisis, Commissioners of Supply curbed prices
and the worst excesses of the profiteers and proclamations were
read at market crosses all round the countryside.

There were lean times as late as 1847 and these again brought
trouble. Out of Port Gordon, round the coast, created by the
fourth Duke of Gordon in 1797 as part of his great improvement

plan, sailed the grain cargoes grown in the seatown's hinterland, and tempers fanned to a high fury in its wind-scoured streets as the rumour spread that the Duke was collecting and storing grain. Special constables, quickly sworn in, were unable to prevent the irate townsfolk from laying siege to the home of the corn-dealer, who had to be protected by armed coastguards until troops arrived from Huntly.

But, those dark days behind it, the north-east coast resumed its business: out of even such small ports as Newburgh, on the Ythan's estuary, sailed schooners and steamships creaking under their loads of autumn gold. And even Port Gordon, quietened by the lull of history, continued its flow of grain exports almost to the dawn of the 1900s.

Wheat, its domain down in the east-central heart of Scotland and in the south-east, both kindlier landscapes, was little grown round the north-east. It was the kingdom of the oat and *girdled breid*, and the concentration was striking in the ballad counties with Aberdeenshire, as late as 1934, producing 930,000 quarters, far ahead of the oats output of any other Scottish shire. That year the county, now lost in the bureaucratic conglomerate of Grampian, grew 173,631 acres of oat crop, a mere 154 acres of wheat against Angus's 18,605, with barley accounting for a further 12,248 acres.

By then the Scottish oat had come a long, long way from its humble origins, far indeed from the old grey oat, sometimes called the sma' oat, that was the main crop of the early 1700s. Its unhealthy look when ripe, an unwholesome pasty-grey colour, had done nothing to give folk any confidence in it and forecast what they all already well knew: its lamentable inability to provide anything but a meagre amount of meal. It was by far the poorest in the Europe of its time and persisted in the lonely outposts of the Highlands until after the Forty-five, when it was finally pensioned off to the cattle-pen.

The white oat, reaching the region about the same time as the Great White Sheep, the Cheviot, but with far better results, gave more than twice the amount of meal, and had the kind of perfection that pleased even Stephens: "Plump, short and beardless," he called it.

For long, as the new one-tenant farmtouns evolved, *tattie corn* (the potato oat) was the most common variety, developed, it was thought, from an Essex oat that had once misjudged its venue, though neither that nor its nationality were held against it. Its grain quality was tolerable and reliable and on anything like fair ground it gave a reasonable yield of good straw for feeding, a fact of more importance then than now. By the mid-1930s, however, things had moved on considerably. Then, in the last days of the traditional farming associated with the old touns, there had come the kind of frenzied cross-breeding that would not have disgraced a racing stud. The Scottish Plant Breeding Station, south at Corstorphine, outside Edinburgh, was unveiling about then two new varieties: Elder (resistant to lodging, that nightmare of a wettish *hairst*, but a bit of a late-ripener in northern fields) and Bell, which did well in the thinner soil of upcountry parks. The Station had also just come up with another new variety, Early Miller. Its Certificate of Registration was notably more fulsome and a lot more respectable than many a cottar bairn's. It was a

> white-grained oat which is in general character intermediate between its parents, Potato and Record; an early ripening variety suitable for general cultivation and high-yielding on fertile soils. The grain is short and plump, well-filled, and of an attractive colour; not thick in the husk, gives a high bushel weight, and shows promise of being a high-class milling oat. The straw is of good fodder quality and of medium length, and possesses a high degree of resistance to lodging.

About the old farmtouns there were men who took on wives knowing far less about them. It was the climate, Stephens claimed, that brought the oat to its greatest perfection in Scotland and it was natural enough that in a landscape that had once weighed a man's worth in grain — as late as 1780 the gardener at historic Cawdor House was paid twelve bolls, the maltster ten and the poor shepherd only five bolls — that the latter-day farmtouns should face the same judgement. They counted their success or failure in quarters-to-the-acre, a yield equation that rarely matched the farmer's hope or the sweat wrung from men's shirts in trying to achieve it. Mostly the old touns settled for modest returns, happy to get ten quarters from ley land, always the better crop, willing to take seven from the clean-land corn. The later target of twelve quarters would have been considered an exceptionally good run of grain.

Such was its hold and continuity, the grain in the fields transcended tenancies. When a crop, like the toun, changed hands, the exchange was ratified in that old, immemorial measure. Auctioneer and valuator met to stride the toun's corn parks, heads thoughtfully bowed as they walked, their hands caressing the heads of the standing grain. Their assessment set the yield the incomer would pay for — and hope to harvest.

In the circumstances the old touns were jealous of their corn, roused by unaccountable loss from their grain lofts and seldom unmoved by damage caused to their stackyards. There, at first, the number of ricks diminished slowly, their sheaves needed to get bedding straw. And soon after *hairst*, there would be the more concentrated thresh of a few ricks to give the toun its cottars' corn, grain to send to the miller to make perquisite oatmeal, and maybe another early flurry to get 50 quarters to foot some outstanding bill.

The weekly thresh had its inviolable ritual. The barn operation about a modest-sized toun would occupy the greater part of an afternoon's *yoking*, from one o'clock to shortly after four, when it was time for the toun's bailies to return to their byres to "sort their nowt" before *lowsing*-time. Just two stacks would be threshed usually, sometimes only one: as little as would keep the toun going, or as much as could be carted into the barn beforehand.

The flail, though it lingered round the crofts as a threshing tool until the turn of the present century, had passed largely into the realm of folklore before the one-unit farmtouns came into their own. From the early 1800s right up and into the 1900s, the barn mills were mainly powered by horses: a pair, or sometimes three, according to the size of the thresher. But if there were some hope that a dam could be created that would fill up regularly so that a good head of water could be built up, the mill might be water-powered by bucket-wheel.

The farmtoun dam, alas, never quite lived up to the promise of what seemed a predominantly wet climate, with the result that the threshing in this case would have to be done in inconveniently small doses since the power quickly dried up. Mostly the touns were content to rely on the proven pull of their Clydesdales, yoked to the outside capstan of the horsegang — in Aberdeenshire, the mill-*coorse* (course) — on which the horses walked round and round while their horseman walked a contra circuit. His role was important in getting a "good thrash", as Stephens explains:

Lagging [by the horses] causes the machine to take in the sheaves with difficulty, and at every start the sheaf will be drawn through suddenly, and escape the beaters. Now, a steady driver walks the course in an opposite direction to the horses, and he meets every horse quietly twice in every round of the course. Irregular action of the horses injures the more complicated parts of the machine, and makes bad work in the threshing and dressing of the corn.

Only the arrival of the temperamental oil-engine with all its tantrums would release the Clydes from the monotony of their threshing afternoons.

Dressing the corn in the farmtoun loft was no easier task. Here on dark mornings before the horsemen could get to the plough, and at the end of the short afternoons when they left it, they were gainfully employed by time-conscious grieves in putting grain through the fanner, the *winnoster*, a job, as the bothy songs will tell you, that could leave you with a very sweaty *sark*. Once the dressing of the corn had been women's work. Says folk historian Helen Beaton in her uplands recollections of the mid-1800s, *At the Back o' Benachie*:

> [they] helped to winnow the corn between the barn doors when there was wind, a method of procedure which accounts for the two doors often seen in old barns, placed opposite. Later, however, the barn fan or "fanners" came into use, which was at first rather clumsy and stiff to drive. After the noise of the flail had ceased for ever, and a horse or water mill had taken its place, the corn-chaff and short straw were all mixed under the mill in a rough state. The fan was used to separate the corn from the chaff, and had to be "fed" into the hopper by hand. This was termed the "first ca' throu'" and when the corn was put through the fan the second time, it was called the "dressin' oot".

About grander touns they called the corn loft the granary. It was a thing of their time, born of the fever of those high improvement times and the frenzied rebuilding of the mid-1800s, and under-lined the growing emphasis on a more sophisticated, commercial farming. It was located usually above the long run of the cart-pends and at times gave a most pleasing loggia'd look to the sterner lines of the new toun's architecture. The stored grain would not be contaminated by the breath of beasts from the stable or byre below, a consideration that never influenced the placing of the bothy lads' domain above the Clydesdales.

Before the granary's appearance, the corn of the old countryside took its chance in *bykes*, beehive-shaped "ricks" of unthreshed sheaves built with a hollow down the centre. The grain was poured into this and, provided it was dry at the time and the "rick" adequately thatched, kept well enough. It was a ploy that much took Pennant's fancy in more northerly Caithness, where they had "neither barns nor granaries".

The afternoons of the barn mill, though, were but a prelude: what the cornyard with its groupings and its well-ordered symmetry awaited was the *mull*, the steam-driven portable threshing-mill. Its appearance about any toun brought on a state of extreme tension, not to say, at times, an almost uncontrolled hysteria. As much as *hairst*, and in some ways maybe more so, it was a culmination, the supreme moment of the year: it sprang as surely from the sowing of spring and had gathered momentum in the flurry of harvest. And if one could be heartbreaking, the other was back-racking.

The steam-mill endlessly travelled the end-of-year roads, from one toun on to the next, its headquarters stance through the slacker months of summer a clearing in some old quarry or among the roadside trees. On its winter rounds its progress was imperious. Other traffic deferred to it, going willingly into the ditch to be out of its way. Nervous Clydesdales would jump the dyke or hedge for it, terrified, taking cart and horseman and all. Its processing indeed was almost triumphal. Down from it as they passed by, almost disdainfully, gazed its sootie-faced crew, black as Dixieland minstrels the pair of them. In the din of their small platform, under the canopied hood, their communication was a series of gestures and nods and in time they grew like a long-married couple, each knowing what to do and when to do it.

But just as often the mill and the traction engine — their names reflecting their roving and heroic existence, with a strong run to Scottish patriots: Wallace, Bruce and the like — moved by night, showering sparks into the sky but otherwise maybe not as well lit as they should have been and sometimes not even lit at all — something you could not always say of the driver. For it was the custom at the end of a thresh that had shown any respectable yield to give the mill-men and the mill folk a dram to take the dust of the cornyard from their throats before they dispersed.

If the folk did not need it for that reason, they welcomed it for another: the chance that it might keep them on their feet until they reached home and their beds. For the threshing mill was savage work.

In the cornyard it took its station between two of the parallel rows of stacks, always at first with some difficulty and with the kind of lurid curses that rent the evening gloam and kept the womenfolk to the house. It had to be level to work efficiently and to thresh as the toun had a right to expect. The machine itself was a marvel of riddles and belts. Connecting rods pumped back and forth in a disciplined fury; pulleys spun, fans whirred. The noise was stupendous, its *stew*, its dust, asthmatic. From its throb and vibration the cornyard trembled. Bearings got suddenly overheated and so did the mill-men and the grieve. Corn and cavings were secretively sifted through the mill's dark intestines: shuffled and shunted with a diabolical skill to emerge in time from their appointed orifices and from its underbelly, on to the chaff-sheet. The corn, the yellow gold of autumn, came scuttling down its spouts at one end into the gaping mouths of the waiting sacks; at the other an endless stream, a tangled web of straw spun from the shakers, spilling into the cornyard. The corn bags were seized as they filled, like unwilling hostages, torn from their hooks and thrown bodily on to the *stalyart*, the steelyard, beside them. The ritual was remorseless.

Ask an old farmtoun horseman or bailie his most persistent memory of the hard tasks of the farming year and he will hardly hesitate: "Oh, the mull—the thrashin' mull. She wis sair wark richt enough." The visit of the mill was more than a gathering of folk and a day of droll stories. A day's *thrash* was a test of human stamina and, in its ancillary job, the heaving of heavy sacks of grain, probably broke more men physically than any other single task. Sir Maitland Mackie, a man closely identified with the farming of the ballad touns, recalls in *The Book of Bennachie* the steam-mill *thrash*, its tasks and its commitments:

. . . it took a minimum of fourteen workers to have a good thrash. Two good men to fork off the rick on to the mill, two men or women to lowse or cut the twine on the sheaf and hand to the man who fed the mill. He was one of two who alternated between looking after the steam engine and feeding the mill. It took two good men to weigh the grain and carry it away to a suitable spot for loading. Then the chaff and the cuffins had to be kept clear of the mill by one man or boy. The building of the straw soo was an expert job that took one builder and three assistants. Lastly, the hungry engine had to be kept supplied with water and coal, which took another man. To gather a squad of fourteen to sixteen people together . . . was beyond the capabilities of any one farm, so the policy of neighbouring or neeperin grew. It became an unwritten obligation for several farms to join together on thrashing days and as a result there was great competition between farms to see which could put through the greatest number of quarters of corn per day. Herculean feats of labour were accomplished, specially by the grain men when two hundred quarters of oats or more were bagged, weighed and stacked during one day. Since they lifted each bag at least twice, they were lifting and carrying some sixty tons by sheer brute strength, which today is of course all done mechanically.

The feeder's job may have been less back-breaking but it was unquestionably the most dangerous. It needed an attentive skill and carelessness down the farmtoun years took a punishing toll in mangled and torn limbs. Rhythmically he swung, working from one side (with its waiting sheaf) to the other (where another sheaf was waiting), fanning the sheaves ears-first into the mill's drum. It was an action superb in its economy of motion, giving the highest possible throughput, and it emphasised yet again that the orchestration of farmtoun work was far, far from being clod-hopping and unsophisticated. In method study, as we have repeatedly seen, the touns had little to learn.

But in its precision and in its concentration it was tiring work, numbing the arms after a time and, because of that, increasing the hazard. For this reason, the mill-men regularly took over from each other, and where the feeder was a horseman the grieve, for once, would give him a rest from the work.

The role had its crucial responsibilities: feeding too fast, for instance, meant that the crop would not be properly threshed, with a consequent loss of yield, the only benefactors being the byre beasts that would get the unexpected titbit of a corn-ear or two in with their feeding straw.

The smoothness of the feeder's work in turn depended on the skill of his *lowsers*, the men or women who were preparing the sheaves for him. When they were women — more nimble-fingered and therefore often faster at the task — they would probably be recruited from the nearby village. Day long, in their Edwardian long skirts and enormous brimmed and flower-bedecked hats (old, yet unquestionably *à la mode*) anchored by scarves tied under the chin, they stood on the high mill-shelvings up to the full blast of the wintry wind, and often with snow on the ground.

Some could cut so unerringly close to the binder's knot that the sheaf string was re-usable to tie the thresh's corn sacks, though latterly the *mull* became so insatiable there was no longer time for such economies.

The *lowsers* on the mill-shelvings were in turn supplied by the forkers working off ricks at either side of the mill. It was possible with sufficient labour to thresh out eight ricks, four on either side, without moving the threshing-mill, which was time-wasting. Sheaf went to shelving in a clever relay, an extended human chain, men on the outer ricks forking on to the inner ricks on each side, where the sheaves would be forked-on to the mill.

The corn that danced down the mill's corn chutes filled bags collected earlier from the toun's corn merchant; the straw that cascaded like candyfloss from the mill's shakers at the other end was carried away elsewhere in the cornyard to become straw ricks, or, as Sir Maitland Mackie suggests, to be built into a *strae soo*. Latterly the *strae soo* had something of a vogue round the bigger touns. It was the size of a house and pointed, rising to a height of fifteen feet at least. Mostly though, the old touns put their straw into ricks.

Every stack of it would be wanted. Even the chaff and the *cuffins*, the corn husks blown out at one side of the mill and the rough waste, broken bits of straw and so on blasted out at the other, had their value. About modest touns they would be strewn in the muck midden to enrich it, first used even to eke out the beasts' bedding straw. Only about the crack touns with their largesse of dung could they afford the expansive gesture of throwing the chaff into a neglected corner of the stackyard.

Once it started, few things stopped the din and the frenetic activity of the threshing-mill. But a downpour of rain did, or an onding of snow. High wind too might cause havoc and final abandonment of the work by persistently blowing the straw back down the shakers and "choking" the *mull*. Even that though did not always stop the ingenious men of the farmtouns: they simply turned the mill the other way round to give it the wind at its back. A howling gale, however, made the straw handling impossible. Then the threshing *had* to stop.

Straw then was valuable, but never more than the grain itself, the corn-gold of autumn. It went to the corn merchant's or the railhead by the cart-load; each load of ten sacks arranged in a traditional order that balanced the cart and the weight on the shafts. The long convoy of carts setting out from a toun in the morning light was an impressive sight. And even here there was the kind of method study that marked all the touns' rituals. One man, when his carts were loaded, would set off ahead of the rest in order to have his carts off-loaded and be ready to assist the turn-round of the other horsemen when they arrived. All returned home together, through the still of the winter landscape, getting off the main turnpike road at least before darkness overtook them — carts and Clydesdales silhouetted in the last gleam of a red-streaked sky, each horseman hunched on the shelving of his lead cart, the reins slack in his fingers as he swayed with its motion, the parks quiet then, their silence broken only by the sound of the horses' feet, the slither of iron-runged wheels and the jingle of harness. It was a sight lost to us when the merchant's own steam lorry began to pick up the grain from the cornyard as each day's threshing ended. And now too the heyday of the *mull* and its legends and the passion it once drove men to, has passed into the mists of folk history.

XII

When the Potato was King

SUMMER LONG THE potatoes lay deep in the drill, dark with history: they had in their time precipitated tragedy and altered destinies. Their field, in the farmtouns' later days, was — sometimes still is — the last bastion of the countryside's casual labour force, the final refuge for the cottar-wife now that she was no longer needed at *hairst*, in the hayfield or, in any numbers, in the dairy. Maybe that is emancipation of a kind though some, undoubtedly, would call it a harsh redundancy. In its needs the *tattie* park has always posed something of a problem, social and educational, and became in its employment of child labour the dominie's eternal dilemma. It was not that the children minded, far from it, but society as a whole as it became increasingly town-based. It troubled the conscience. Yet the need remained, apparently insurmountable, well into the age of intensive farm mechanisation.

If it did nothing else, the problem underlined the potato's importance.

Humble it may be but it has rejoiced in taking its name at times from the highest in the land. With all the hallmarks now of a native, it is in fact an interloper that swapped the shade of the South American sombrero for a much colder clime and the comfort of the farmtoun bonnet. Drake or Raleigh — and no one is authoritatively saying which — brought it to Britain from the Indians of that continent, where it had grown wild for 2,000 years.

It came north from England with the drovers, who by the very nature of their calling were unable to travel empty-handed, and across the sea from Ireland. It was not an instant success: a garden rarity at first, it graced the laird's table and then the minister's while the common folk partially-boiled it to fill their hungry horses' bellies and push down that day's helping of crushed whins — hardly an auspicious start for the root that would become king of the cottar's board and everybody's friend: the improver's, the Highlander's and the peasantry's country-wide.

According to Robert Chambers in his *Domestic Annals*, the potato was first heard of in Scotland in 1701. Its early cultivation was by the lazy-bed method or, simpler still, the crofter's one of scooping a hole, popping the seed tuber into it, and putting the turf back like a lid on top. Its delicacy was such that for the cultivated palate it sold in the capital by the ounce and by the pound. It was when it came out of the kailyard into the field — a Stirlingshire man in 1728 apparently being the first to so transfer it, planting a half-acre that brought spectators thronging from miles around — that a new element was added to the cropping pattern of the farmtouns.

The potato was known in the North-east by then. Says J. E. Handley in *Scottish Farming in the Eighteenth Century*: "In Kincardineshire the potato was first cultivated about the year 1725 in the village of Marykirk by an old soldier who had brought it from Ireland; but he remained only a season there and the potato was not reintroduced until 1760." Thus was an early lead lost to an area that would become an important producer, an example, perhaps, of how unpropitious were the potato's early days.

On its return, not even its most fervid champions would have predicted how close the alliance would become or foreseen the Scottish predominance in seed-growing in later years.

The early potato, in fact, did not enjoy the vigorous good health hoped for it. So sickly was it that men flocked to its aid in the hope of helping it and thereby adding lustre to their own names by breeding livelier varieties. In Edinburgh, about 1750, Potato Wilkie of Ratho, a kenspeckle academic whom Henry Grey Graham dubs "that grotesque lout of genius", came on the scene and was soon absorbed in its culture. By then the potato was being grown as a field crop in the north also, mainly by the improvers, and by the early 1800s east-coast men were pursuing potato perfection as avidly as Wilkie had done, William Paterson of Dundee with some claim to pre-eminence among them.

But there would be others: Archibald Finlay, for instance, the *tattie* impresario from Fife who became none the poorer by filling the fields with such prestigious varieties as the much-grown Majestic, Up-to-Date, and Eldorado and British Queen. In contrast, the Arran grocer, Donald McKelvie of Lamlash, with patient devotion, quietly put his island on the northern potato map with a whole string of successful varieties such as Arran Pilot,

Arran Chief, Arran Crest, Arran Consul, Arran Comrade and so on. The modest grocer could not have realised the impact he would have on those distant acres of the farmtouns, where "Pilot" particularly became a favourite with such astute growers as Keith of Cairnbrogie, a man who was never far away when the inspectors came yearly to hand out their Stock Seed certificates.

By the time the touns came out of their boom years between 1840 and 1880, the national acreage in potatoes would be 190,000, having risen from 25,000 in 1775. That would dip during the depression years — with 134,000 in 1939 — but quickly and vitally re-establish itself at 236,000 acres in wartime 1943.

There were good reasons for the mid-1800s expansion, not least the rising town populations and the fact that, unlike the grain crop, potatoes as yet faced little competition from abroad. But there was, too, another factor: the seed market. The farmtouns, especially those of the central eastern seaboard, were to be the cradle of a Scottish seed trade that would spread its influence worldwide. Potatoes slid increasingly into the rotation, going on to the stubble as well as breaking up the ley. The *tattie*, far from home on Scotland's plain, was brought to a fine perfection and promptly re-routed to the outposts of empire, significantly to the Mediterranean ports and even back, enhanced out of all recognition, to its homeland of South America.

The triumph is one too little sung. It had to do with soil characteristics and climate as well as with men and good farming. The names of the new varieties were indicative of their breeders' assessment of their standing — and of their own achievement. Royalty featured widely and Queen Victoria was honoured in the drills. She may not have been amused. We cannot say now. King Edward (1902), only now fading from the scene, was a good cooker, and has endured longer than his yield potential may have deserved.

Sometimes a perfectly respectable potato travelled under an alias, and King Edward was a grander re-christening of a Northumberland variety. The cottar's and crofter's favourite, Duke of York, had changed its identity and come grandly north from the Lothians to find its large early-potato following. Up-to-Date, Finlay's long-stayer, it is said, was sold at various times under 200 names. There were other varieties, more practical and prosaic, that held the love of the country consumer and concentrated on colour: the cottar's Kerr's Pink (the creation of a man of Dumfries who came to grow his potatoes in Banffshire and lived to be ninety), Edzell Blue and Golden Wonder. None had the least cosmopolitan lustre, but Kerr's Pinks were widely grown for the cottars' perquisite potatoes and some cottars would not have "flitted" had they been offered anything less.

With little else to be connoisseurs of, they knew their potatoes and the horsemen and bailies of the touns in their "yards" kept their old loyalties regardless of international trade, their only criteria the look of well-being on the plate and the taste on the palate. Men, at their relaxed Sunday *denners* as they visited each other, admired each other's potatoes much as they extolled each other's wives, with an excessive politeness and the assurance (as was only good manners) that they were indeed without blemish. And their interest went deeper even than culinary assessment: it was also economic, for the cottar's kailyard "earlies" had to carry him through to the delivery of his perquisite maincrop load. There was concern always in a cottar's house until he had settled his Whitsunday *fee* and it was known in which "yard" he would be planting his seed potatoes.

Like the turnip field, with its similar initial tillage, the potato park had its distinctive rituals: in spring, with the corn sown, the planting; a summer of cosseted growth; and in the days of autumn the gathering that sometimes got in the way of the corn harvest. The patterns of labour would survive down the years as that great recorder Stephens saw them, the cameo of the planting in his *Book of the Farm* as valid in the 1930s as it had been in the mid-1800s. One ploughman sets up the drills on the well-tilled ground, another carts dung to the ridges, where it is spread along the drills by women — cottars' wives doubtlessly riven from their endless washtubs. Women planters follow, stooping to place the seed. Finally comes the drill plough again, the final movement, closing earth once again, over dung and potatoes. Truly little changed, except that maybe the women of the later *tattie* parks were more rumbustious lasses wearing their men's breeks or dungarees and sometimes their old cloth bonnets. Those who did not hold with such things appeared for the day heavily jumpered and scarf-wrapped, tammied and wellington-booted.

Besides the women, the planting squad of that later time would have at least an equal number of schoolchildren in their early teens, there on that grey April or early-May day with or without the dominie's consent. All were hired by the day and, whatever their age, were expected to justify their presence there.

In line abreast, seed-laden bags slung satchel-like in front of them, they dead-marched down the dunged drills as though to some solemn funeral dirge unheard on the wind, heads bent, seed potatoes dropping from mittened fingers into the drill-bottom to nestle there, each in its turn nudged with the heel of one boot against the toecap of the other, that sequence endlessly repeating throughout the long day: foot/potato/foot/potato. It gave the necessary equal spacing between each.

The tedium was lifted only by the coarse jokes and farmtoun drollery, for the days of the planting gave an old grieve the opportunity to be a "big man". It was seldom that he had so many folk about the place. Back and forth behind the work-gang he strode the drills, inspecting, looking for fault and easily finding it, cursing more than praising (which was always bad policy), spurring his troops — quick with the quip that could put a plukey-faced *loon* in his place and with the kind of riposte that would bring the blush to a young cottar-wife's cheek. There were grieves who were especially strong on sexual innuendo, so that the day might turn into a bizarre education for any young lad, away and beyond his years and long, long before he had the functional need of it.

The bag-slung-before-you, however, was the easy method, permitted only about the placid touns where they took life more stoically. There were more pernickety men who boxed their seed potatoes and — maybe taking their cue from Stephens — insisted that you placed each tuber in the drill (if into a dollop of dung, so be it) and with its gaze to the sky. Their work-gangs had to bend their backs, dragging the seed-boxes along the top of the drill beside them. In the end of the day such men had better potatoes, though they might be damnably short of friends. Planting for such touns was back-breaking work and you were thankful for the *yoking*'s end and *piece*-time, the midday break, when you could sit down and put your sore back against the dyke as you ate your oatcakes and cheese. (You would marvel whiles at townsfolk's penchant for picnics.)

The following weeks brought to the potato fields the kind of hoe-husbandry associated with the turnip parks and, uniquely, that most sedate of farming patrols, the rogueing squad whose destiny it was to stalk the summer drills stripped to *semmits* under a burning sun (and sometimes to the bra as lady-student roguers got more daring) or as oil-skinned as Peterhead fishermen.

Their prey was the "rogue", the cuckoo in the nest, the eccentric plant that dared to be different. They were a bad influence, like all such species, and for the seed-grower disastrous. The search was relentless; fugitives were found, fault was uncovered wherever it lay: leaf-roll and mosaic, blacklegs far, far from all industrial contention, all the flaws and diseases the poor *tattie* had suddenly fallen heir to. The patrollers halted from time to time in their magisterial tracks, each in his or her row, to debate this or that, incipient traces: should it go, should it stay? They discussed, took counsel, argued and fell out among themselves over what was the acceptable cull in a field for which they had some prospect of a cherished Stock Seed certificate.

Rogues were dug cleanly from the drill, expunged from all contact with their healthier well-doing neighbours and carried off in the sack of the bag-man, who walked two paces behind the roguer's back so as not to crash into him every time he stopped suddenly.

Yet the contention was worth it, not only financially to the toun concerned but to the man in charge. A promise of "Stock Seed" when the inspectors came sent him home to his supper that night like a champion from the jousting arena. The price he paid was a ceaseless watch. Rumour of the Colorado Beetle, too, woke a vigilance in the land that could not have been greater had the *Wehrmacht* been spotted suddenly in the *neep* parks of Buchan — and as suddenly led to the mass-capture of innocent ladybirds and the swamping of small country post offices with carefully-addressed matchboxes going registered post to Edinburgh.

Autumn and October brought another work-gang to the toun: the gatherers, often the same folk who had so solemnly and ceremoniously committed the seed to the ground those few months before. They came, as before, recruited from far and near, by personal canvass and the whisper on the country grapevine, in an assortment of sizes and abilities. Again a large number came out of the schoolroom, their presence this time at least with the blessing of the education authorities and sanctioned as the "*tattie* holidays", long a hallowed tradition of the Scottish rural school. Many came who would not have been chosen. All by the end of the day had something in common: an aching back.

Wartime squads were lifted in the early light like dawn commandoes from all surrounding villages by van, lorry and tractor bogey, half-awake folk who came running from the shadows clutching Thermoses and *piece*-bags and fell asleep again as soon as their backs touched the support of the bogey's shelving. Once, with food less critical, folk had made their way on foot or two on a bicycle to the field.

It took, by Stephens' estimate, 20 to 24 gatherers to keep the spinner digger going in a moderate crop, with a lifting capability of four to five acres for the day. The touns of the 1930s and of the World War Two years were usually happy to settle for less: say, a squad of 20 or so which managed to keep the digger circulating comfortably and maintain an output of at least three acres a day, though that, as always, depended on the weight of the crop as well as the expertise of the gatherers.

The *tattie*-gathering is a sharp memory still in the minds of all those who share the experiences of a Scottish country childhood. Like Ramsay MacDonald, that sad, doomed premier, they worked to augment the household income. Yet it is a task, strangely, that awoke in Lewis Grassic Gibbon an apathy unexpected. Of the potato-gathering, he says in *The Land*: ". . . somehow they are not real harvests, they are not truly of Autumn as is the taking in of the corn. It is still an alien plant . . . an intruder from that world of wild belief and wilder practice that we call the New, a plant that hides and lairs deep down in the midst of back-breaking drills."

So it did. The ritual that harvested it and brought it again into the light took the old grieve back to the field at the head of his troops, a general deploying unknown forces. Work started from the gate, when he had paced the endrig to mark off the number of drills estimated as that day's acreage: it was land he hoped to gain ere that day's end. He paced then the length of the drill, counting from one endrig to the other. There, dourly incommunicado, he would take an old envelope from his pocket and the stump of a pencil and, wetting it with his brose saliva, do some blunt arithmetic. Mathematics stood in peril of its life; the folk at the mercy of the grieve. As he paced back down the field he placed the markers — small branches torn from luckless trees — at appointed intervals, each a section of the drill surrendered to one gatherer's sovereignty.

It would be his or her responsibility to stay ahead of the game, to have that portion of the drill gathered always before the digger reappeared on its clockwise rotation of the field. The day would gradually narrow the work-strip the grieve had chosen; the digger was relentless, foiling all attempts at surreptitious sabotage. As it passed your first marker, flinging the dirt in your face, you flung your scull or box in behind it, pushing it aside and grabbing another as it became full, not lifting your head or straightening your back until you reached your top marker. There ended your responsibility; beyond lay another's domain.

It was, as all grieves knew, a remarkably fair system. As they also well knew, it strongly stirred the competitive element, if not directly at least in the sense that the quicker you gathered the crop the longer was your seat as you waited for the digger to reappear.

That was the belief. There was, however, in the potato field a great deal of treaty and amalgamation, of tampering with territorial allotments. The slow lass who was hindering the pace of work could suddenly find her commitment much shortened (and herself the subject of gossip). The subtle reality was that the faster you worked, the sooner the digging-machine returned. The grieve, pleased with his ploys, went home chuckling.

Hit by the depression years up to World War Two, the old touns clung mainly to the old method of storage: the clamp. It was the easiest, cheapest and most satisfactory method available in the absence of the specially-built sheds so few could afford. The "*tattie* pit", as it was called, could be made in any corner of the field: the old touns for once were not over-fussy about alignment or about the desirability of working off the south-facing end of it. Well earthed up, and with a heavy insulation of three inches of straw, the clamp — about five feet wide at the base and three and a half to four feet high and as long as you liked — kept out all but the most savage of frosts.

The later dressing of the potatoes from the clamp was something akin to the threshing of the grain crop, but without its frenzy. The dressing by machine was usually the prerogative of the special work-squad and, especially as time wore on, of the travelling gang organised and made mobile by the potato merchant or contractor, and paid a weekly wage that compared with that of the farmtoun workers. Piece-work, it was thought, might be an incentive to reckless work and ultimately to the detriment of the company.

Nonetheless, a daily throughput on the machine of ten to twelve tons was expected of the team, except where a crop was bad or when there was difficulty caused by hitting a damp spot in the clamp.

Six men were needed to operate the potato-dresser, though it was possible with five. Even by farmtoun standards it was a cold job; standing at the face was like being exposed on the Eiger and the *tattie*-workers muffled themselves in several layers of clothing before taking their stations round the machine. Items could be discarded as the sun rose, and reassumed as the afternoon sky grew cold.

The potato-dresser was not high technology, more a cabinet of shuffling screens and clattering elevators that sifted and graded with human assistance and delivered the crop in three categories — seed, ware and chats — and bagged the first two. The ware, the large potatoes destined for human consumption, were shaken off the top riddle without ceremony; the seed fell through it for further grading and the chats, the potatoes so small that they were not worth the scraping, sank to the lower depths and spilled out at the side of the machine as pigs' potatoes and usually the squad foreman's "perk" should he be fortunate enough to find a pigman willing to carry them away.

The seed was bagged into one-hundredweight sacks, new and fresh-printed from the jute mill, emblazoned with the merchant's name, taking his goodwill to wherever they were going. They left the toun in the last of the afternoon light, collected by the contractor's lorry as the *tattie*-squad closed down the clamp for the night, put out their brazier and went home to their villages under the canopy of another of the contractor's vehicles. They were not folk of the farmtouns. Where the potatoes went, nobody quite knew.

Increasingly with the war and after it, in the final days of the old farmtoun era, an extension of the arrangement began to operate. Contractors took more to renting the farmtouns' fields, letting the touns prepare the ground, set up the drills and so on and close them after planting; do the horse-hoeing of summer and provide the straw of autumn for the clamp. The contractor's labour committed the crop to the soil and later lifted it and "pitted" it, supplying tractor and digger and, in addition, the squad for the later dressing of the crop.

By then the expected tonnage per acre — seven or eight tons through the 1930s — could be as high as fifteen tons. And on prime seed-growing touns such as Keith's Cairnbrogie ware represented only five hundredweight per ton against the often half-and-half ratio of earlier times and lesser touns. The secret lay in "burning off" the shaws, the haulms, to arrest the tubers at their optimum stage of growth and when they were mainly seed-size.

The seed-potato trade had become that sophisticated. And more and more it would become mechanised, needing fewer and fewer of the village's schoolchildren. Their potato-gathering had been more strongly marked in the country calendar, the last harvest of the land. With it, the farmtoun year came to an end. The clamp in its corner lay quiet and waiting, huddled under the bare autumn trees. And until another year the fields emptied, of folk and voices.

XIII

The Roots of Wealth

THE TURNIP WAS the last green of summer: it lingered on in the drill, a last gash of colour after the corn was home and the *tatties* were tombed in their clamp. It had come north like a godsend into a country that sent its beasts to fatten in the south, and it would be impossible now to over-estimate its impact in a land so desperately short of winter keep. Out of it grew an agricultural industry, that plethora of winter feeders' byres and skilful bailies who could put weight on a *stot* with little more than a kindly word. And not only that: the turnip took its place in the rotation cycle, the last missing link of that magical chain of fertility and decay, giving the farming of the time a vast new dimension.

It *hurled* by day (and sometimes by night) in bailies' barrows the length and breadth of the land to satiate bellowing *stirks* in whose impatience lay the ultimate irony. The *neep*-shed became suddenly an important part of the toun's *biggings*, incorporated into the steadings of the improvers as a special domain at the byre's end where the *hasher* sat Buddha-like in the gathering gloam of late-winter afternoons, the bailie's barrow below it. That farmtoun men should have worshipped the turnip — even, if but half-jokingly, called for a memorial to it in every country parish — is hardly astonishing: it would sustain the ballad touns' beef reputation through many long years. The growth of that trade, from its first real upsurge of interest about the 1820s, through its rapid expansion in the next 30 years, grew only with the increasing reliance they placed on the *neep*.

It had never lacked champions: lairds of improvement chorused its dramatic and beneficial effects; that Jacobite rebel in prison for his loyalty to the Old Pretender espoused the new turnip instead and from his cell proclaimed its virtues. It was, as Stephens suggested, the basis by which the beef trade turned from being an English monopoly into a Scottish one. Now the Scots would keep their beasts at home until they were ready for the market and, unarguably, improve the product at the same time. The beasts' diet certainly was enhanced by more nourishing grasses but it was the turnip, in that hallowed partnership with oat-straw and the later addition of oilcake and maybe bruised corn, that put the market bloom on an animal. Thus was made possible the retention of beef wealth in the countryside where it originated. It was a fine and seemly revenge.

Of the *neep*'s place in the farmtoun economy Stephens has not the slightest doubt: "The turnip crop has, to a large extent, given to Scottish agriculture the eminence it has attained, and it has made the eastern half of Great Britain the greatest cattle-feeding district in the world." An unequivocal statement by a man who stood close to its impact.

Still and all, the turnip's coming is somewhat clouded by the veil of history, not to say the contention of conflicting claims. The Earl of Rothes gets credit for introducing the *neep* to Scotland in 1716. About 1754, only eight years after Culloden, Robert Scott, an MP and therefore a member of that oldest of farming clubs, enclosed his fields at Milton of Mathers, not far from St Cyrus, and grew the first field crop of turnips in the Mearns. By that time, however, Sir Archibald Grant was pioneering something else. A disciple of Tull's, it is said that the Monymusk laird had a well-thumbed copy of the Englishman's *Horse-hoeing Husbandry* in his bookcase by the end of 1736. He was planning turnips in rows by 1738 and in the year of Culloden, his Forty-five apparently being a singularly uneventful one, was ridging both turnips and potatoes into their drills, something the rebel William Mackintosh, incarcerated in Edinburgh Castle, had been advocating since 1732.

Yet again, then, the North may have been marginally ahead, though there are indeed counter-claims from the southern counties, where improvers like Lord Kames, said to be the first in Berwickshire to grow turnips in drills for cattle-feeding, was a devout advocate.

Those early drills had to be made with the plough, a two-way task, since the *dreeler*, the double-mouldboard plough, had not been devised. The credit for being the first tenant farmer to raise *neeps* in the ridged drill in Scotland, on any sizeable scale, is said to belong to a Kelso man who had earlier worked on English farms. Stephens, writing around the mid-point of the 1800s, with

nearly one hundred years of hindsight, tends to corroborate the
claim:

In Scotland, Ireland and the north of England, turnips are now
universally grown in raised drills. The method, it is said, dates
from about 1760, when it was begun by Mr Dawson of
Harperton, Kelso. For districts with a moist or moderately
moist climate, it has long ago proved itself to be superior to all
other methods of root culture.

The early drills were an astonishing six feet apart, though the
Scots farmtouns soon saw the waste in this and settled for a width
of less than half, between 24 and 30 inches, just enough to let the
Clydesdale pass comfortably along with the *neep*-barrow and the
shim, the horse-hoe. By Stephens' time the width had settled at
about 27 inches, and there it largely stayed.

Not everyone in that earlier time was convinced by the
argument for drilling, nor even about the potential of the *neep*
itself. Grant, in a fury that so few were following his example —
and in quite the broadest of hints imaginable — in 1756 had sent
each of his tenants turnip seed as a Christmas gift, and with it his
Memorial to the Tenants of Monymusk in which he spoke with
something less than seasonal goodwill: "Your misfortunes," he
told them, "are not for want of good soil but from your
mismanagement of it. Those of you who are diligent won't take
advice from those who know better, but prefer the old way. As to
your poor living, I am sorry for it, but it is your own fault." Sir
Archibald was not the man to mince words when they needed
saying.

In neighbouring Kemnay by then, however, one tenant farmer
at least was growing turnips in the field, a Mr Burnett, who had
been cropping them since 1750 — the first farmer in Aberdeenshire to do so, says William Alexander. Soon, by 1763, they would
be growing in Alexander's home parish, Chapel of Garioch,
introduced there, along with sown grasses, by the toun of Mains of
Inveramsay. The man responsible was better-known as a character
than the shrewd improver he also was. Unlike Grant, he was at
first an implacable opponent of drilling the crop. Alexander, in
Northern Rural Life, his review of the countryside of the 1700s,
fills out the character of a man who was a rabid Jacobite long

inured to the habit of sleeping with his boots on; who after the Forty-five went into hiding in the area yet somehow managed to marry himself to the heiress of the Inveramsay estate. "Laird Hacket of Inveramsay," says Alexander, "was decidedly in advance of his time in his general notions of agriculture. . . ."

In fact, he did all the usual forward-looking laird's improvements, yet boldy hung the Pretender's likeness over his fireplace and persistently worshipped as an ardent Episcopalian. A small-built man, he strutted his estate in brown coat, knitted worsted breeches and with his "docken" spade invariably in hand. Alexander again:

He sowed turnips first about 1750 and in those days people came from the next parish, when harvest was over, to buy them by the pound and stone weight from his farm grieve, to be used as a dainty dish at the clyack supper and other fit occasions. He sowed at first broadcast, a practice which, although given up earlier in some localities, prevailed pretty commonly in Aberdeenshire down to the close of the century and even a little later. And he believed in the broadcast method for the time, though not impervious to argument on the subject. When drilling began to be advocated, Hacket saw fit to forgo the old practice for a season in favour of it. The crop disappointed his expectations, however, and in hot ire he exclaimed, "Deil drill me aff o' the earth if ever I drill again." Yet he did drill again, not once but frequently, having seen reason to change his opinion, while the arch enemy took no immediate advantage of his rash utterance.

The kenspeckle laird had some interesting ideas about the singling of the crop, too, including the use of hoes with shafts only two and a half feet long — so that his farmtoun folk could see their work and keep close to it.

It was probably the bad *hairsts* in 1782 and 1783 that gave the North-east's farming the spur it needed. Turnips were being grown of course — incorporated into the crop rotation — but despite Grant and men like Hacket still largely broadcast. And results in the region as the 1800s dawned were more than encouraging. The Earl of Aberdeen, farming Mains of Ellon, reportedly got a yield of over 50 tons an acre; in 1809, a Mr Pirie, in Waterton "near Aberdeen", had a similar triumph with 47 tons of white globe turnips to the acre. Freakish though they seem, such results may have been enough. Now the whole land, from the Wash to the stormy Pentland Firth, was in the grip of turnip fever.

Men never noticeably hot on the subject behaved as though they had found water in the desert. Norfolk, in 1768, when Arthur Young, farmer/writer and later the first Secretary of the Board of Agriculture, made his so-called Southern tour, was rapidly adapting:

> The culture of turnips is here carried on in a most extensive manner, Norfolk being more famous for this vegetable than any county in the kingdom. . . . The use to which they apply their vast fields of turnips is the feeding of their flocks, and expending the surplus in fatting Scotch cattle, which they do both in the stall-feeding method, in bins in their farmyards, others in pasture fields; and others again hurdle them on turnips as they grow, in the same manner as they do their sheep. By stall-feeding they make their crop go much the further, but the beasts so fed are apt to founder on the road to London. . . .

What Norfolk could do, the farmtouns could do better. It was a time agriculturally, as we have seen, of a remarkable coalescing of many factors: in changing rotations, enclosure and the formation of consolidated single-unit touns.

With the arrival of the turnip (and cultivated hay) the Northeast dramatically quit the long and not undistinguished past of its stock-raising and turned to the future of stock-fattening. From about 1820, or so, the turnip spread through the region like wildfire. Sober churchmen, penning the *New Statistical Account* of the mid-1800s, were favourably impressed. The ministers of Ellon, the Garioch and uplands Alford were much in favour of it, and the man in the pulpit of Old Deer with its plethora of meal mills and the plague, still, of thirlage, was ecstatic. "Nothing," he said, "for many years back has contributed more to improve the farming interest in this part of the world than the discovery and general use of bone manure for the raising of turnips."

Turnips and progress indeed hung together in a quite remarkable way. That inter-relation is underlined most succinctly by T. Bedford Franklin in *A History of Scottish Farming*: he pinpoints precisely the significance of the humble *neep* in the great arena of improvement:

Turnips and potatoes were excellent allies for the improvers. As soon as their use as a cleaning crop in place of the old unremunerative fallow, and their worth as winter food for animals and men was realised, no farmer could afford to neglect them. So the abolition of the common rights of grazing the stubbles and of run-rig came naturally, and the fencing of the arable fields to keep out the roaming hungry black cattle was an obvious necessity. Very soon these two crops assumed a considerable importance in the production of that farming pre-eminence for which Lowland Scotland became famous.

There were those who gave the turnip something of a grudging welcome: the farmtoun men themselves. For all the long years of its unchallenged reign the *neep* put its stranglehold on the work pattern of the winter touns. Farm servants remember that time as a period in which they did little but "pu' neeps, ca' neeps and full the mull and thrash". Travel where you would through the ballad counties, you would hardly find a winter *neep*-field without its lone, stooping figure.

Round the North-east Lowlands, the yellow turnip was king; its nutritive qualities were held to be greater than those of the white turnip and it had other properties that endeared it to the hard-pressed touns: it stayed fresh in store, though maybe not so well as the swede, its closest challenger and a stranger in the land until sent home from Gothenburg by the son of Mains of Dunn in Forfarshire.

His father, most appropriately a Mr Airth, cultivated it in 1777, sowing the seeds in his garden and then transplanting them into rows in the field. The yellow turnip, it is thought, originated as a cross between the newcomer and the white turnip, a liaison arranged in Aberdeenshire, hence the strong bond of loyalty.

For all that, the turnip always did better elsewhere, in the Lothians particularly, and in Dumfriesshire, and over the ten years up to 1933, even the touns of neighbouring Mearns were much better rewarded. Indeed, one year the Aberdeenshire figure was under ten tons an acre, a sad return for such persistent affection. The turnip would grow (in Stephens' estimate) to have a girth of 30 inches and weigh up to eleven pounds; the ballad touns were pleased with smaller mercies and their *neeps* were never in any danger of embarrassing them with such proportions.

A well-run toun sowed its yellow turnips about the middle of May, after the corn seed was in, and was in dèep disgrace if the task was still uncompleted as the May Term came round. Yet even the forceful places it seems had sometimes to endure such disappoint-ment.

> 'Twas on a Monday mornin'
> I gaed hame tae Sleepytown,
> And he ranked us in good order
> To lay his turnips down.

The "making" of the *neep grun* was painstaking; it needed weather and men and curses, and all at the same time. With the winter-grey furrows torn down by the grubber, the ground was harrowed and cross-harrowed, teased to a tilth, *growth* gathered and the clods frightened finally into submission if need be by the passage of the roller. It was an obsessional frenzy of work capped at last by a fine friability of soil that fell before the drill-plough like a calm sea from the prow of some stately ship. The drills, under the auld regime, were heavily *muckit* before being split, again by the *dreeler*, to form the turnip-drills.

The *neep grun* was always well-dunged — or as well as the toun could afford — not only in consideration of the turnip crop itself but for all those that would follow it. It got the best of the midden.

For an implement that would crown or negate all the anxious ritual of preparation, the horse-drawn turnip-sower was a singu-larly unimpressive machine. The *neep*-barrow it was called round the old farmtouns, with some justification, for it was basically two small seed hoppers set on a frame with seed spouts to feed the seed down into the shallow drill-top trench created for it (from one inch or so to as little as half an inch, depending on the weather), with a roller fore and aft of each to first flatten the top of the drill and subsequently seal it.

The *neep*-barrow was seen about the bigger touns by the early 1880s, some time later about those of more modest means. It came new home to the touns usually in sharp shades of green (or even blue or red) but was mostly seen after the first season in its more usual livery of rust brown, a sign of its neglect between times and the dismal depression that made so many of the places unable to run to the expense of an implement shed. It sat in hibernation for the rest of the year with the old stone rollers whose frames, like many an old farm man's, had gone in the joints — in a corner of the toun and in a comforting fold of nettles or vigorous docken-leaves.

It had a nodding acquaintance with that first drill of Tull's of around 1700, though the latter might have had some difficulty in recognising its distant descendant. All in all, Tull's genius deserved better.

Before the *neep*-barrow made its appearance, however, the sowing of the turnip seed along the drills had been accomplished by that even humbler tool: the bobbin' john. It was an innovation of the 1730s, a date that suggests (a) it may formerly have been used in the broadcast sowing of the seed; (b) that it had earlier been used for some other farmtoun task that has somehow gone unrecorded or (c) that its inventor, Mr Udny, had a blinding vision of the future. The metal cylinder on a stick, simply shaken along the top of the drill to release the seed, would be updated to roll along the drill-top and it long survived about the later touns as a "patcher" of the gaps left by the horse-drawn machine or to make good the depredations of the dreaded "flea" — the turnip fly.

For the horseman delegated to it, driving the *neep*-barrow was a light job with a heavy responsibility. Trouble with the *neeps* was invariably laid at his door and there was no man about the toun more glad to see the first healthy burgeoning of the green *braird* down the length of the drills a week or two later. Two or three pounds of seed went to the acre and it was prudent to err on the generous side. The thing that most influenced the subsequent yield was the amount of dung in the drill and not every toun could afford the desirable shower of plenty. No more could the crofter men cultivating the marginal land, whose *neeps* often failed on their poor ground. There were years even about a good toun when the *neeps* did not "take", when the drills would have to be harrowed down, re-drilled and re-sown. That kind of failure came usually with a dry summer.

Most years though the turnips were ready for "singling", for *hyowing*, about mid-June or very soon after. That was a task that involved almost the entire crew of a toun and was a fine enough job in its way: there was time for a chat and a puff of your pipe as you moved along; for a coarse joke or two that you could not tell in front of the servant lass (though again, that depended on the servant lass). The foreman led the *hyowing* gang, setting some pace (as he was paid to do); then came the toun's horsemen in their ranked order, with the grieve for once bringing up the rear and with him the bailie who, if he were expected to appear for an hour or two in the morning, could usually find some plausible excuse for his non-attendance in the afternoon. Only the *orra loon*, the youngest member of the gang in his first year at the *hyow*, found no time to light a cigarette let alone take a drag on it. He was usually a bad last, never out at one headland before the rest were heading again for the opposite one.

There was psychology in the *hyow*: a man could be beaten by his own diffidence. There were dainty *hyowers* and rough *hyowers*, bold buccaneers whose flashing blades fair covered the ground but whose work bore no close inspection. Fine *cheils*, they were, all the same, to have in your park when you were a little behindhand.

Good *hyowing* was an art: it came with the years like a growing fondness for good whisky. The eye selected the strong plant that outmatched its peers, the mind instantaneously signalled the utter destruction of its neighbours. Thousands perished that it alone might prosper. Confident *hyowers* slapped gaps in the *braird* the full breadth of the hoe and then teased with its corners. John R. Allan, North-east author and farmer, reflecting in his country-man's column for the region's newspaper, *The Press and Journal*, once confessed: "There were three jobs I hated above all — pulling turnips on frosty mornings, gathering corn behind the scythe and hoeing turnips. The last was the worst, and that says a lot about it." He poses the *hyower*'s eternal dilemma:

> The plants were very thick and bedded in a jungle of weeds, mostly couch grass that had a very firm hold of the earth. That was a remarkable thing because we always took gatherings of weeds before making the turnip ground, three gatherings maybe, and burned them but still the couch came up stronger than the turnips.
>
> At the dense thicket the hoer had to hack until he left just one small turnip plant every exact interval. . . . It took a lot of pulling and pushing to clear the space round the plant that was to survive. Then there was usually the critical moment when I

was left with two plants lovingly entwined. In trying to separate them I often knocked out both and left a blank which brought immediate shame and, sooner or later, derision.

I got very lonely. The rest of the squad, gallant ploughmen, hoed away from me as if it were no bother at all. I felt like a lamb left behind by the rest of the flock. . . .

Such too must have been the feelings of many a young *orra loon* as he first took the field.

It was a task in which the competitive urge of the farmtoun men was subtly fostered. The *hyowing* match was as much a part of the country summer as the ploughing match was of its winter. Often, the committee was the same for both events. The hoeing match, however, lacked some of the glamour of the turn-of-the-year event, taking place perhaps in an evening over two or three hours. Then the bothy lads from the different touns matched their skills and the committee men strolled circumspectly among them not so much to study form as to ensure that none was slyly dibbling back plants they had carelessly knocked out. There would be a prize for the best-hoed row, i.e., one in which the work was tidy and the remaining plants were equally spaced.

By the 1920s and 1930s, that spacing was usually six inches, the width of the hoe-blade then widely favoured, though there were touns that liked to see their *hyowers* with blades an inch less. In Stephens' estimate, a fair rate of work was an acre per man per every 24 working hours, a little better if conditions were particularly favourable. But that was never quite so important as the quality of the work. Bad hoeing, Stephens said, could lose you two to four tons per acre, a sizeable part of the crop, hence the pernicketiness of old grieves and their unusual insistence in bringing up the rear of the squad.

With the *hyowing* behind them, the farmtoun men left the turnips in peace, though the drills would be *shimmed* (horse-hoed) twice and maybe three times during the course of the summer to keep down the weeds. That too was important, as Stephens' English counterpart Young once emphasised: "Everything depends not only on turnips, but on turnips well-hoed. . . ." As they were the cleaning crop, any carelessness in this was reflected in the later crops that came off the field.

The *shimming* too was a fairly easy job for the horsemen ("Jist het on the feet," they will tell you now), covering two acres in the five-hour *yoking*. The so-called second hoeing — by hand hoe to tease out weeds encroaching on the vigorous young plants — was done after one of the *shimmings*. It was the kind of work every bothy lad hated and few were disappointed when its high labour cost made it the kind of luxury that even diehard touns could do without.

Summer came and went; the hurry of harvest passed. And still the *neeps* sat undisturbed in the drill. It would be the middle of October, with its beasts housed for the winter, before a toun turned to its crop, feeding the yellow turnips first, complete with shaws. Later, when these became "blasted" by the frosts, the turnips would be *heided* and fed with the shaws trimmed off. The swedes were held in reserve, sweetening unmolested in the drill, growing daily more apoplectic in hue. There were touns where they considered them still to be growing long after Hogmanay, and that was when they were all of them sober again.

The custom was to feed the yellow *neeps* to fill ravenous bellies and to give the swedes, a firmer root, to fatten up the *stots*. Bailies of most touns had the pleasure of pulling their own turnips from the frosty drill. With their *denners* taken, they set away to the *neep* park — huddled into heavy jackets, with their bonnets and mittens on, and with their *tapners*, kept handy in the byre, tucked into their trousers' belts.

Pulling turnips was not congenial work, nor was it lightsome. But most bailies — most farmtoun folk, in fact — had long practice at it. Their actions had a patterned rhythm, again an ease and economy of movement. The *tapner*, the turnip-knife, flashed; one movement flowed into the next in a stunted disciplined ballet. The body swooped and swung, the hands pulled, "tailed" and flung, all in one uninterrupted sequence.

At first the turnips were plucked from the row by their shaws; later, when the heavy frosts came, they had to be riven from the drill by sinking the hook at the *tapner*'s end into their sides. Then they were topped as well as tailed.

And the ritual of the pulling extended itself into yet another, telescoping into that which facilitated the later work of carting the *neeps*. Four drills of roots (one, two, three, four) merged into one waiting row as the bailie, in the outer rows (one and four) leaned over to *heid* the *neeps* so that they fell conveniently with those of the inner two rows (two and three). It was a method typical of the

way all the farmtoun tasks took account of the one that would
follow.

Cold to the bone, soaked to his *semmit*, the bailie quit the field
about mid-afternoon — in the dead of winter as the chill light
began to fail — to return to the comfort of his byre and the
"sorting" of beasts. Carting home the turnips was the horsemen's
work, something they did when they could be spared from the
plough. Few touns were willing to give the bailie's *neeps* the high
priority they deserved and they could lie in their field rows for a
day or two without coming to harm.

In the horseman's method, the pattern "telescoped" yet again:
eight drills were absorbed as he stationed his cart between two of
the bailie's rows and worked from each in turn, scooping the shed-
ready *neeps* two or three at a time into his hands and heaving them
over the cart's tailgate almost without looking up. Four moves by
the Clydesdale could fill a cart.

Though most touns took their turnips home as they needed
them, careful places (and old-fashioned grieves) found time before
the onset of deep winter to make a *fordel*, a clamp under straw and
a protective tarpaulin somewhere about the steading, against the
time when it would be impossible to prise *neeps* from the
frostbound drill — or even to find them under several feet of snow
as weeks of storm locked the touns into their solitary isolation.
There would be a flurry too, come late spring, to get the last of
them off the ground for the sowing of the clean-land corn, for the
neep-field was always the last to be ploughed.

Tipped thunderingly into the *neep*-shed, the turnips became
again the bailie's responsibility. For the beasts in the head bailie's
byre the turnips were sliced. Thrown into the hopper of the vast
hasher that dominated the *neep*-house dark, they tumbled like
chips into his waiting barrow below. Machine and practice had an
incongruous history, typical of the associations that the heady days
of improvement fostered: the *hasher* had stemmed initially from
the interest of the Society for the Encouragement of Arts, which
had public-spiritedly offered a £20 premium for the invention that
would slice turnips and so prevent the fattening animals from
choking on them. Many of the old farmer men, no doubt, would
have been surprised to hear it: their interest rested mainly on the
fact that the beasts that were given the hashed turnips fed better
and therefore fattened quicker for market.

The beasts of the little bailie's byre were notably less pampered. The yellow turnips for the *stirks* in the lower byre were given whole and, like those of the head bailie's domain, unwashed, the farmtouns being mainly of the belief that by the time the turnips had been pulled, loaded, tipped, loaded again, barrowed, and thrown finally into the trough, there could surely be little earth left on them.

Thriftily, the touns feeding their turnips for the first few weeks with the green shaws on them were taking the good of the whole plant. That was something that Stephens would not have been happy about for he believed the shaws caused a looseness of the bowels that pulled down the beasts' condition. It may well have done so, but if it did, what matter: a toun could always put dung to good use — when it came time again to manure the turnip ground.

The weight of turnips that went down a hungry *stot*'s throat in a day was astonishing: about one hundredweight. That combined with the oat-straw, cattle cake and bruised corn to put it into a mart readiness. In 1877, with the touns at the absolute peak of their heyday, it was considered that one acre of turnips would be sufficient winter keep for only two bullocks, and Aberdeenshire then was growing 95,000 acres to feed an estimated 160,000 cattle and a similar number of sheep. In the 1930s the county was still growing 80,000 acres, an emphasis, were it needed, of the fattening beast in the region's economy.

The sheep of that far countryside, unlike its cattle-beasts, took their *neeps* alfresco, nibbling them from the field row, a practice that brought its own familiar pattern to the winter landscape. If the sheep were never a significant or central element in the old farmtouns' existence, they remained a stabilising factor on the fringe. And if there was a single wandering creature of the ballad touns more nomadic than their bothy lads, it was the sheep.

Their shepherd was a pilgrim in the land, bearded at times and almost prophet-like, a man voyaging from one toun to the next droving his flock before him. "The lazy shepherd", the old horsemen called him, envious maybe of his liberty in a tied world since his was a calling in which he made his own time, quite beyond the grieve's rule or the tyranny of his watch. Though the shepherd might, in the employment of one farmtoun, be asked to *fa' tae* (fall to) at the turnip-hoeing or at harvest, even that was often not demanded of him.

Mostly, the shepherd was the flockmaster's man, a wanderer untrammelled by toun allegiance. He took his flock round the district, blocking the country roads, seriously impeding commerce (the travelling grocer's van, horse-drawn or motorised) and putting the entire work of the day behindhand, his collies darting this way and that, up one side of the flock and then the other to discourage any old ewe with wayward tendencies. For the flockmaster's man it was a life broken only by the pauses for lambing and dipping and the shedding of wool.

In their wanderings, the sheep adroitly filled a gap in the tight farmtoun calendar, occupying the empty spaces of the land and taking over pasture and turnip field as the opportunity arose. As with the wandering grazing *stirk*, the price on their backs was speculative money. The flockmaster, usually with several flocks, ordered their pilgrimages. He was a kind of impresario of the old countryside: tell him of a vacant stage, a toun with a field of turnips to spare, and he could find you a flock for it — his own. He might himself be a farmer, maybe not, but he would at least have a bit *grun* somewhere that his sheep could return to for the dipping and clipping and so on.

He rented grass in the summer and turnips by the acre in winter, to which his flock moved in turn, their schedule such that they were hardly here but they were away again. His sheep, for instance, might take the first flush of the grass after hay, the "second crop", as soon as the *coles* were off it, since it was considered a bit rich, even dangerous, at first for the milk cows and cattle beasts. If they were allowed on it at all, it would at first be only for a couple of hours at a time.

Come the end of the year, the flocks took as readily to the winter roads and the available *neep*-parks. For the toun that had pessimistically over-estimated its needs, there was the chance to turn a penny or two on the unwanted turnips and, whatever else, the sheep would always leave their dung behind them. There was usually an average price set per acre; it emerged from an early, yearly consensus of farming opinion and, short of an exceptional dearth or some powerful private blackmail, was generally adhered to.

The whole arrangement had a system, an established order that made the bargaining brief: the flockmaster supplied the netting and sheep stakes (for folding the animals on the turnips), the troughs and the *neep-hasher* (where the idea was to fatten the sheep quickly). Usually, however, the sheep ate from the drill, raising a tender thankfulness in the heart of the *orra loon* or whoever had the unenviable winter-long chore of "pu'in' the neeps". It was the custom, if not implicit in the agreement and the clasp of the bargaining handshake, that all such equipment would be delivered by the host toun to the next one on the sheep's itinerary, a task that might take two or three horse-carts. Even so, it was always cheaper to bring the sheep to the *neep*.

And if it fed livestock, there were other occasions in that old bare countryside when the toun turnip slipped surreptitiously into the cottar's pot to accompany the boiled beef of the Sabbath day. Pulled from the drill in some roadside park in the bygoing, it succoured the schoolbairn till suppertime, taking the edge off his hunger. Then the swede would be smashed against some sharp dyke-stone and one of its peppery fragments munched as he marched happily homewards. It was a kind of country vandalism most farmers suffered with unusual tolerance, maybe because they too had once been guilty of it.

XIV

Marts and Measures

THE MART — THE weekly auction market — was the Scottish farmer's stock exchange, not only literally so but in the starker reality of his financial resonance. It was here, as in his fields, that he assessed the performance of his livestock and their future profitability; it was here that his own farming skills were tested and sometimes found wanting by critical peers. The week's prices were his barometer and that of his farmtoun's wealth or impending loss. The mart was what owung him from horn to corn and back again; what made him buy store beasts or be urgently rid of them as he responded to the flow of the market's prices.

Even if the old men of the farmtouns might not have acknowledged it so, all, intuitively, knew it. From the mart a man might go home like a king: with a lift of the heart at the prices he had heard round the ring and some certainty at least about his immediate future. Sometimes too the mart sent him home in despair to bury his dreams and maybe with the knell of the roup's unforgiving gavel already ringing in his ear. It was all a harsh and hazardous business that only the frequent sedation of drams could make anything like bearable. And when it was otherwise, what better cause for celebration?

Once there were gallant shelts that pranced the mart road and could be relied upon to get their masters home, drunk or sober. (There was always in the bare North-east Lowlands an unconscionable need for such dedicated beasts.) But their day passed and the motor car when it came was something else again. Anxious mothers, as mart night wore on, gathered their bairns in from the peril of the turnpike.

Yet the day was central to the existence of the old touns; it knitted the country community as much as the Kirk. They could not have functioned without it and a dedicated follower in the ballad heartlands could have had a mart for nearly every day of the week had he a mind to it: Ellon on Monday, Strichen on Tuesday,

Maud on Wednesday with a brief respite at home on a Thursday before the climax of Aberdeen's Kittybrewster and the Grassmarket on Friday.

If the marts now are maybe not what they were — and most of them have lost their old character and the most of their characters — they were never perhaps all that they seemed. The business at times could be a bit dubious. Deals were quietly wheeled occasionally by the seller's friends (who knew they would one day have need of a similar service) to get him something like reasonable prices. Acquaintances were cozened to stand in the crowd as the implements were sold and became bidders of such fearsome determination that one bid had barely been uttered before it was capped by another. Bewildered men squeezed at the bank and wanting only a second-hand machine, were delivered instead into the clutches of the tractor salesmen.

But if the mood was competitive (and it frequently was), it could never be said to be ostentatious. Interest was bland and poker-faced: the casual pull on the peak of a bonnet, the fingering of a lapel, the protrusion of a single, solitary index finger under the ring rail — bids so sly and surreptitious, you would never have seen them — was all that proclaimed the fervid contention. It was a secret society, a subtle freemasonry of men intent that day on bewildering their fellows for purposeful gain. It seemed whiles as though the auctioneer were picking his bids from the air, and there were folk who swore that he did.

For all that, the mart had its magic: men who had never held a plough or mucked out a byre or calved a cow, came with their dream of country air from the city's outer suburbs to sample its sounds and immerse themselves in its clamour, the exciting cantata of its long-established rituals. Into the sale ring at one side of the auctioneer's rostrum tumbled men and protesting beasts — black bullocks hesitant, glowering, butting and nervously flicking their tails across each other's faces. Herdsmen bellowed, incensed by all stupidity of man or beast, impatient to get away to their *denners*. Gates clanged on their wards. Sheep poured in, apprehensive, pathetically bleating, as though in foreknowledge of the day's dark outcome. All had their entrances and their inglorious exits.

"Now then, now then. . . . Fa'll start me. . . . They're fine beasts aff a guid braeface. Twenty, twenty . . . twenty-five . . . thirty . . .

thirty . . ."The auctioneer that day was prince and cajoler, the mart his kingdom. Beside him sat his clerk, a secret understudy with dreams of greatness, strangely detached from the mêlée of men and beasts below him, studiously recording, waiting for the great man's heart attack (and his commission).

"*Oh aye,*" folk said of the ringmaster, "*he would sell his auld mither gin he got a guid price for her.*"

A sale did not hinder him long; he hammered them through and the gate to the side of him clanged behind them, leaving their toun with some profit or a sad disappointment.

Many of the old country auctioneers were characters; they had the kind of charisma that transcended their calling. Some were actors without an Equity card and occasionally of Falstaffian dimension. Mostly they were men with a liking for fine tweeds, good whisky and high conversation. They would come out from the city to talk business and stump your plough-rig without the slightest of qualms, giving their stout brown brogues a wipe on the grass by the roadside before stepping back into the gig and heading for town. A few were themselves farmers, which cannot in some circumstances have inspired confidence. Larger than life, they would come out to the country on an early-May evening to roup-out a toun — beasts, implements, stacks, furniture . . . lock, stock and barrel — and think nothing at the end of the evening of marching the fields to value the grass, the growing crops, the fences, and of measuring the midden to take the worth of the toun's dung. At such times, the man became an entertainer, more of an actor than ever, as he held his audience in a cold cornyard and tried all his arts of persuasion on folk who were never parted easily from their *siller*.

He would as soon come out to sell-up the last belongings of some poor widow when she no longer had need of them, bringing his toun's horsemen as assistants (at half-a-crown for the evening) and stirred by compassion give his highest performance for the smallest reward. Many of them were like that; it was the stage that mattered. Beneath the patter of his trade and the propelling of bids came circumspectly and *sotto voce* the voice of concern as a piece of furniture emerged from the house:

"*Roon tither wye, loon — dinna let them see the scratches.*"

But it was in the mart, such Lowlands centres as the Kittybrewster Friday market, that the auctioneer came into his own as his gaze swept the serried circle of faces before him. Week by week, into his

animal kingdom came the livestock of the old countryside to
parade before a critical farmtoun audience: *stirks* and *stots*, store
cattle (from as far as Canada) and cast cows, heifers with calves at
foot, weaned and suckled calves, bulling heifers and pigs for every
purpose; gimmers and wedders, hoggets shorn and unshorn, cast
rams and ewes with lambs at foot, half-bred lambs and cross lambs
of tender and utmost timidity, clean sheep (not washed wool but
ones that had avoided the ram); bantam cocks and pet rabbits,
ferrets and guinea-pigs and hens of all persuasions: White
Leghorns that could have done with the sun of Italy, Minorcas
without a word of Spanish from homely Cauldhame, Scotch Greys
strutting regimental, Plymouth Rocks and Orpingtons so far from
home and Wyandottes and Dorkings and sad ducks that had never
seen Aylesbury. . . .

Singularly and collectively, to the mart in its season came nearly
every mortal thing under the northern farming sun. The parade of
the ring faithfully reflected not only the turn of the farming year
but its triumphs and its tragedies. There was the financial health of
the countryside truly mirrored; there slow prices marked a slow
year or a hesitant *hairst*.

Beyond the bustle of its sale-ring the mart company could sell
your barley or oats where they stood in the field, naming their
acreage and variety as inducement but stating such codicils as
"straw to be retained". Bale your barley straw and they could find
you a buyer.

It was in the mart that you heard, undiluted, the strange tongue
in which the touns did their business. It was complex and
colourful, the terminology of an older landscape, so that a stranger
might have thought himself lost in a Disneyland of odd and
fabulous creatures. It was the language of the old fairs and markets
and known intimately by Scott and Burns, one well sprinkled with
the argot of old measures and so full of subtleties it could grossly
mislead you.

Stirk, for instance, covered both genders as a rule between one
and two years but a *stot* was distinctly a bullock between two and
three, usually black and bound for the butcher, as was all fatstock.
Store cattle, however, sold usually about eighteen months, could
confidently look forward to pastures new and a better diet than
they had known, albeit for the most sinister reason. All beef beasts
round the ballad touns tended, collectively, to be called *nowt*, *kye*

distinguishing a toun's milk cows. And the sheep world was even more bewildering: a lamb could be a *ewe lamb* or a *ram lamb* or (with less to live for) a *wedder*, progressing to the *hogg* or *hogget* stage and, in the case of a *ewe hogg*, to become a *gimmer* or a *ewe* after its first lamb was weaned. A mature *ram hogget* progressed to the rank of *ram*, *yearling*, or *shearling tup*, becoming with the years a *two-shear tup*, a *three-shear tup*, after which, it was thought, he might have lost interest. In the cause of time-saving, however, and keeping their breath to cool their brose, most old farmer men called their flocks simply *the yowes* (to rhyme with howes).

The word "mart" itself was out of the past and one with roots in that earlier time when meat was little eaten and folk each winter and often co-operatively salted down a carcase for the hard months ahead before the level of winter keep could guarantee their beasts' survival through the end of the year. The obliging *Jamieson* says of the word and the custom: "a cow or ox fattened, killed and salted, for winter provision; a cow killed at any time for *family* use; and originates from Martinmas, the November Term, the time about which the 'beeves' were killed for winter store." It was into the 1790s before the first fresh butcher meat was sold in Perth in winter.

Long before the auction ring became the focus of farmtoun commerce, gathering to it the function of the old fairs and slowly diminishing and extinguishing them from the country calendar, the "mart" must have given its name to a selling-place, most likely for the benefit of townsfolk laying in their winter meat. It was out of such small gatherings that the auction mart grew.

It was in its infancy a Border bairn but in its beginnings can be seen the transitional stage that brought it ever more firmly to the centre of the farmtoun scene. It was initially the brainchild of Andrew Oliver, the son of a Kelso tenant farmer; the venue was Hawick, centred in the Border sheeplands, and it was, it is claimed, the first in Britain. Oliver set up his business in 1817, while the landscape was still in the turmoil of change, advertising his sales by handbill or by the town's bell-ringer. Fat sheep were brought in from the surrounding hills in the autumn and in the familiar phrase "exposed for sale" lying, feet-tied, on straw along the side of the street. The breakthrough was neither instant nor highly successful and for a long time after fatstock continued to be sold almost entirely at the great fairs — in Oliver's countryside, that at Newton St Boswell's, an occasion that Hogg, the Ettrick Shepherd, was unwilling to miss for anything.

And there were other impediments to the mart's development, notably the auction tax, at one shilling in the pound, on any farming auction held elsewhere than at the farmtoun itself. It was its repeal, in 1846, by Peel, the controversial Corn Laws premier, that paved the way for Oliver's method of disposing of farmtoun stock and goods at a centralised point. Real success had to wait for the railways, the decline of the droving days and a more serious approach to the fattening of beasts by the touns themselves. But little by little there grew and spread the network of markets that would weekly draw the farmer to town with plausible excuse, and now and then with serious intent. In time the mart became so central to the farmtoun economy that folk could not think what they had done before its existence. Though the old fairs might live on, their real function now had been usurped.

The mart came north to the ballad touns when John Duncan set up his stance in Aberdeen's King Street. John was primarily a cattle-dealer bringing his beasts in from industrious Orkney and the evolution of his mart, though predictable, is interesting in that it must surely typify the development of many. First he erected *flakes*, portable fencing, to mark stock divisions, then came the rostrum and, finally, more permanent structures took shape. John knew a good beast when he saw one and like many old auctioneers expected the same skill in others. He was, it is said, the fastest seller in the North — maybe it didn't do to give folk too much time to think about what they were buying.

In time, however, with the erosion of all competition, the main focus of mart-day moved to Kittybrewster on the town's northerly fringe. As the cattle-market it shared the day with the corn market in the city's Grassmarket, a mile or so away in the town centre and just down-level of the city's grand thoroughfare, Union Street. There, weekly, came the croft wives and those of the small farmtouns to sell their produce, mainly butter, eggs and farm-made cheeses, though there were also vegetable stalls and folk selling plants and flowers.

There, in the afternoons with the stock sales behind them, came farming men to meet their grain and manure merchants on neutral ground. With New Year well past, and when they judged the price

The farmtoun men, *above*, who went to mow in the late 1800s: note the scythes, old-style and new (on left), some preference apparently for knickerbockers and the quite distinctive headwear. *Below*, roping the hay load for its journey from field to farm, a picture, like the one above, from a more peaceful countryside.

Dragging the hay coles, *above*, by means of a rope round the base of the haycock, was light work for a Clydesdale, and it brought a farmtoun wife to the field in her summer frock. Sometimes, *below*, a hayrake would be used for collecting the conditioned hay for ricking into trump-coles that would safeguard the crop in the event of bad weather.

A pause at the hoe, *above*, the singling of the turnip crop, about a 1920s' toun. It was a field task in which the foreman led his squad and the orra loon often came a bad last with the farmtoun dog. In a bleak landscape it could be a cold job demanding thick waistcoat and jacket. *Below*, the desired, later result: the neeps coming home to the toun by cart and Clydesdale pair in the late-autumn afternoon to fatten the beasts in the feeders' byre.

Days of harvest: *above*, redding the roads — clearing a path — a preliminary necessary to let the binder into the field to start work, drawn at first by only two horses. *Below*, binders in action, each drawn by a team of three, in the final days of the old farmtoun life. Driving the binders was usually the prerogative of the first and second horsemen.

Days of harvest: the hairst-ale break at Mains of Haddo, in Aberdeenshire, in the summer of 1911. The crop of oats is being cut by two five-foot-cut machines drawn by three-horse teams. The bucket (centre) is what the ale came to the field in and was hardly set down before thirsty men gathered round it. *Below*, the way ahead as the touns of the region turned increasingly to tractor-power and the stables that had housed the Clydesdale pairs finally fell silent.

The old pattern of harvest-time, no longer part of the late-summer landscape: the stooks, *above*, that stood after the binder had gone, to dry in the wind, were all set at the same angle to the sun. *Below*, the sheaves leave the field, forked out of the stook and on to a farm cart bound for the toun and the greater glory of a well-built cornyard with its autumn gleam of gold.

The look of a champion, *above*, as the judges make their assessment before an equally critical audience. The occasion: a lamb show and sale at Aberdeen's Kittybrewster mart in the 1920s. *Below*, market day crowd scene at a northern sheep sale of the 1930s at the same mart, a strong focal point for Scotland's farming region of the North-east.

The way it would be: the days of highly-mechanized agri-business foreshadowed at the farmtoun of Overton of Memsie, in Aberdeenshire, in 1916, as the chain-driven Mogul tractor, *above*, took to the harvest fields. Ten short years later design had moved into the shape of tractors to come with the American-made Case, *below*, from Wisconsin. The massive wheel-cleats tell the story of early tractor difficulty: traction. It was a problem that rarely troubled the old Clydesdale pairs.

to be about right, they "threesh-oot" their seed-corn and brought with them their corn samples — in tattered envelopes and string-tied small "baggies" that they produced from their pockets as they took out their tobacco-pouches.

The sample would be carefully inspected, offers hazarded and a bargain struck. Such deals were a matter of trust, though, in any case, inferiority in the delivered grain would have been detected immediately and the consignment most swiftly returned.

Yet it was "news" that was the great thing on market day: from their often lonely touns, men comfortable only with their kind united in groups, dourly abrasive of each other's egos, outdoors on a fine day, inside the corn hall perhaps on a wet one. Relentlessly through and among them (avoiding the pernickety and the bad-payers) stalked the agricultural salesmen, those masters of casual accostment, quietly back-stabbing each other in pursuit of trade and in the hope that a man who had just won a good price for his oats might at last be persuaded to pay what he had so long owed on a new binder.

Into the mart year came the special show and sale idea that heightened the competition and punctuated its calendar. There were, latterly, stock sales of such wide and riveting importance that they became the sole focus of the day   or several days. William Duthie's was one of them. It fell to such men to put the seal of greatness on the cattle-farming years. In a countryside of cattle-kings, his reign comes nearest our time and stretches into the dying days of the old farmtoun life.

He was a different kind of man entirely from the ballad-singing John Strachan, whose Aberdeenshire countryside he shared. But his skills too brought the world to his door. On the morning of one of his famous stock sales at his toun of Tillycairn the road out from Aberdeen was thick with the traffic of speeding brakes, gigs, phaetons and four-in-hands, all of them filled with expectant passengers.

The night before one of the great man's October bull sales, his stockmen and horsemen got barely a wink of sleep so frantic was the commotion as they prepared the prize beasts. The animals were groomed like beauty-queens: shampooed with soft soap and water, their coats then combed by the toun's bailies. When they paraded in the sale-ring before a gallery of international breeders, it was as prime examples of their kind. It would have been surprising had it been otherwise, for Duthie was the undisputed Shorthorn king—a tall, well-built man, by then silver-haired in his seventies, with a liking for hard hats and the kind of sober attire suitable for the local banker, which he also was. He kept his touns as tidy as his beasts and his horsemen carried their Clydesdales' bedding straw from the barn in a chaff-sheet (manure bags sewn together) so that no single solitary straw could escape to blow in the wind. The sales started at eleven o'clock, to give all the buyers time to get there, and business was never delayed by the pressure of drams. Willie Duthie did not believe in the drink and folk took home with the thirst they had brought with them.

Beyond the marts and sales though, there was another market-place never to be missed: the local newspaper, *The Press and Journal*'s columns. There men without time to spare for a convivial mart-gathering might offer bulls for hire, their in-pig gilts (telling when they were expected to farrow), tups for outright sale, *neeps* for sheep and fields for grazing. You could be offered, in the battered kitchen chair, so sad in the springs and losing its stuffing, after you had gulped down your kail brose or the high delicacy of mince-and-potatoes, calves, cows, heavy grubbers and part-used binders, young pigs and store pigs. Beside them, in an attendant column, men gave notice of their urgent needs, maybe suckling calves or a willing boar, or put forward pleas for hay or straw.

There, too, you could read the record of mart day: the numbers of stock forward, the prices that could cause mid-day consternation. And as autumn drew on a man exhausted by *hairst* had hurried decisions to make: how many calves to keep through the winter, how many to let go?

In the slow speak of the marts and the corn markets there rang the indelible echo of the ways in which the northern countryside had long and traditionally counted its output and measured its efficiency. The acre was the farmtouns' unit of extent, in which they reckoned the area of their respective kingdoms. But it was more than that: it was the constant, the unit, against which man and beast, machine and crop yield were judged. Only the acre itself gave no guarantees for acres that one year gave you abundance, next year took it back with unkindly grace. The acres of poor land were eclipsed always by the good, the fields of Buchan, for instance, statistically disgraced as a rule by the richer soil of Moray and Angus.

The number of a toun's acres determined the number of Clydesdale pairs in its stable and the size of the farmtoun crew in its bothy, though there were farmer men who consistently tried to work too many acres with too few folk. Theirs may have been a false economy though they little thought so. Output and through-put were the notorious variables on which such tight touns foundered.

The horse-ploughman's stint was traditionally an acre a day; in fact, through the short dark days of winter it was rarely achieved and at other times seldom exceeded. There was more accuracy in the formula that united the acre with the pace of the Clydesdale as the basis of machine calculation: i.e., a foot per acre per *yoking*, so that a five-foot-cut binder might be expected to harvest five acres in a five-hour *yoking*. The same rule applied, essentially, to mowers and corndrills and favourably so to broadcasters and bone-davies.

Crops could be difficult and all too often disappointing. Through-put altered with the state of the crop, and yield with the weather and the condition of the soil. Hay and the *neeps* were a heartbreak, one year largesse, the next acute dearth.

Round the ballad touns, in a decade when they were in the deep trough of depression, from 1924 to 1933, the yearly county averages for hay swung from a little over a ton, a lowly 23.8 cwt per acre, to 38 cwt per acre. Potatoes in the same period were low by later standards, never topping an average of six and a half tons, and taking turnips and swedes together, the farmtouns yawed wildly from 14.8 tons per acre (for cattle-rearing Aberdeenshire, by far the largest grower) to 19.1 tons on the kindlier redlands of the adjoining Mearns.

But it was in those leg-buckling bags of corn that the old touns computed their real wealth, sticking dourly to the measure of "quarters per acre" in the face of official and statistical preference for the hundredweight. The quarter was based on the immemorial bushel (reckoned eight to the quarter), oats being bagged for the seed merchant's in half-quarters in one-and-a-half-cwt sacks, barley also in half-quarters in two-cwt sacks, an apparent anomaly accounted for by the differing natural bushel-weights of the grains, which ran lighter (40+ lb against barley's 50+ lb) for the then still dominant oat. The better the bushel-weight, the better the grain.

The problem stemmed from the fact that the bushel was a measure of volume rather than weight, regulated by the old corn-loft container of the same name, a shallow wooden vessel (oak hooped with iron and with a handle at each side). It was, says Stephens, with a not-unusual magisterial turn of phrase, "the standard measure of capacity in the country for dry measure, it forms the basis of all contracts dependent on measures of capacity when otherwise indefinitely expressed". The hooped bushel measure came — like a fiddle with its bow — with the *straik* (the strike), which was used to level off the top of the measured grain with the lip of the bushel. Oats and barley averages for that sadly depressed decade of 1924–1933 fluctuated as strongly as the yields of other crops, barley from 33.4 bushels to 38.8 bushels, oats from 39.1 bushels to a high of 50 bushels per acre, predictably enough in Angus, where good soil in a good year could return up to twelve quarters to the acre. If the figures now are unimpressive, they point up the uncertainties of the old touns in that time before science got a foothold on the land.

Yet there were other measures that had their currency in the stable talk: the *lippie*, for instance, always somewhat loosely used but a quantity that governed the horses' bruised corn on some touns. It was a quarter of a peck (about 3 lb). And with Term Day just past, the "boll" got an airing. It had itself once governed grain, but mainly it was the miller's measure and like the man himself its past was occasionally disreputable. Supposedly standardised in 1696, the boll continued to vary from region to region even as the farmtoun era ended. It was, like the bushel, not a weight but accurately a dry volume measure. Says Enid Gauldie in her study, *The Scottish Country Miller*, ". . . a boll was as much as the miller said it was, and there was very little his customers could do about that".

It was in the context of his perquisites that the cottar's interest was engaged. His *fee* was for wages plus an allowance not only of potatoes and milk but, more importantly, oatmeal, six and a half bolls a year usually, a ration that percolates through Scottish history and got a nod of near-official recognition from the great Sir John Sinclair, instigator of the *Statistical Accounts*, in his *General View of the Agriculture of the Northern Counties*. The man the *Times* unkindly called the "Great Scotch Rat, with tail and whiskers" ruled that quantity the yearly consumption for a man, allowing the working lass four bolls and a bairn only one. In the 1920s the cottars' bolls of meal (at 140 lb each) were worth about 30 shillings per boll, so that a man new-wed and as yet without family might take half-yearly only "twa bows and a firlot" (two bolls and a quarter-boll) and accept the money in lieu of the missing boll — that is, if the farmer could ever be persuaded to part with it.

By then the chalder had died out of the language. But, a collective of bolls (sixteen of them), it had been in use right up to the time of Improvement in William Duthie's countryside, where the minister of Methlick as late as 1792 was happy to have, besides his stipend of £27 14s 2d, his three chalders of meal and five bolls five pecks of bere meal. In 1842, the then incumbent was in somewhat improved circumstances, for he had £80 with 64 bolls of meal and a similar quantity of bere meal. The chalder had been displaced.

But "thrave" lingered on, casting the mind back to the not-so-distant day of the sickle-wielding reaper gangs, when it had been the piece-unit of their payment. The word accurately described two stooks each of twelve sheaves and seven or eight threaves cut (a total of 192 sheaves) had been considered a good day's work. The word, however, fell loosely into the thirties' talk of old men round the Friday mart-ring to substitute for "stook," a reminder perhaps of a past that some of them hungered for.

The weekly mart would continue the hub of farming commerce but there would come a day of disillusionment as later men saw that auction selling sometimes put at hazard their reward for months of work and long investment. The mart, after all, was sensitive to so many factors: the number of butchers there that day; whether they had given preference to another market in another town; the number of other touns flooding the market with their beasts.

These were the imponderables that buffeted the touns, and in the face of such things there would come a time when the sealed contract with the supermarket chain buying its beef out of the field beckoned with its cut-and-dried certainty. Yet the direct-sell too had its ironies: in separating the farmer from the dangers of the market, it isolated him too from the sudden benefits of its booms.

It is unlikely that those old men by the auction ring of the 1930s would have foreseen the changes to come or dreamt that the mart would become a little less of an occasion. In their time a town's market day brought a lowing of cattle to the streets and a parade of Clydesdales bound for new farmtouns. Soon the beasts would be prosaically driven in by motor-float. The sedate shoppers would be undisturbed. And one day the kilo would be king.

XV

The Song of the Clydes

THE DANDY BRUSH that lay in the hall of the cottar's house was strong and vigorous. A broad band of leather spanned its back that the hand slid through, and splines along its sides took the fingers so automatically that it seemed that nature had always intended it so. It might have been a prize once, in the harness class, or simply bought of the travelling folk who came regularly to the door. In such circumstances it never groomed horse flesh, but it brought up the navy nap of a hand-me-down school coat to perfection and gave the cottar's "scuddler" suit a brisk rub as he took through the door for the inn on a Saturday night. The brush was a symbol, like nicky-tams, of the horseman's trade and a reminder of the closeness of a way of life that never strayed far from the stable that was its centre, or much beyond the echo of the Clydesdale's clop that was its indelible music.

The Clydes were the draught horses of Scotland, in the fields and in the city streets. They pulled with equal ease the ploughs of Buchan and carter Wordie's lorries along the Granite City's harbourside and up the hard tug of Market Street into Union Street, that grand avenue of northern commerce. As likely as not the man who clattered his way over the city's causey-stones had once held the country plough. But whether or no, they were the same kind of men under the skin.

The horsemen of the farmtouns — the men who drove the Clydesdale pairs — left school too soon (the sad source of their dominie's despair) to plunge into a career of ploughing and sowing and constantly carting turnips. If the bothy ballad, the cornkister, was their song, its thump the matching rhythm of their horses' feet, the plough-rig was their kingdom. And there they strove to excel. Good men passed from toun to toun with each passing Term-day, going from one grieve to the next on the strength of strange and cryptic testimonials to their worth: messages that never seriously strained credulity or the grieve's grammar, and

penned laboriously on the kind of coloured notepaper that
proclaimed that it was not the bossman himself who was his family's
main correspondent:

> I hereby certify that —— was here as 2nd horseman for 2 years.
> I always found him a Honest Sober & trustworthy man he
> attended his horses well. I have every confidence in recommend-
> ing him to anyone who may require his service.

So the grieve's signature smoothed a man's way from one place to his
next, to fresh fields and a new bothy, both of which looked
remarkably like the last. The plough-horses too might seem
lamentably familiar, as they did to that versifying horseman newly-
home to the Alford toun, the Guise of Tough, one Martinmas day:

> I gaed to the stable
>   My pairie for to view;
> And, fegs, they were a dandy pair,
>   A chestnut and a blue.

But things, alas, at Jamie Broon's toun were not all that they seemed
and the horseman, on closer acquaintance, was due for disillusionment — like many another.

The "pair" was the power-unit of the old Scottish farmtouns,
seldom augmented as it was in England, except for pulling the
binder at harvest-time or the heavy cultivator of early spring, when
the two would be added to by the inclusion of the oddly-named *orra*
beast.

For such tasks as carting or leading in the *hairst*, the pair worked
separately, each pulling its own cart. For hoeing — the *shimming* —
sometimes for sowing and for many other jobs the ploughman
needed only one of his pair and would leave one in its stable stall or in
the field, changing over the beasts at midday. Only the heavy-
clawed grubber that tore the stubble apart for seedtime interrupted
that general pattern: it took *two* pairs to pull it, each pair hitched to
the implement with its own yoke and swingletrees — an uneasy
alliance that could put a strain on stable camaraderie.

If the relationship between man and stable beast was a close one,
there was never any doubt as to their relative standing. To reach the
bothy, the *chaumer*, of most of the ballad touns, you had first to

enter the stable, where the men's quarters were then reached by a rickety wooden stair in the corner. The bothy lads took their very air second-hand from the stable below them, along with all the other smells that filtered up to them through the boards.

Often the bothy was cheek by jowl with the hayloft, divided only by a slim partition and sometimes even with a communicating door. If the occupants were not kept awake by the scrape of stable hooves, their sleep was certainly disturbed by the night-scurrying of the stable rats. Where the bothy led off to the side of the stable the division was often by the flimsiest of partitions.

Always the stable was the more hospitable of the two, and many a *fee*'d lad stumbling home from the inn tumbled in through its door and was content to lie where he fell. In the case of the loft *chaumer*, its light and the breath of a warm night came in through the skylight, a hinged glazed frame let into the roof-slates; with the other, a window was provided, uncurtained at times though that mattered little: it was so rarely cleaned it was seldom in danger of revealing its occupants. Spiders spun their own gossamer lace in the window corners, unnoticed and almost unmolested for such was the pace of the farmtoun day and the tiredness at the end of it. Inside, the *fee*'d men slept two to a bed with their socks, *semmits* and drawers on with no nonsense about consenting adults and, as the rate of impregnation of kitchen maids shows, were remarkably little affected by it.

The size of the stable, like the number of its cart-pends, told you a lot about a toun, not only its probable viability but the extent of its acres. A pair plus the ubiquitous *orra* beast could work 60 acres even in a fairly hilly district. And at that size the toun's horseman might well be the farmer himself, a man taking his first tentative steps on the farming ladder who had mastered the art of doing without sleep and had so become the nearest thing to perpetual human motion — a man hanging on by his finger-ends and living for the next good *hairst* or the death of close and rich relations.

His stable complement was a workable arrangement that always gave him a *lowse* horse for his three-Clydesdale binder team and at other times a beast with which the hired help could cart home turnips without interrupting the winter plough. At the other end of the scale, untroubled by such considerations, were the crack places, those legendary touns of the cornkister ballads never tired of boasting their status:

If ye want to learn high farmin'
Come ye to Beenie's big toun;
It tak's fourteen pairs and some orra
To work it the hale year roon.

Behind the heavy stable door as it squealed back on its pulley and overhead rail was a closed world. Women had no dominion there; they entered only on the most urgent errand and stilled voices at once for it could only mean an emergency. It was an enclave of restless hooves, the smell of harness and horses' urine; of coarse talk, abrasive humour and occasional high tempers, its silences punctuated by the sound of bodily functions of man and beast. Deep and earnest conversation gathered itself round the cornkists, the horses' feed-chests; rosettes and prize tickets, yellow, red, white . . . almost of every hue, prizes from the ploughing matches and country shows, marched up and down the travis posts giving each beast the credit due to it for its style of walking, build and so on. Their faded colours were a remembrance of past glories. It was a man's domain and men's affairs were settled there. John R. Allan, North-east Lowlands farmer, journalist and writer, remembers it as "almost sacred".

It was a world that almost every country boy and bailie *loon* longed to enter. John C. Milne's "Nae Nowt for Me" perfectly voices that dream, and, coincidentally, manages at the same time to list all that was involved when it came time for the ploughman to tend his beasts or, in the older language of the touns, "sort his horse".

Nae nowt for me;
For aince I leave the Memsie skweel,
I'll be a strappin foreman cheil',
And drive a bonny weel-matched pair,
Big fite horses wi' silken hair,
And milk-fite manes ahingin doon
Fae their smooth curved necks like a bridal goon,
And fine lang tails te swipe the glegs
Fae their snaw-fite flanks and their clean straucht legs.

I'll buy a dandy brush and kame
Te groom them weel at lowsin-time.

I'll rub them doon wi' a cloot that's saft,
And feed them on bruised-corn fae the laft,
Swaddish neeps and bran and hay,
Linseed cake and winlins o' strae;
And baith my beauties will lie and sleep
On fresh clean beddin twa feet deep.

Though the horsemen of that wind-scourged bulge of the North-east Lowlands were as attentive to their horse (like the Queen's Horse, the Clydes of even the most threadbare touns were referred to always in the singular) as their East Anglian contemporaries, few touns fed their beasts with the high indulgence that Milne promises.

In Stephens' survey, *The Book of the Farm*, in the second half of the 1800s, the Clydesdales' feed came under his scrutiny. Now, over a hundred years later, his words emphasise how little routine changed round the farmtouns:

From the beginning of October to the end of March, hard-worked horses in Scotland are fed three times a day. The morning feed in some cases, where high feeding is the rule, consists of 5 to 7lb of bruised oats; the mid-day feed 4 to 5lb of bruised oats, and 3lb crushed linseed cake; in the evening from 5 to 7lb bruised oats and as many raw Swedish turnips, well-cleaned and given whole, as they will eat, oat-straw being given as fodder. . . . In spring, when farm horses are doing hard work for ten hours a day, many Scotch farmers give full supplies of hay instead of straw.

Stephens knew what he was talking about, since he had earlier, between 1820 and 1830, farmed the toun of Balmadies, in Angus. In fact the custom of feeding hay became increasingly the rule and led to the nearest thing to automation about the old steadings: the openings above each stable stall into the hayloft above, so that each horseman had only to stand on the forestall to pull down the bundle he had prepared for his beast.

Four bushels of corn per week was the recommended measure for each Clydesdale. Few touns, however, stretched themselves to that unseemly extravagance. Auld Luckie of the famous ballad, with her dire insistence on only "six bushels a week amongst the five" is far from being the only farmer castigated in the bothy songs for the poor treatment of plough-horses, and only about a "guid toun" of the 1920s and 1930s would a Clydesdale get about three pounds of bruised corn from the cornkist at each feed-time, the corn being measured out in the *cog* or, in the upcountry parishes, a *leepie* or *lippie*, significantly, a word that regionally came to mean a small quantity.

Meanwhile, two other things had changed from Stephens' day: double-feeding had become the rule at midday and the period of winter stabling seems to have been lengthened. Few of the later touns let their horses out to grass before the middle of May, and then at first only for an hour or so in the middle of the day until their stomachs grew accustomed to the change of diet.

Stable life had its patterns, its hallowed rituals, daily and throughout the year. A toun's daily time-keeping for instance was from the stable door and it was uncompromisingly rigid. To observe it, the horsemen tumbled down the bothy stair at five in the morning to have their pairs ready to yoke at six. In the afternoon the yoking time was one o'clock; then, with his beasts in the field for the midday break, a man had to "catch his horse" in his own time.

Any fluctuation of the timetable brought a ripple of some consternation to the toun: when the foreman's watch went wrong and kept the horsemen in the plough-rig after *lowsing* time (discipline was such then that the "second", in a neighbouring furrow, would not have dared to draw attention to the fact) he would return to the steading to face a waiting inquiry of farmer, grieve and interested spectators and, curtly, a demand to know what-in-hell he thought he was playing at — along with some strong words about his watchmaker.

The horses' working day was ten hours, the horsemen's considerably longer for its hours were extended not only by the pre-yoking stable-work in the morning but by the same kind of schedule at midday, and in the winter dark they would return to the stable about eight to "sort their horse" for the night.

Each horseman refilled his own cornkist, carrying the bruised-corn from the corn loft in a two-cwt bag (the kist's capacity though not the corn's weight), and carried his own bedding straw from the straw-shed. It was the grieve's job to bruise the corn: he might do

fifteen-cwt or one ton at a time, working the corn-bruiser himself
or with an assistant, and leaving the bruised corn loose in a corner
of the loft. Everything about a farmtoun got bruised corn at some
time or other: horses, cattle, sheep and sometimes, surreptitiously, the horsemen's hens. The cornkists were not locked though
a suspicious grieve might well keep a watch where their contents
seemed to be diminishing a little too rapidly. Each man, unless
illness prevented him, "muckit" his own pair; each had his own
graip for doing so, though seldom a fork for hay or straw, which
would be brought through from an adjoining shed by the armful.
In the short days of winter, when the Clydesdales were at work for
only seven hours or so, the poorer touns fed them straw, to save the
customary hay, along with their bruised corn and a *neep*. Said one
old horseman: "There wis naething a horse likit better nor a swede
in its corn box."

The grooming that made a Clyde's coat gleam was a matter of
pride not only for the toun but usually for the horseman, and
farmers, through the prize-giving of their local agricultural
societies, shrewdly heightened an interest in it. A horseman of the
1920s and 1930s groomed his pair morning, noon and night,
putting the dandy brush over them, down back and sides,
brushing and combing the mane — always down the right-hand
side of the horse's neck. On crack touns of the time the
Clydesdales' legs were washed down with soap and water at least
once a week, usually on Saturday, and once, it seems, there were
even touns that gave their horses' legs a touch of grease just to
swacken the joints. Rascally "John Bruce of the Corner" was one
who lost no time in inculcating this particular ploy, for obvious
reasons, as his newly-*fee*'d men soon discovered:

> The first Sunday mornin', oor temper to tease,
> Oot cam' aul' Johnny wi' a flagon o' grease
> To rub oor horse legs frae the queets to the knees,
> For they're a' cripple nags at the Corner.

The leg hair that was washed weekly was combed with every
grooming and the horses were clipped, to show that plimsoll line so
distinctive of the show-winner, twice-yearly at least, more often if
competitive showing or the ploughing match merited it. The
clipping, just after *hairst* and before the onset of ploughing and

again at the back of the New Year, was done by the horseman himself, with the hand-clipper, and the line ran the length of the horse's belly from breast to rippling flank. The determining factor, however, was not the look of the animal but its comfort, since it sweated in periods of heavy work.

Much the same consideration governed the clipping of the horse's tail: this was "plaited up" into a ball like the bun on the schoolmistress's neck for hot weather, with the stump clipped over. At other times the Clydesdale, so to speak, let its tail down and it was allowed to grow. His beasts' clipped hair often brought a little bonus for the ploughman: it was sold to the travelling packman or tinker who traded also in rags and rabbit pelts (illegally poached). The bonus, alas, was not always in cash for such traders liked dealing in kind and the horseman's reward, like as not, might be just another dandy brush.

The stable beasts got to the horse-trough to drink as they left the stable and before entering it, and many touns put a pail in each stall so that they would not have to be let out at the last eight o'clock feeding time. It saved the horseman's time, too, and kept the night-chill from filtering into the stable. Other touns were less concerned. One old horseman recalled:

Well, ye see, gin there wisnae pails in the sta's ye hid tae tak' them oot at echt an' gie them a drink. Och, there wis some places ye ken that they jist let the horse oot on its own tae tak' a drink. . . . An' they jist walkit oot and syne traivelled back in again when they had gotten their drink. . . . An' the lads jist stood in the stable. . . . Waited for them tae come back in. . . . The horse cam' tae ken. . . .

In the stable stall the Clydesdale was approached up its left-hand side. Outside, it was led from the left and, riding to the plough, always mounted, or *breisted*, from the left, the horseman seizing mane or collar to hoist himself up. It was not a difficult feat, as any old horseman will tell you (surprised that you should even ask). For all that, out of kindness to short horsemen some touns had a stone by the stable door from which a man might launch himself on to the Clydesdale's back. Failing this, there was always the edge of the horse-trough: it afforded the same, if slightly more hazardous, facility.

On the turnpike road a Clydesdale pair kept to the left, the horseman riding on the left-hand animal. This was his lead horse, always the left-hand one of the pair. It was the "land" horse, and by far the better-educated beast. The one in the furrow, after all, could hardly go wrong but a good "land" beast, like Burns' auld mare, Maggie, had to know to keep its distance from its partner unvarying. It was aware of its rank and privileges and wanted to be accorded them. Yoked in its cart, as at harvest or in carting home turnips, it took the lead automatically and in the stable it expected to be fed first and groomed first and would not be well-pleased were it otherwise.

Even the horseman's Sunday was not always his own. His turn as tounkeeper came round with a rigid regularity, part of the stable tradition. There was no later day in lieu, even if the duty day were New Year's Day. On that date, as on any Sunday, all those who could stand upright were expected to tend their Clydesdales in the morning before leaving them to the tounkeeper's care for the rest of the day. There were horsemen who welcomed their tounkeeper turn as a chance to miss the kirk, still others who liked to take guests, visiting horsemen from other touns, round the Sabbath fields — through the grazing cattle as well as the horses' park in summer — as though the farm belonged to them. Additionally, there was the expectation about modest touns that while he was doing so, the tounkeeper would drive in the cows for the milking and afterwards drive them out again. Even a toun's bailie took a tounkeeper turn, at least in the summer when he did not have to "sort the horse".

The two *yokings* per day, each of five hours, was fairly standard round the touns by the mid-1870s and was considered the optimum work pattern for the horses, which got no rest period at the plough. Not a sanctioned break, anyway. Old horsemen ridicule the notion: "The mannie [the farmer] wid hae been chasin' ye. Na, na, nae rest. But of course it was up tae the foreman . . . he stoppit tae fill his pipe noo an' then. . . ."

If a toun's horses were not all that the farmer in the *feeing* market claimed for them, the Clydesdale in its prime and in its purer strains *was* a beast with some nobility of head and stance and the farmtouns through their heyday never really looked beyond it. It was, with the Shire, with which it had affinities, and the Suffolk Punch — few of which crossed north of the Border — one of the main horse breeds of British agriculture. It had a foot action, a briskness of step, that delighted the show judge and connoisseur and gave it, in some opinion, the edge over the other breeds. First harnessed as a three-year-old "clip", probably with an older horse, its working life would be from twelve to fourteen years before failing strength or ailment forced it out of the plough. Mostly (and ideally in terms of breed characteristic) bays and browns were favoured, frequently with a white blaze on the face and white about the legs, which were feathered with the kind of silky hair many a plain kitchen maid envied.

On average it stood a little over sixteen hands, the geldings, like stallions, weighing about a ton, the mares a little less. It was no coincidence that the rise of the breed, between 1830 and 1880, corresponded with the rise of the new, single-unit farmtouns.

Stallions in particular could bring their touns prestige and give their names a lustre in the show-ring. Men squabbled in the courts to claim a favourite's fame. The *staigs* travelled the spring roads from late-April on — as soon as the ground was sown — eyes glittering, dancers on a short rein, their necks arched and their hooves striking sparks from the road-metalling. They were all of them dangerous and wild-eyed beasts that put the wind up home-going scholars of the old countryside who had to meet them on the narrow farm roads. Their attendants, the men who "travelled a *staig*", were men apart, droll men and loners all, with unsavoury reputations that often matched those of their charges, and were said to be wanted for paternity through several parishes.

The arrival of both about a toun "kittled it up" as much as the arrival of the threshing-mill. In Flora Garry's earthy, broad-Buchan words in "Figures Receding":

Charlie traivelt a staig.
They rampag't up the closs in cloods o styoo.
The sma' steens skytit aff the barn sklates.
Dogs bowfft, hens keckl't an flew.
Meers nichert i the clover park, took roun' the dykes,
The bairns war dreelt to the hoose.
The kitchie lass tichent her stays.
The gweed wife lat doon her broos.
The sma', reid-mowsert chiel, I min', wi a mad look in his e'e,
Far ben i the Horseman's Wird.

Fin suppert he'd roar an sing,
The melodeon on his knee,
The Dowie Dens, Drumdelgie, Lang John More,
Syne mak' for the deemie's sleepin place wi' its open door.

Folk-myth surrounded the stallion man of that old landscape and
credulous schoolboys would listen wide-eyed to tales conspiratori-
ally told (and therefore all the more believable) of their horny
masters' conquests and of kitchen maids made insatiable by
innocently accepting a sticky sweet stained lightly with the *staig*'s
saliva. But maybe these, after all, were but stories to intrigue
young and gullible *loons*.

The coupling the *staig* itself came for was less widely broadcast.
It took place on the blind side of the steading where neither the
kitchen maids nor the toun's small boys could witness it. It was
man's and stallion's work sometimes achieved, it was rumoured,
only through the intervention of human agency, the groom, so to
speak, becoming hand-servant to his impetuous charge. Maybe it
was inevitable that the beast himself and his journeyings round the
touns should fund a wealth of salacious stories, none of them
printable, all of them unsuitable for the roughest of mixed
company and one at least involving the legendary Mae West.

There were legendary *staigs* too, their prowess still verifiable in
the stud books. One of the greatest in the 1920s was serving 300
mares or more per season and his success cannot have been only in
numerical terms since his fee, finally, rose to over £120. At the
peak of his career, Willie Dunlop's great stallion Dunure Footprint
was selling his services every two hours of the day and night at
60 guineas a time, with a like sum payable whenever it became
evident that he had done the job he came for. Mares were arraigned
for him at the rate of eighteen a day; some had to be woken in the
middle of the night to go and see him. His prowess was proverbial.
And there were others of near-equal reputation and with the kind
of potency that would have left a pop-group green with envy.
Humbler beasts, however, averaged only about 80 mares a season,
travelling a more restricted area.

A good stallion continued his life's work for 20 years or so. Many
were tinged with a royal reverence, their titles advertising the
quality of the blood: princes abounded and barons proliferated.
Famous figures were honoured: Lord Raglan and Sir Walter

Scott, for instance, and the then Prince of Wales. What they thought of the compliment is not known though it cannot have been unflattering to manly vanity, surely, to have such work done in their name. Other beasts were more prosaically named, though sometimes just as aptly: Conqueror once regularly took the spring road as did the equally competent Satisfaction. Mares took their cue from their masters, their high pedigrees given prominence by the wide sprinkling of queens and princesses among them, with Lady-this and Lady-that again pointing up the quality of the breeding.

The cornkisters though are strangely silent about the stallion's role and it was left to an unsung poet, Will Ogilvie, to observe his majestic progress round the countryside:

> Beside the dusty road he steps at ease;
> His great head bending to the stallion-bar
> Now lifted, now flung downward, to his knees,
> Tossing the forelock from his forehead star;
> Champing the while upon his heavy bit in pride
> And flecking foam upon his flank and side.
>
> Save for his roller striped in white and blue
> He wears no harness on his mighty back.
> For all the splendour of his bone and thew
> He travels burdenless along the track.
> Yet he shall give a hundred hefty sons
> The strength to carry what his kingship shuns.

Hefty sons indeed he gave, always to the benefit of a toun for if a foal was future power it could also be *siller* in the bank. Good mares could throw foals regularly as well as pull the plough and that was the kind of bonus the tractor could never give you and just the thing that could put a young farmer on his feet. Working the ballad touns, their offspring were at the very heart of the farmtoun story and an intrinsic part of the great farmtoun era from the mid-1800s, the start of the boom years and the time when the breed really came into its own. After some early confusion there was a fining of strain, with an acceleration in values until around 1880 when £250 was being asked for a pair, a fortune against the lowly *fee* of the man who drove them. There was a time when horsecowpers traded at the pace of used-car dealers, buying and selling as though the beasts were hot property and with pedigrees quietly blurred: their animals went to London where they took things at their worth (caring little for antecedents), to feed the market there. And, ironically, they crossed the Atlantic in increasing numbers to break up the prairie cornlands that would hasten the doom of the farmtouns.

The Clyde's value was always wedded to farming's wealth and declined to as little as £50, even for a good gelding, as the century closed, reaching £100 again only with the needs (and the wealth) of war.

A horseman seldom had direct responsibility for foaling the mare of his pair, simply working the beast until it was thought advisable no longer to do so, when she would be put into the loose-box to await her foal. Touns where the breeding interest was particularly strong would work a mare lightly for a long time beforehand, having always an extra horse or two to make up a broken pair until such times as mares could be returned to work. If she foaled in the spring it might be *hairst* before a mare was back in harness, having run with her foal all summer long.

Foals not needed by the toun, or where they made do with poorer quality in the plough, were sold at fairs like the famous Aikey Brae in Aberdeenshire, probably *the* fair of the North-east Lowlands and one that came finally to an end as a horse market in 1952. The end had long been foreseen though as late as the mid-1930s Aberdeenshire still had 17,000 farm horses, the largest number of any county in Scotland, and 49 stallions, again the highest number. But the tractor age loomed and was being constantly nudged nearer by the county's yearly toll of between 200 and 300 beasts that died from grass sickness, something unknown until about 1880. If it was seemingly an insignificant percentage, it was nonetheless a body blow to the touns concerned.

All the same, it was the sad end of an old song. Fittingly, among the folk there to witness it was Jack Webster, the journalist son of one of the region's best-known auctioneers. His autobiography, *A Grain of Truth*, which movingly records much of the area's later history, relates the death throes of the once-famous fair:

In 1950 I was there as a young reporter to find that the gathering of horses was down to a mere hundred. The following year it had dropped to sixty. I should have been better prepared in 1952, for the end came more suddenly that anyone expected. Back I went with my notebook and pencil to find that no one had yet arrived except Peter Grant, the hotel keeper from Old Deer, who was also the feuar of the Aikey land. His refreshment tent was already in position, stocked for a moderate day's business. A few buyers arrived from the south on the forenoon train to Maud and came on by hired car to Aikey Brae. Policemen turned up to regulate the traffic, as had always been the custom. Ten o'clock became eleven o'clock and by noon only one piebald pony had been presented for sale. . . . In such ludicrous circumstances and after centuries of high spectacle the great Aikey Fair came abruptly to an end.

The day of the farmtoun Clydesdale was finally over. Though mainly docile, it had sometimes been less than biddable. Some, grazing the summer fields, had walked to meet their horseman when he appeared in the field for them, most waited for him to come up to them — and others took some catching. They could be nervous at times, kittle in the plough and dangerously unpredictable if frightened in a public place. For all that, and in spite of the derogatory verse they sometimes inspired, they stirred a dogged loyalty among the men who drove them. If *puir guidship*, bad usage, of a beast could send a man from the toun, it was equally true that a horseman's stubborn care for his pair could lead him into conflict with the grieve, a man always with his own considerable pressures. Such dramas indeed were constantly played out in the stables of the old touns as a horseman resolutely refused to yoke a beast lamed, say, by bad shoeing or other injury.

Yet ultimately it is not the bothy ballads, the songs of the men who drove the heavy horses, with their down-to-earth record of farmtoun things as they were, that is the song of the Clydes. It is the work of that little-known poet Will Ogilvie that distils the wonder and affection felt for the breed:

> Blue blood for him who races,
> Clean limbs for him who rides,
> But for me the giant graces,
> And the white and honest faces
> The power upon the traces
> Of the Clydes!

Another, greater poet was to share the wonder, perhaps even more deeply, and to transform it. Stumbling in *An Autobiography* to trace the source of his poetry, Edwin Muir confesses:

> I must have been influenced by something, since we all are, but when I try to find out what it was that influenced me, I can only think of the years of childhood which I spent on my father's farm in the little island of Wyre in Orkney, and the beauty I apprehended then, before I knew there was beauty. These years had come alive, after being forgotten for so long, and when I wrote about horses they were my father's plough-horses as I saw them when I was four or five. . . .

An early childhood terror, when he stood trembling "seeing only their great bearded feet and the momentary flash of their crescent shaped shoes flung up lazily as they passed", had given way to an understanding of the plough-horse's ponderous grace.

Few of the men who once filed in and out of the old landscape's stables morning, noon and night would have expressed it so profoundly, yet to them too the Clydesdale's step was a pleasing thing: clean, clear and, within its own class, surprisingly swift. They would be saddened by such things as the demobilisation and widespread slaughter of worn-out beasts after World War One: they had lived within the thunder of guns and trampled their way through carnage and the dead, and retirement to grass was their due. A rapid decline in the numbers needed after World War Two again sent beasts, many in their prime, straight to the knacker's yard. For most of the old horsemen that was the unacceptable face of progress.

XVI

The Horseman's Word

IN THE NORTH-EAST Lowlands village of my childhood the name of the saddler was Stables, a conjunction so apposite that it delighted the young mind. It had it seemed an irreproachable logic. He was a kindly man careful not to show it and if pressed would sew a schoolbairn's torn satchel strap with the same sweet care he would have lavished on a broken breeching. With the tractor years already upon us, time had diminished his old trade and doubtless some of his standing. Maybe he was glad to take the penny or two the broken bag-strap brought him and you didn't grudge them, though it was money you had hoped to put to a better use.

Gone, to be sure, were the times when he might have had three hired men working with him half into the night, peering at each other through mounds of waiting harness, lips pursed in the poor light as they forced stitches into recalcitrant leather and the urgency of *hairst*, with its deluge of binder canvases, came on them. Then the saddler's shop had been vital to the community of hard-worked farmtouns, a thronging place in which circumspect folk were careful to keep the right side of him for there was nothing like broken harness to hold up a toun's work.

His flow of trade would be steady through the year, with its highpoint in that lull between the haymaking and the harvest when the touns traditionally took stock of their affairs and their harness and sent their horsemen to wash the carts and their feet in the burn or the mill-dam. The carts went to the joiner for repair and for re-painting three-yearly; flawed harness found its way to Mr Stables' door.

Saddlers as a rule were a superior kind of men inclined to look a little down on you if you were not come of better folk. There was one in every village; their shops were like the souter's or the blacksmith's, only a bit more select. Everybody got a welcome at the shoemaker's and was invited to take a seat and a smoke and their boots off, and the smiddy was far from class-conscious. In the saddler's, though, it was usually only the grieves, those bossmen of the touns who had a say in where the harness went for repair, who were encouraged to stay and have out their speak. The stories were less coarse and the gossip, after the souter's, genteel by comparison.

Maybe the reason was that the saddler, unlike his trade colleagues, was a relative newcomer to the country scene, a stranger in fact until the start of the 1800s. Leather harness was still far from common in the countryside as late as 1794, when the farming commentator George Culley reported:

I have in Scotland many times seen a horse and cart conveying peats or turves, when the whole apparatus contained neither iron, leather nor hemp. The collar . . . was made of straw, the backband of plaited rushes, and the wheels of wood only, without bush of metal or binding of iron.

That most readable of Scottish social historians, Henry Grey Graham, in *The Social Life of Scotland in the Eighteenth Century*, confirms that state of affairs in the 1700s: "The harness consisted of collars and saddles made of straw, and ropes made either from hair cut from horses' tails or rushes from which the pith had been stripped."

Good harness in leather arrived with the fresh century, an immediate boon which, with the lighter ploughs, gave impetus to the use of horses through the countryside — and would in time bring a new competitive element into stable life. Oxen indeed often assumed the new type of collar-and-traces harness before they finally quit the plough. Thereafter, improvement was more in quality and embellishment than in revision of the essential arrangement.

Even so, the equipment that harnessed a farmtoun Clydesdale to its work was skilfully adapted to the job. Yoked to the cart-shafts, for instance, it gave an exceptionally wide use of the beast's brute strength, not merely in pulling the load but in bearing some of the burden of it as well as the means to manoeuvre it. Its main components were the bridle, the collar, the saddle and the breeching. The first, a confining series of headstraps, most importantly kept the steel bit — the vital means of control — in the horse's mouth and consequently its guidance, through the reins, securely in the ploughman's hands. There were touns — most in fact — that favoured the "blin' bridle", which was fitted with side-shields designed to give a nervous Clydesdale tunnel vision and a heavily blinkered view of the world so that it could remain unstressed and undistracted by any activity on the edge of its sight.

The collar went over the beast's head to take the thrust of its powerful shoulders and was used in all the farmtoun tasks. For the beast's comfort, the fit was crucial, though not all the small touns could afford a deep concern. Locked on to it were the hames, the steel frame (usually detached from the collar in the stable) on which were anchored not only the hooks that took the strain of the traces, the pulling chains, but the rings through which the reins were threaded on their way from the mouth-bit to the horseman's palms.

The saddle, put on to the Clydesdale's back for all tasks with shafted implements or cart work and anchored by the girth or, more colloquially, the bellyband, was partnered by the breeching — the *britchin* — casing backside and haunches. Together, and with the collar, they formed an ingenious system of checks and balances that enabled a Clyde not only to brake its turnip load going downhill but to back it into the turnip shed when it got it home to the steading.

Support for the load came from the saddle, specifically by means of the chain that ran over the saddle's centre steel channel or ridge and hooked to the elongated inverted-U loops on the top side of the shafts. Pull from the collar was transmitted by short chains from the hames hooks at either side to the front of the same inverted-U loops, while similar short chains between the breeching and the other end of the shaft-loops kept the whole arrangement taut and stable. There was just one complication: when a yoked beast bolted from home or the field it had to take a valuable cart with it.

Plough gear was less complex; it put less on the beast's back and gave it a kind of freedom that was evident in its stride. This comprised bridle and collar with hames, complemented by the broad backband through which the traces, the *theets*, threaded on their way to the swingletrees and yoke. The dragpole of corndrill, binder, mower or potato-digger conformed and fell in with this harnessing arrangement.

Considering its complexity, the stable ritual that put the appropriate array on a Clydesdale for its working day was a remarkably swift one. It was also highly methodical, beginning

usually with the saddle and concluding with the collar, which went
over the horse's head the wrong way up and then had to be twisted
right way up into position on its neck, the turn being made always
the way the mane lay.

Such was the Clydesdale's workaday gear that took it to the
plough, the *neep*-park and the corn rig. About most touns it was
maintained to a fair standard and it engendered a particularly
fervent possessiveness that kept a keen *fee*'d man up late and into
the cold hours after the bothy fire had blinked out, peering in the
poor light of a guttering candle as he polished it for show and
ploughing match.

It was another competitive flame the farmers themselves, ever
careful of their own interests, fanned with praise and threats and
the prizes of their local agricultural societies. Medals were also
struck by the then Highland Society to lend added support on a
national basis and to mark the supremacy of one man against his
fellows. It was a safe investment for it made the harness last longer
and in the pride instilled probably helped to keep it out of the
saddler's shop.

Harness-cleaning, though, was not only confined to the approach of show-days and the onset of the winter's ploughing
matches. However undistinguished his talent in the plough — not
all could be artists and the mediocre were always in demand for the
poorer, lower-paying touns — a man could always be expected to
keep his pair's harness clean. And if nobody made the slightest
move to stop the bothy lad so keen that he did the task in his own
time — not the foreman and certainly not the farmer — most touns
did give their men the chance to do the job on a wet afternoon.
Then, while the rain danced beyond the stable panes on the
midden-head, the horsemen took down their *bleck* (harness
blacking) and their brushes, the foreman rising occasionally to rub
the inside of the misted window and make sure the weather was
still such that he could not yoke them again to the plough.

Each horseman was given his own tin of *bleck*, and with it, two
brushes, one for applying the blacking, the other for raising the
polish to a presentable shine. That was the rule for working days;
for such social and important occasions as the day of the games or
the Sunday school picnic there was concentrated frenzy. The
Clydes that would be drawing the carts would be preened like
queens; manes and tails were plaited with raffia and ribbon, small

flags marched the high arch of the necks. Ear-covers, or *lugs*, were worn, knitted likely by some lass knowing that the way to a horseman's heart was through an interest in his pair, and the long hair of the Clydesdales' legs was painstakingly shampooed.

Whether or not the heavy horse is the remote descendant of the warrior steed — and the link is tenuous — its staunch and well-haunched form once encouraged the kind of beribboning and caparisoning that might well have heralded a more martial display. The Scottish horseman was never scared of decoration and there were times indeed when it ran to excess. Brasses crusted leather facings wherever an inch of space could be found; flying terrets, like ear-*lugs* once mainly to ward off flies, were fitted into the bridle's headstrip.

The craze for brasses, unlike the harness incitement, lay with the horsemen themselves, its highest tide paralleling the heyday of the touns in the 50 years or so up to the 1930s. Worn mainly on the forehead and on the martingale (the strip stretching from the bottom of the collar to the lower girth) these covered the field in motif and design, from busts of a stern Queen Victoria, a figure of some esteem round the touns perhaps because she loved that countryside so, to masonic insignia, less surprising in the strong-hold of the Horseman's Word. Brasses begat a following indeed that continued long after the Clydesdales had left the scene and, copied as the covetable reminders of a rural and more restful era, would become the curios of the sitting-room and the genteel bar lounge that had long forgotten the rougher clamour of a cottar's Saturday Nicht.

Yet the accoutrements that converted the working Clydesdale into the power unit of the farmtouns were but half the story. The beast's strength was transmitted and the Clydes joined irrevocably to their implements, through the *theets*, and the wooden yoke and swingletrees, a linkage system that cleverly self-equalised the strain of harrow and plough. That union, the hitching, took place in the field, in *yoking*, the word that described the action also giving its name to the work-period itself, morning or afternoon.

That yoke linkage gave several permutations. With a single Clydesdale yoked, say, in the horse-hoe or for dragging *coles*, one swingletree was sufficient (for any self-respecting horse these lightsome tasks were like having a day off). But the "pair" was the real unit for the plough, harrow, cultivator and so on and here the arrangement was invariably a swingletree taking the trace-chains from each beast, these (the whippletrees of the English landscape) being in turn connected at each end of the longer, stouter yoke that united their efforts. (There was yet a further sophistication of adjustment for the plough, the yoke being anchored on the hake, at the front of the plough-beam, an attachment that allowed an even finer adjustment to regulate the behaviour of the plough in the soil.) Similar swingletree arrangements hitched the mower and the binder of harvest as well as other equipment.

When the pair had to be augmented, say, for the binder, by making the unit a three-horse-abreast team, the *lowss* horse was hitched on the right, to the outside of the pair on the binder pole, exerting its pull only through its traces, which were commonly wrapped round with sacking so that, off-centre as it was, the animal would not have its legs or haunches chafed by the chains in turning at the end of each bout.

The grubber, the big-toothed cultivator in its heavier versions, brought the uneasy amalgamation of two pairs yoked side by side and hardly ever in harmony. Each pair was driven in this instance by its own horseman, a fact that usually heightened a day of contention between men and animals: as the monster implement hit one unseen boulder after another the bothy colleagues fell out about whose turn it was to wrestle with the lever to lift the implement out of work.

There were grubbers that managed with a three-horse team. They were a more feasible alternative for a middling toun and needed only one horseman, who then was master of his own destiny. He walked alone and took his own counsel.

It was seldom that the men of the old touns yoked their Clydesdales in tandem — "tracing", as they called it — as was so frequently done in England for heavy work. In the city, though, the practice had its following.

Ye got it in Aiberdeen wi' the cairters' horses. Ye hid aye a tracer in Market Street tae tak' the load up on tae Union Street. We're speakin' aboot the Shore Porters' and Wordie's men. . . . They wid jist unyoke the extra horse at the top o' Market Street an' it was taen awa' back again. . . . That's the only place I ivver saw't. Aince they wir on the level twa ton wid hae been naething tae a horse tae pull on the causeys.

Yet it was the *theets*, the trace-chains, that took the main strain of a farmtoun's work, absorbing and transmitting the power of the Clyde as it leaned daily into its collar.

It was the flick of the reins on the Clydesdale's rump that started a toun's field work of the day. These varied in length and weight according to the task: the reins for the carting were the thickest and shortest, the horseman walking to the rear left of his loaded first cart with his second horse in the following cart on a short rein. The plough reins were lighter as well as longer, finer in the plough-man's hands and wound round his wrist.

It was the foreman's job to see that a toun's Clydesdale pairs kept up their pace through the *yoking*; to "haud on the twine" — keep them going by the insistent ripple of the reins. In his key role he left the stable first and at the end of the day was the first to re-enter it; inside, all took their cue from him: even in the hurried blear-eyed morning of a "crack toun" none lifted a collar or a saddle from its wall-peg until he had done so.

The work hinged on that important relationship of a horseman with his pair. Besides the usual words of command, the *Hi*, *Whissh* and *Whoa* and the urgent imprecations to *Hup*, *Haud* and *Back, back* (as he reversed his loaded cart into the turnip shed) a man's rapport with his beasts was strengthened by such sympathetic encouragements as "Come on, lass" — much the same kind of incitement as he used to his women in more intimate moments. And however they fared with the latter, there were men of that old landscape of the Horseman's Word, undoubtedly, who had a way with horses. Some might say a sinister power.

Helen Beaton, in her folk-record, *At the Back o' Benachie*, identifies a character, crippled and dependent on crutches, who attended all the old markets of that uplands region to buy up old horses. The dealing done, the animals he had bought obediently followed his gig home, unfettered by bridle or tethering rein. The lame dealer was known as Sticky Yernin', a name that came from the oddity of his other sideline, the selling of *yerning*, the rennet needed for the making of the farmtouns' cheese.

Even Sticky, however, would have found himself outclassed by another of that period's great characters, a horse-trainer called Rarey — "the first good horse-trainer who came north", says Mrs Beaton. Men walked miles just to see Rarey show his skills and put a horse through its paces, and it was from him, the Garioch folklorist believes, that the concept of the Horseman's Word, and all the magic that the term implies, filtered down. She is informative if not too specific on the methods of horse magic seen in the old countryside:

> Sometimes young men who called themselves "horsemen" used most culpable methods, taking a horse out of the stable, and "lounging" it and "dosing" it with spurious powders and the like, unknown to its owner; and it was not until long after that the owner would have a suspicion of the practice by observing that the horse's coat became brown, and that the animal had an unnatural depression of vitality. . . . Of course, much loss and trouble resulted to the master from such practices, and it was not uncommon for a farmer to lose two or more valuable horses from the effects of the drugs.

Mrs Beaton describes for us the kind of gathering — boldly canvassed at the kirk door on the Sabbath, as then were all meetings of the countryside, secular and holy — that passed down to the chosen candidates the sought-after word, and with it, the secrets thought to be the gripping power of such men as the remarkable Rarey. A young horseman showing no signs of coming forward, it is said, might receive a horsehair through the post, a reminder to him of where his own best interests lay.

> Tuesday evening duly arrived, and a large number of young horsemen was collected at the farm of Bishopton. A quantity of whisky and a loaf of bread had been brought to the "chaumer" on the sly. Those who "cam in aboot" brought rum and other kinds of drinks, and as each came in sight and within hearing he was welcomed in the rough phrases which are the speciality of that class. People who had no knowledge of farm servants would certainly believe that the words of welcome used would have been more suitable for their enemies, and in spite of advanced education, the same profane and coarse language continues to be used by the majority of farm servants in addressing each other at the present day.

She sets the scene for the ceremony:

The window of the "chaumer" was closely blinded, and the door barricaded. Several young lads, who were to be initiated into the mysteries of "the horseman's word", were to be pitied. On such occasions the lads were frequently subjected to much horse-play and the torture, which were believed by them to be part of the "swearing in" to the horseman's word. Certain facts were told them, which, under great pains and penalties, they must not divulge. The drink, loaf and sweet biscuits were freely partaken of from time to time, and willy-nilly, the raw young lads had to pay their "whack", and had to drink their share also. Next day those young lads were more dead than alive, although they made an appearance of doing some work on the farm. But sometimes they were too sick to be able to leave the "teem sta' " in the stable, where they had gone early in the morning.

If Mrs Beaton is less than forthright about the detail of the ceremony, that is hardly surprising for a lady writing on the subject in the 1920s, when some of the touns at least were trying to live down their raw past. And it is likely that neither oath nor ritual were known to her. The "pains and penalties" of which she speaks, however, had become clearer in the early 1900s when an old farm-toun horseman, defying all the taboos, sent north a copy of the horsemen's oath taken at such gatherings — from the safety of London. It is now with the National Museum of Antiquities of Scotland in Edinburgh, a relic of an earthier past and something of an embarrassment still, since none can quite judge its authenticity.

It is an oath quite precise, indeed over-elaborate, about the punishment for infringement. Forswearing all or any divulgence, the recipient acknowledges that

. . . if I fail to keep these promises may my flesh be torn to pieces with a wild horse and my heart cut through with a horseman's knife and my bones buried on the sands of the seashore where the tide ebbs and flows every twenty-four hours so that there may be no remembrance of me amongst lawful brethren. . . .

There is on reflection a touch too much of the burlesque about the whole business, not least in the initiation itself: the scene inside *chaumer*, barn or, about a big toun, the more usual venue of the chaff-house. It was conducted by four horsemen. Before the oath was administered the candidate was taken before an "altar" improvised, perhaps, from a full sack of corn and the bushel measure by which it had been filled; questions would be put to him, to which he was expected to give satisfactory answers. The ceremony ended when the enrolee got to shake the Devil's hand, a stout stick bound with hairy sacking, and was given The Word. John R. Allan in his *North-east Lowlands of Scotland* says of it:

> It certainly did have great force in the minds of those of us who were boys then at the beginning of the century. Whenever we were allowed to lead the horses to the water or ride them home from the plough, the men said we would not be any use till we'd gotten the horseman's word. If we showed a fondness for a servant girl who gave us jelly pieces, the men teased us and said we must get the horseman's word before we tried our hand. But when we asked what the Word was, we ran against an impenetrable secret. The men looked at each other and winked and laughed at us in a way that made the secret all the more real. More real, and more desirable, for the Word gave its possessor a power over horses and women and was the proof that he had become a man.

Edwin Muir was sure that his father knew it and assumed it to be a shocking one: it was a word "which will make a horse do anything you desire if you whisper it into its ear".

In fact the initiation itself may have been much more shocking, since it visited considerable indignities on the person of the entrant, "some of them sexual, according to the humour of the court", says Allan, a man who has chronicled so much of the bitter-sweet story of the region's past. For all that, during the early years of the century the ploughboys of the ballad touns would willingly pay up to £1 from their meagre six-monthly *fee* for entrée to its secret magic:

> First I got on for bailie loon,
> Syne I got on for third,
> And syne of course I had to get
> The Horseman's grippin' Word.
> A loaf of breid to be ma' piece,
> A bottle for drinkin' drams,
> Ye couldna get thru' the caffhoose door
> Without yer Nicky Tams.

The old song, much sung in the bothies, charts the typical rise of a young farmtoun lad from the status of lowly bailie *loon* to the eminence of the horsemen's ranks.

Allan's knowledge was imbibed by the bothy fire in his boyhood, sitting in the circle of the touns's *fee*'d men 70 years ago. Few of the horsemen of the later years of the 1920s and 1930s will confess to knowing much about it. By then perhaps the Word and its supposed magic had begun to pass discreetly into the folklore of the old touns.

Yet not entirely: something of the kind, a ceremony of serious freemasonry or an initiation and high-spirited revelry that took a hesitant halflin into the horsemen's ranks, continued about some of the farmtouns for as long as there were Clydesdales about the place. *Gaun throo the caff-hoose* was the usual name for the ritual: the *loon* had to strip (or be forcibly stripped) and the toun's kitchen maid was kept to the house, maybe for her own protection for the midnight ritual ended invariably, as did all things, with great *wachts* of whisky.

By then, there was likely little substance behind the bacchanalia, little, indeed, of that old horse magic that had once given the Scottish horseman a power much envied as far south as Suffolk — and in particular, it is said, the ability to *reist* (arrest the movement) of a beast, making it immobile and immovable by another's command.

But there were other qualities that made a good horseman and they may have been even more widely valued: handling skill and understanding — an empathy — were all necessary in some degree. And these were inculcated long before a lad was old enough to go through the chaff-house or to have his own pair in the stable. An old horseman, denying all knowledge of the Word and its magic, recalls that time when such qualities were almost inborn:

> Young loons, like today's generation an' tractors, wir brocht up among't. Ye kent it a', the words o' command an' sicc-like. Mercy aye! It wis a' natural tae ye. An' when ye got een — got yer ain pair — ye jist thocht that wis fit ye'd dae a' yer life. There wis nae ither thing. . . . Naething else in yer mind.

In the latter days of the old touns a horse that stopped immovably in the field was merely indicating its superior knowledge, that its understanding of the task it was about was something better than that of the lad driving it. Mainly, the men who worked the Clydesdales were content just to "let them wauk". That speed suited most jobs. It was the pace at which a toun's work was done. As night came down in the late afternoon the men in the winter ploughs would turn their implements a few yards into the start of a fresh furrow, light their pipes and *lowse*, unhooking the trace-chains from the swingletrees to loop them up on the backbands of their Clydesdale pairs.

Coming home, it was their jingle with each step of the tired beasts that haunted the gloam of that now distant landscape and signalled the end of the farmtoun day in the fields.

XVII

The Lore of the Land

THE LAND WAS filled with voices, with the small echoes of history.
Put your finger on the Ordnance Survey and you pinpoint a cameo, a
moment in time, a toun or croft or mill that lives on in legend. More
than that, the Ordnance map picks out in its names the past of a
parish, all the elements that made it once a rural entity: croft names
where the croft is no longer, mills that no longer mill and long bereft
of their millers, cot-touns without cottars. Let the exploring finger
glide and there jumps to notice the toun where the rebel hid, where
the king came, where the Devil once appeared to help out the
gudeman behind-hand in his flail-threshing. In the fields linger the
names that betoken past purpose or stirring deed and between them
still run the roads the cadger took and the fishwife with her creel.
Beyond them stirs the presence of ancient man, his stone circles
looming in the dusk, dark with secrets, a hindrance to the man who
yearly ploughed round them and an eternal puzzle to the scholar.
For the land had a soul; it sang to you in the silence of the night — a
sough in the wandering wind for all that had been, long and before,
for its long-forgotten folk and lonely places — and smiled on a
summer morn, some strange indefinable thing, close to the heart of
you, that encompassed the throb of the centuries; a matrix on which
man had imprinted his patterns and implanted his legends, one that
pulsed still with the march and countermarch of history. You would
have to hate it, not to love it. Few poets have peopled it as well as
Charles Murray. In his verse his love of the old countryside comes
down to us. He is sure in the role of all its characters, the farmer, the
miller and especially "The Packman", that itinerant trader in trifles
who once so closely knitted not only the folk of the farmtouns but the
entire fabric of rural society.

> He kent wha got the bledder when the sooter
>   killed his soo,
> An' wha it was 'at threw the stane 'at crippled

Geordie's coo,
He kent afore the term cam' roon' what flittin's we
  would see,
An' wha'd be cried on Sunday neist, an' wha would
  like to be,
He kent wha kissed the sweetie wife the nicht o'
  Dancie's ball,
An' what ill-trickit nickum catched the troot in
  Betty's wall,
He was at the feein' market, an' he kent a' wha
  were fou,
An' he never spoiled a story by consid'rin' gin 'twas
  true.

Whatever the quality of his work against Milne's or Flora Garry's, Murray's spectrum is broader and he deserves to be more widely read.

There was a time in that dour landscape of the packman and the souter when the seasons brought the power of the old pagan gods into the fields, their worship at times a joyous thing and far, far from the fearful evangelism of the Kirk and its canticles of holy praise. Then was the rule of darker deities that decided destinies and fretted over the fruitfulness of man and crop and beast. Like the old livestock and hiring fairs, their festivals followed the ties of the farmtoun year and the Kirk, finally, came to live with them where it could not absorb them. Maybe even the ministers understood the need for them, for they too had usually crops to win.

Their time was before science and technology entered the agricultural arena and they immeasurably enriched the rural year. Few of them survived in anything like their intense, original form into the great days of the farmtouns though they lingered still on the calendar as a date for frolic and feasting. Halloween, like Hogmanay, hung on. Though it was little involved with the crops, it brought the breathless dread of darker superstition to the fore round the touns much as it had done in Burns's day. It was a night set by for the supernatural, for such "spaeing" of fortunes as "trailing the rope". Its rituals were half-fun, half-fearful but still full of portent.

That it was so is less than surprising. Shut in their end-of-year quiet, the touns could be lonely places. Folk came home from the fields to "sneck" their cottars' doors against the night, and only the stable would take a man from his fireside. Snow spread the long hush of winter on the land, a silence, under vast star-filled skies, that muffled the familiar and comforting sounds of the country-side. At night the dark steading of a small toun — maybe without even the glimmer of a bothy lamp — could be an eerie place, a cluster of unaccountable stirrings and deep, inscrutable shadows. Folk waited in the dark round a winter toun: beggars and lovers on illicit encounters, and men on sinister errands. Footsteps were heard but their owners never encountered; presences sensed but never explained. Ghosts lurked there, shadows of deeds known and unknown — a history that raised the hair on the back of your neck as you went round the silent toun on a black night with a playful wind brushing the dead leaves of autumn to heel behind you.

Then the past came close and with it that earlier time when witchcraft flourished; when pilgrims had flocked to the saints' wells to implore favour and to hang rags on to the surrounding bushes, a kind of holy bunting that fluttered in the breeze until its threads rotted and lost their hold. When a man's stacks heated, when his cow went unaccountably dry or his sow fell sick and died, he patiently scoured the corners of his mind to recall who it might have been who praised them and so brought his misfortune. Then as now the phlegmatic men of the region were loth to hear praise and in the face of such things took their counter-spells: the twig above the byre door (elder, ash or ivy, but most usually rowan); the dead horse's ear clipped from the corpse to hang in some out-of-the way corner of the steading to ward off further deaths in the stable. The combined magic of "rowan tree and reid thread" as a safeguard lay with the anxious milkmaid.

> Lest witches should obtain the power
> Of Hawkie's milk in evil hour,
> She winds a red thread round her horn
> And milks her thro' row'n night and morn.

The rowan twigs were sometimes tied to the cow's horns. Tucked under the beast's tail they apparently ensured an abundance of milk. They might be in the form of a cross, though for milking they would usually be bent to form a circle. Bennachie milkmaids strengthened their counter-magic by putting a shilling in the bottom of the milk *coggie*, and by milking the first few strains through a wedding ring, and in the parish of Pitsligo right up to the 1900s there was one toun where a George III silver sixpence was similarly used in the milkmaid's pail to keep the fairies from "stripping" the cows.

Superstition fairly flourished round the dairy. Butter too was a problem and sulked in the making from demonic agency. It was thought unlucky to wash the churn and hair was allowed to meld the butter to the right consistency. Belief in such things died hard. Witches, in their final examinations, confessed smugly to taking the milk of their neighbours' beasts by means of the "hair-tedder" (hair-tether) made from the tail hair of every cow — a kind of fairy pipeline that magically siphoned off the abundance of a distant beast's udder. The evil eye that thinned the milk and made the cow go dry could be damaging in the butter churn. Thus Burns, himself no stranger to misfortune, in his "Address to the Deil":

> Thence, countra wives, wi' toil an' pain,
> May plunge an' plunge the kirn in vain;
> For, Oh! the yellow treasure's taen
> By witching skill;
> An' dawtit, twal-pint Hawkie's gaen
> As yell's the Bill.

The belief was as prevalent on Deeside as in the poet's Ayrshire, though soon the farmtoun wives would come to know that the lack of success in butter-making was more a matter of temperature than devilish interference. For all that, it didn't do to upset the Devil and it was considered prudent to give him this due: it was at least the mid-1600s before some of the holdings in the shadow of Bennachie broke their trust with him by no longer leaving corners of land untilled as the "guidman's fields".

A witch with a down on a toun could blight its corn or make its *kye* cast dead calves. Such things had given credence to the rituals of Beltane, still not out of mind as the farmtouns began to take Scottish farming into the days of its high prosperity. Beltane began the pagan year, the start of warmth and fertility; it had its counterpoint in Samhainn (Halloween), the first day of winter. It was connected with fire worship and the propitiation of the sun in order to ripen the crops—though the Highlands had folk who swore that the moon ripened the grain faster. No barley would be sown in the Highlands before Beltane, which was also when the beasts went out to pasture.

Fire was the powerful agency and as the day came round—May 1 on the old calendar—the herdsmen of the old landscape gathered to light the Beltane fires and put their flocks through the yearly ritual. They danced, says Henry Grey Graham in *The Social Life of Scotland in the Eighteenth Century*, "round the flames and spilt a libation of caudle on the ground; they took their oatcake, having on it quaint knobs, which they flung in turn over their shoulder saying, 'This to thee, protect my cattle,' 'This to thee, O fox, spare my sheep,' 'This to thee, O eagle; this to thee, O hooded crow, save my lambs.' ". Pennant, on his celebrated tour of the Highlands in 1769, was more specific:

> They cut a square trench on the ground, leaving the turf in the middle; on that they make a fire of wood, on which they dress a large caudle of eggs, butter, oatmeal and milk; and bring besides the ingredients of the caudle, plenty of beer and whisky; for each of the company must contribute something. The rites begin with spilling some of the caudle on the ground by way of libation; on that, everyone takes a cake of oatmeal upon which there are raised nine square knobs each dedicated to some particular being, the supposed preserver of their flocks and herds, or to some particular animal, the great destroyer of them: each person then turns his face to the fire, breaks off a knob and flinging it over his shoulders, says "This I give to thee. . . ." When the ceremony is over they dine on the caudle.

Cattle were made to pass through the smoke, or even the flames, on that opening day of the Highland year. For fire was the great protector as well as the great harbinger: baby as well as beast was submitted to its magic by being passed to and fro three times across the hearth with a soft incantation to the fire-god before being carried three times sun-wise round it. Man, in some secret compact with the dark gods, carried fire round his corn and his steading, sun-wise, always *sun-wise*.

But there were prohibitions too in the old Highlands that seemingly had less to do with pagan things: the plough, for instance, never entered the ground on Good Friday. There was a horror of iron then and the blacksmith temporarily forsook his forge in the belief that the nails of the Cross had been fashioned that day. Sowing of seed at that time was as heavily frowned upon.

It is hard now to assess, precisely, how much of such belief percolated down to the era of the single-unit farmtouns. Probably very little, for there is no doubt that the supernatural would have held less sway with the hardy folk of the Lowlands. Yet, a century and a half ago, the boundaries of Gaeldom impinged more strongly on much of the uplands of the ballad counties, imposing still a residue of Highland custom and belief. And there may have been other factors that carried old rituals beyond their normal, regional bounds. Folk of the sickle had passed south in the old landscape as the *hairst* came on, bound for the hiring fairs — gangs of mixed sexes travelling whiles on the Sabbath to the great wrath of ministers — to bargain and *fee* their skills, to cut under contract and lodge in the harvest bothies. Most were Highland girls, queens of quern and churn, heading for the lush Lothian harvests; there the grain was earlier than in their Highland glens, where their folk were relying on their *siller* to put them through winter. Is it likely that they left nothing of their culture and customs behind them when they returned home? And given that reminder of an earlier Gaelic time inherent in the names of so many of the Lowlands farmtouns (far-famed Collynie, for instance, in the Gaelic, *a green hill*) isn't it possible that the crust of their hardy lifestyle overlaid a more Gaelic culture? For the farmtoun men stooking in the *hairst* parks of the 1920s and 1930s, the rule would still be "follow the sun" — which meant a clockwise direction as it rose in the east, moved south and sank finally to the west. Most farmtoun operations took place clockwise: ploughing, stooking, cart- and stack-building, hay-cutting and potato-harvesting. Coincidence perhaps, yet however tenuous the link, worth noting. Round their steadings the touns like the old crofter men grew one *rodden* (rowan) tree at least, its presence unacknowledged — and the byre twig was common elsewhere than in the Highlands.

Witches once had been sought out to calm the northern plough oxen when their control went beyond their goadman. William Alexander, in his *Northern Rural Life*, says of the 1700s:

Belief in witchcraft generally, and in the existence and *can* [the knowledge] of the fairies, held wide sway among the country population till the close of the century; and, indeed, for a good while after. The merry little folks with their green coats were the "gweed neibours", who seldom did serious harm. . . . They would do many a good service when the humour was on them; and happy was he who, when some sturdy male fairy took a bout of thrashing on his barn floor of an early winter morning, could creep quietly up behind, and getting hold of the flail souple, "catch the speed!". Such cantrips as an old wife converting herself into the form of a hare, and hirpling about from "toon" to "toon" at uncanny hours; or in other guises "trailin' the rope" to deprive a neighbour's cow of its milk-giving powers, transferring them to some other cow, or inanimate object even, for her own behoof were regarded as serious contingencies, against which protection was needed. . . . The more pleasing superstitition, which had respect to wonder-moving tales of Elfland and its inhabitants, got gradually attenuated and died out with the wooden plough and the small oats; the grosser and less ethereal one lingered much longer; and, indeed, in regions where primitive ideas are allowed to have some footing, the notion that certain occult powers, derived from an evil source, might be exercised on man or beast by people of sinister antecedents and reputation is hardly more than extinct even yet.

An old crofter man could always use help at the flail and if there is just the suggestion, here, that Alexander is writing with his tongue tucked into his cheek, there is little doubt but that the "flinging tree" inspired its odd beliefs and its own kind of country wisdom. It dwelt long in the farmtoun folk memory and with it remained the kind of doggerel verse that obliquely stressed an underlying need for good threshing:

> Tremmlin straes maks kickin owsen,
> Kickin owsen maks barket lan,
> Barket lan maks puir corn
> An puir corn makes thin pottage,
> An thin pottage maks weak men,
> An weak men mak "tremmlin straes".

Such lines describe the old circle of dependence that once was farming man's. The "tremmlin" or rustling of the straw was an indication that it had not been adequately threshed and "barket", in this sense, would indicate poor tillage.

Round the old Lowland touns the plough was as widely honoured. In its symbolism it outmatched even the flail as a primitive motif whose potency stretched out from the earliest days of man's long conquest of the soil. The image endures for still, mainly, the country year begins with the plough though much recently has changed in the old rituals, never to be revived, as the operations of the farming year are increasingly telescoped by machines: the automatic planter, the forage-harvester, the root-harvester and the all-pervasive "combine". Yet still it is the old-style ploughman who walks the furrow of song and poem and story; his is the figure that haunts the old landscape.

The plough could not have remained immune from the taint of magic. Nor did it. That first scratch of furrow, the *feering*, had once been marked by its own ritual, "streeking the ploo", a ceremony that gave food and libation to the ploughman — and, apparently, sometimes to the implement itself — in the field and was followed, later that night, by a farmtoun supper. It was an observance of hope rather than celebration, a considered precaution in a countryside where famine had once been a close neighbour and the memory was long. It was in a way a christening of the farmtoun year. John W. Fraser in "A Ballad of Buchan" commemorates the custom and its time-honoured responses:

> "Gude speed the plough," the maiden cried —
> The Ugie sings as it rins to the sea;
> "Speed weel the wark," the man replied,
> And the sun glints bright on Bennachie.
>
> The owsen pause on the furrow so red
> The Ugie sings as it rins to the sea;
> The lark sings loud in the blue o'erhead
> And the sun glints bright on Bennachie.
>
> She has brought him bread right sweet and brown
> The Ugie sings as it rins to the sea;
> And clear bright ale to wash it down
> And the sun glints bright on Bennachie.

The verses beautifully unite plough and nature and landscape and in the places upland of the ballad country "streeking the ploo" was still practised well into the 1800s. That it was ritual rather than festive custom is emphasised by the fact that with the first furrow drawn, work ended for that day, beginning in earnest the day following. The ploughman traditionally ate his bread and drank his ale seated on the ploughbeam, toasting the farmer and his family.

But if the plough feast died out of the northern calendar it would be wrong to assume that the old landscape of the farmtouns and crofter men, even in its hardest days and despite the normal austerity of its tables, did not have its feasts. Tame though they might appear to our sophisticated time, they once loomed like beacons in the year as country folk supped down their usual diet of kail brose (with oatcakes, of course) and brought a momentary respite at least to the monotony of farmtoun days.

The feast of Fastern's E'en (Shrove Tuesday) was one such occasion. Meat, but rarely seen beyond christenings, weddings and the New Year, came to table and the excitement and excess were proverbial (relatively speaking). The gastric juices positively dribbled. There are folk around still who recall "beef brose and bannock days" as highlights of the year if not, quite precisely, the reason for such celebration. Helen Beaton, however, delightfully describes the occasion in *At the Back o' Benachie*, her folk-record looking back to the mid-1800s in that upcountry district:

Beef Brose and Bannock Day in the middle of the nineteenth century was looked forward to for months. In the early morning of the day the guidwife of a farm would tie up a large piece of fat beef and put it in a large pot, full of clean boiling water and salt. Dinner at a farm then, as now, was at noon; consequently the "weemen folk" had a busy forenoon, looking out dishes and spoons etc., for the festive occasion. About half-past eleven the mistress would bring the newest milk plate to the meal girnal and neatly fill it with oatmeal, and then adding some salt to make it taste, she put in a ring and a button. The pot meantime would be boiling, and, with the assistance of another woman, the beef was removed and set beside the large peat fire, while the guidwife was careful to skim the boiling fat from the "lytheside" of the pot, and afterwards, pour it on the meal and stir well. When a plentiful supply of the boiling stock had been poured on the meal, the brose was made and placed on the centre of a large deal table which stood in the middle of the "kitchie fleer". Sometimes the table would be covered with a white cloth but oftener not, as, owing to the dish being in the centre of the table, it was difficult for those eating therefrom to keep "frae blibberin' an' spullin' a' owre the table".

Neighbours would be invited and an old grandfather perhaps coaxed, for once, to say less serious grace:

> Grace be here, and grace be there,
> And grace be on the table;
> Ilka one tak' up their speen
> An' sup a' that they're able.

It was a bidding that never needed repeating. The merriment was self-distilled and even allowing for the nostalgic mists that now separate us from that time the feast was one in which master and servant seem to have combined without strain. And with the future so excitingly at stake, the communal supping — as at the toun's meal-and-ale later in the year — was fast and furious. The finder of the ring, it was thought, was soon to marry; the unfortunate who drew the button would have long to lie between cold sheets. Afterwards . . . "came a large piece of beef and it was served to each on a plate, and likewise potatoes. If knives and forks were not forthcoming fingers would be used."

But if the beef was sweet the morrow brought folk back to earth and brose again, probably until harvest-time. A "good *hairst*" was a joyous thing and in turn brought its own open-handed hospitality. Harvesters were well-fed as well as well-paid. Except about the most niggardly touns, the farm men and the extra *fee*'d hands fed like fighting cocks, their brawny strength at a premium for often enough it was that, only, that stood between a farmer and financial ruin. It was the rule throughout *hairst* and for as long as it lasted — even on wet days spent rope-making in the byre — that the men got a *piece*, morning and afternoon. Then too, if at no other time, the rabbits flushed from the corn and killed were the harvesters'. They lay on the dyke till *lowsing*-time, and for once went home to the cottar's house. At *hairst* most farmers got in a barrel of frothy *"hairst* ale" that went to the harvest field in bucketfuls even supposing the master himself had taken the pledge. Like the celebratory harvest supper, it was a tradition that endured in the North-east into the 1920s.

"Entering morning" was the designation of the day when cutting began. It never started, Helen Beaton assures us, without refreshment instantly available and frequently

> A waught o' ale fae the grey pig
> That was aye handy on the rig.

The "pig" was a large whisky jar, complete with cork, that could be later used, with only hot water in its innards, to warm the winter beds. About Mrs Beaton's Bennachie countryside, morning *piece*-time was around ten o'clock. There appeared then at the field gate the *kitchie deem* — the servant lass — laden with a basket containing "many quarters of oatcakes, some spoons and bowls, a ladle, etc., and a sweet clean towel covered them all up. The girl also carried a pail containing curds and cream, or rather yearn't milk."

Dinner might be taken in the field in much the same way but mostly the touns took a midday break even in the middle of harvest. Afternoon again brought the kitchen maid to the field with her basket crooked on her arm and, under its plaided teatowel, the hot teapot and jammy scones and maybe big brown, gingery perkin biscuits, hot on the tongue, that slid down a treat with the hot milky tea.

Her arrival was like the lifting of a siege; folk gathered and sat down, sore backs to comforting stook. Men with bald pows took their bonnets off and laid them on their knees for a pause, a picnic, in mid-afternoon, an occasion suddenly of much delicacy and banter and social chit-chat that showed none of the strains of the day.

That was the jovial side of *hairst*. Their suppers taken, there had been a time when the crew had danced the evening through (or what was left of it) to a tired fiddle or the traditional melodeon.

But that had eventually died out with the century and by the 1900s the real celebration was reserved for the end of the task, either the cutting or the carting-home of the sheaves. Both were moments of thankfulness, the first, once, much qualified by ritual.

If the task of cutting the last sheaf, the last stalks of standing grain, attracted little significance to it in the Lowland plain, it was not always so in the uplands where it met the presence of the Highlands. There the past was always less easily shrugged off and there endured a ritual that had its own inescapable logic, which completed the "magic circle" of fertility, and doubtless at times infuriated the Free Kirk.

The cutting of the last sheaf was a thing of consternation, at times a task to be avoided. To be absolved of all guilt the shearers threw their sickles at the last standing stalks of grain. In the Highland glens that last sheaf was called the Cailleach, the old woman, and sometimes the Maiden. Either way the sheaf would be dressed to resemble a woman and given a white cap, a frock, a small shawl sprigged with a bit of heather, and an apron suitably pocketed to take bread and cheese and with a *heuk* tucked into its tie-string at the back — in short, an effigy of the woman shearer. At the harvest supper that followed the Cailleach took the head of the table and was toasted as the drams went round. When the dancing began one of the younger men swept her gallantly into the reel or strathspey. But then, the supper past, the Cailleach like Cinderella was shorn of her finery, to be kept, in some regions at least, as a "tasty morsel" for the plough horses as they drew the first furrow of the following season.

The end of the cutting about the ballad touns, however, was always less traumatic. For all that, the ritual that followed seems hardly to have differed, except that in the Lowlands the cutting of the last sheaf was a joy unalloyed. The sheaf, if not called the *clyack* sheaf, was designated the Maiden and the harvesting of it was considered an honour and fell only to the worthy. Helen Beaton, as a later medium for *folklorico* might say, has the details:

At the end of the cutting of the crop it was customary for a little girl or some preferred person to gather the last sheaf. This was called the "clyaack she 'f", and was bound with several bands, and was very often decorated with ribbons, being finally borne home in triumph and kept safely until Old Yule, when it was set out to feed the birds. If a large sheaf had been gathered it was given to the milking cows instead of the birds, but nevertheless all the beasts and birds got something extra at "Aul' Yeel".

Around Cuminestown, the creation of that initially much-scorned improver, Joseph Cumine, the *clyack* sheaf of the mid-1800s was dressed by the lass who gathered it. Coming close indeed to Highland custom, she bedecked it with her sunbonnet, apron and anything else fashionably becoming that could be brought to the field. The sheaf was tied, again with a great plurality of bands, and taken home to the toun in a mood of victory to be set over the door, the hearth, or the kitchen bed (depending perhaps on where there was most need of good fortune), where it stayed until Yule (the old New Year). Then it was divided among the plough horses in the stable or given to them on the first day of ploughing. Sometimes, less reverently, it was thrown into the rafters of the barn, forgotten, and maybe finally given to the hens.

The celebration of harvest was universal; its customs transcended borders and cultures. The dressed *clyack* sheaf was the corn dolly or kirn baby of the English counties where, as in the Highlands, there was dismay about cutting the last sheaf and the reapers lined up to throw their sickles at the last of the standing grain so that the final executioner might never be known. There too the continuum of fertility was jealously observed with the *clyack* sheaf being buried at times in the first furrow of the new farming year.

There was, after all, something mystical about the corn. Even a man as steeped in the harsh realism of his native countryside as Lewis Grassic Gibbon recognised it and in his essay *The Land* he nods to the old gods and acknowledges that the corn "is so ancient that its fresh harvesting is no more than the killing of an ancient enemy-friend, ritualistic, that you may eat of the flesh of God, drink of his blood, and be given salvation and life". A strange amalgam of pagan and Christian thought, uncertainly rooted, but one that demonstrates above all how the old creed lingered on the land, its magic never discounted.

Round the ballad touns, though the cutting of the *clyack* sheaf might be marked, the lass who brought it home from the field dancing with the farmer perhaps at a special supper that night, the real celebration, the toun's meal-and-ale, was latterly reserved for when it had "winter" — i.e., when all the sheaves were safely in the stackyard. Then the melodeons and the fiddles sprang to life, the trump (the jew's harp) and even the paper-and-comb, and so began the fearsome foursome: "mak' the figure eight, trok deems

and furl" (make the figure eight, change partners and whirl).
Burns was no stranger to the frenzy of the harvest home:

> They reel'd, they set, they crossed, they cleekit
> Till ilka carlin' swat and reekit.

Men cleared their barns more willingly for the meal-and-ale than
they ever did for the Free Kirk's travelling sermons. The
centrepiece of the harvest supper however was the meal-and-ale,
the dish that gave its name to the feast and indeed paid its respects
to the old gods in its ingredients, which came mostly from the
"corn parks". It was a deadly brew, made somewhat beforehand in
a big bowl or basin, that had the old talismans, rings, buttons,
thimbles, silver coins (sixpenny pieces usually), stirred into it. Its
other constituents were fine oatmeal, beer, whisky and sweetening
syrup or sugar. There were meal and ale makers who were a lot
more reticent about their precise recipes than they ever were about
their love-lives; they passed them down almost like a secret code
when it came time for them to leave the stage — at the very last,
and by word of mouth. In the Highland regions, the thickening of
the meal-and-ale with oatmeal was a propitiation to ensure a good
crop the following year; round the farmtouns of the Lowlands
plain there was always more concern with the dish's alcoholic level
and its guarantee of a lively evening. Though its creation was
certainly individualistic, Helen Beaton in *At the Back o' Benachie*
gives the recipe from her own uplands area:

> A bottle of stout, half a bottle of whisky and two bottles of brisk
> ale were poured into a large milk plate, and a bowlful of sugar
> stirred into it. The oatmeal was strown into the mess gently, till
> it was of the consistency of not too thin porridge. A ring and
> button were put in. . . . Sugar put on the top finished the
> "meal-and-ale" making.

Others mixed the ingredients together, letting the liquid come to
the top.

The dish, again, was supped communally from a big bowl set in
the middle of the table. "You dove in wi' yer speen tae see what ye
could get," reflected one old female participant. "Gin ye got the
ring ye were likely to get a man and gin ye got the button there was

little hope for ye . . . an' a saxpence was still a saxpence in those days. It could pit a ribbon in yer hair or gin ye were a man pit a bittie o' tobacco in yer pipe."

After the first course came the more substantial part of the menu: beef or fowl followed by plum-duff maybe, though there were small hard-pressed touns where they were tactless enough to serve sowens. About a sizeable place the supper might have its formal side, its toasts and its traditional responses, with the farmer thanking his *hairst* crew for work well done and a crop snatched not a moment too soon. But then the tables were cleared for dancing and for a night of fun and flyting past all remembrance the morning after, with many folk far from sober and some of them under the table. Neighbours were invited, of course, and every toun had its meal-and-ale in turn. Once upon a day you could be worn out by the time they were all of them put past.

It is hardly to be wondered at that a *hairst* so hardily won should be so riotously celebrated. Behind that night lay the long shadows of history, the old knowledge that in that land of the grey touns harvest had been known as late as Yule, when the corn had been riven from the crusted snow, threshed into the cart and taken to the drying kiln at the mill. The meal-and-ale was, by the 1920s and 1930s, in Gibbon's words, a

> relic of the ancient fun at the last ingathering of the sheaves —
> still a genial clowning and drinking and staring at the moon and
> slow, steady childes swinging away to the bothies, their hands
> deep down in their pouches, their boots striking fire from the
> cobbles; still maids to wait their lads in the lee of the new-built
> stacks, and be cuddled and warm and happy against brown dank
> chests, and be kissed into wonder on the world, and taste the
> goodness of the night and the Autumn's end. . . . Before the
> Winter comes.

If the old rituals by then had disappeared, the mood was the same, one of deep thankfulness. That joy, when there was "winter" or at least certain hope of it, was reflected too in the plain little kirks up and down the farmtoun countryside. Thanksgiving Sunday then was a more movable feast, a difficult *hairst* a matter of suspense for the Kirk as well as the touns. The minister for once was forced to take advice from his farmer elders about the end and outcome of harvest and set past an appropriate Sunday. That day the house of God wore its autumnal adornment of golden sheaves — one on each side of the kirk door, at least while the binder reigned — and its long polished table was laden with the offerings of the hens' cruive, the dairy, and the cottar's garden — eggs, kebbucks of cheese, vegetables and so on — and the melancholy scent of chrysanthemums hung briefly over the pews. Whatever the heart could give, the poor of the parish would receive.

It could be the end of October, even into November. Hallowed hymns were sung and beyond the lancet panes the stackyards were full, a token of His goodness to the folk who lived by the land. The year finally had come full circle. . . . And the Kirk, after all, had outlasted the pagan gods.

Once such things, the festivals of the land, were intertwined with the destinies of its folk. The old feasts were their social scene; from them and their meetings sprang the great events of their lives: their follies, their loves and their sometimes unsanctified unions. So the pattern of the year was interwoven with the pattern of life.

XVIII

The Mystique of Muck

WALKING THE SPRING morning parks of his native Mearns,
Lewis Grassic Gibbon, that champion of ploughmen and
peasants, paused to reflect on "What a fine and heartsome smell has
rank cow-dung as the childe with the graip hurls it steady heap
upon heap from the rear of his gurling cart". Gibbons was not
squeamish about dung, for unsavoury though it sounds, a
farmtouns's wealth was largely based on it.

You might suppose then, that all countrymen would have been
tolerant of it. Alas no. One grieve, but shortly home to the big
estate's Mains, grievously offended and fell foul of the factor by
building a "park midden" too close to the Big House's sequestered
avenues where the laird's nose, when he was at home, could have
wind of it. He had to lift the midden forthwith to a more
inconvenient location — and managed in time to live down the
misjudgement.

His error, though, is understandable for much more desperate
than muck's omnispresence about a town was the dire lack of it.
Earlier farming had suffered dreadfully from the want of it — so
much that in its shortage in the Highland landscape the crofter folk
had to be restrained by their lairds from periodically ripping off
the thatch of their poor dwellings in an attempt to enrich their even
poorer bere rigs. And that dung, after all, had been a puny thing
against the pungent product of the latter-day Lowland touns.

Usually it came from under the same roof as the crofter folk
themselves, where it had lain winter-long under the hooves of their
housed cattle-beasts, festering and coagulating its essences. From
time to time, when its odour became unbearable, a scattering of
soil would be thrown over it, and as it went to the croft rigs there
would frequently be added to it, to the laird's consternation, the
sooty thatch of the but and ben that had harboured it — along with
anything else likely to enhance it. . . . For the search for that
mystical element that guaranteed good crops was never-ending.

If dung had a champion it was Lord Kames, that compulsive improver; writing as late as 1776, he still doubted whether any branch of husbandry was less understood than the vital contribution of manure. In that time, as farming began to stir out of its dark and impoverished past, only the in-toun — the close-lying fields — had gotten the manure, the outfield and *faulds*, as we have seen, being cropped for as long as they would bear corn and then left again in grass or "growth" to let the years re-enrich them. Folk then had lived close to the margins, fearful of life's uncertainties and an ill-*hairst*. Only the spread of the new-type farmtouns could quiet the qualms of such a hazardous existence and distance them from its perils.

It was the matchless partnership of the growing *stirk* (steer) and the spread of the turnip that put an end to the dearth and neglect that had so troubled Lord Kames. That looseness of the bowels among *neep*-fed *stirks* that so troubled Stephens can hardly have bothered the farmtouns since their life, like their future, revolved round it. Artificial fertilisers would complement it, enhance it but not yet be a substitute for it. And when it travelled from a toun it went with a price on its head: about 3s 6d a cubic yard around 1860, a figure that seems to have varied little over the next 70 years.

Such was its importance that when a toun changed its tenant, auctioneers and their assistants, at the end of the out-goer's roup, would hold their noses and measure the midden's volume in valuation for the ingoing man. It was a realisable asset and it fell, as always, to the redoubtable Stephens to delineate its constituents: "Farmland manure consists of the solid and liquid excrements of farm livestock and of the litter provided to them" — as succinct a definition as has ever been penned. Stephens was not the kind of man to hide anything under a euphemism. The only thing he forgot to mention was the richness of its odour, which was sometimes all-pervading and regularly filtered through the bothy's windows and sometimes even those of the farmhouse itself. Of its elements, the urine — the *strang* as the ballad touns, equally unsqueamish, unhesitatingly called it — was of more value in fact than the solids, being richer in both nitrogen and potash.

Traditionally a toun was built round its midden: its quadrangular layout encompassed byres (with their abutting *neep*-shed and straw-shed), the stable and almost certainly the cart-shed. Whichever door you opened into the inner sanctum formed by their walls it led on to the midden, and whenever you had to it was to wheel a barrowful of dung — or to throw a reeking shovelful of the stuff — into the fermenting heart of it.

Dung came from both stable and the byre. A Clydesdale, it was said, made twelve tons of manure in a year — for the statistically-minded three-quarters of the weight of its feed over the same period — and paradoxical though it may seem to talk of quality in such a context, the byproduct was considered superior to that of the earlier oxen, which had produced a like quantity when housed for the same months of winter and fed on a not-dissimilar diet of turnips, corn and hay.

For all that, the muck midden was, and remained, mainly the bailie's kingdom. Day in, day out, after the horsemen had quit the toun for distant fields, he rolled out the barrowloads from his byre that filled it, a fine abundance that stirred a new ingredient into the great cycle of soil fertility. The black *stot* was the catalyst in the new equation. There was never a better muck-*maker*, or muck-*spreader* for that matter. The steer was always more than tomorrow's steak: you fed turnips and straw and maybe bruised corn and oilcake in at one end (converting to beef) while it effortlessly made you manure at the other: one ton a month from a fattening bullock. If the beast left you nothing else when it went to the fatstock mart, they said — little profit, that is, for all the *neeps* you had put into it — it always left you its dung.

It may have been an odd testimonial, but when it had done so man and Clydesdale stood up to the *queets* in cow-*strang* in order to transfer its fertility to the waiting fields.

A toun's muck was carted out in the fall of the year, in October through into November, in that strange indeterminate season when the farmtouns began to gather their momentum again after the crescendo of harvest. It was a task that turned grieves into kings on their own midden-heads. Not since *hairst* had they played so central a role. Up and down the ballad counties they seized graips and forked dung as though their lives depended on it. They hurled command at man and beast, hardly making distinction. That was the way of it when it came to carting out the muck: it always heightened the grieve's blood.

The task, like every other about a toun, had its peculiar pattern, its ingrained ritual that ensured a high efficiency and would have delighted today's method-study expert as much as it did the dedicated grieve. For it was he who orchestrated the work and its pace was relentless. Day long, Clydesdales and carts came and went from the field and his often-scurrilous instructions with them. Each horseman drove both his beasts, yoked in their carts. For a start, both grieve and horseman loaded first one of his carts, then the other as it was backed through the ankle-deep *sharn bree* (call it what you would, it smelt not one damned bit the sweeter) against the banked dung, until the midden was emptied sufficiently to let them load two carts simultaneously.

There the job took a sinister turn, for if it was sore on a slight frame it was also one that allowed a brawny, well-built grieve to show his prowess with the muck-graip. Such a man would enjoy the competition of the midden-head, and the thinking behind it, so diabolically simple yet so typical of the life of the old touns that one needs hardly to explain it. With the grieve setting the pace, the horseman who wanted to stay on at the next *feeing* time would think it prudent to match him, throw for throw. It all made the turn-round that much faster. . . .

There were variations on the theme though: where the distance to the field was less than would strain both the horseman and his pair, he pulled his loads out of the midden, left them there, and returned to the midden-top to give a hand in filling the next pair of carts before driving his own loads to the field. It always made another man filling instead of idling his way to the field, and that, too, helped to speed the muck-carting.

So, to and fro as the day went on, in an endless shuttle of carts they deposited the heaps of dark steaming dung on the stubble in an ever-widening pattern. Only as the November gloam and the cold night air came down on him, when he could no longer see the cart in front of him, did the grieve quit and allow other folk to do the same.

In the "muck park" the horseman had a helper, a man who never left the field — or the stink of dung — till dusk relieved him. He took the second cart of each pair as the carts came to the field and unloaded it, again speeding the turn-round.

The dung, pulled reeking from the ungated tails of the carts with the pluck (a hook-tined handtool understandably no longer fashionable), formed a dotted grid on the yellow stubble, each mound five or six paces apart, the rows each at a similar distance one from the other. Even in this there was method long and tried:

it was the optimum spacing that ensured that the subsequent spreader — a man with his graip — could distribute the maximum amount with the minimum of unproductive walking. It was a pattern as familiar in the fields of Suffolk and as old as Tusser, that poet of farming wisdom.

The mucking of the fields differed from toun to toun and from year to year. The number of loads or tons to the acre varied according to need, the farmer's whim (and sometimes the grieve's guesswork), and what the midden would provide — especially the latter. For despite the number of black *stirks* housed in its steading, few touns of the old landscape ever had enough. Crucial decisions had to be made about muck. Traditionally the ley parks, the arable grass fields, got none since they had benefited from the summer bounty of the *stirks* and had also their own humus. The concern was always for the *neep grun*.

By the day of the farmtouns, the muck-spreading was mainly man's work and usually the bailies', who thus became men twice-blessed. Things had moved on from the days of the old cot-toun when the womenfolk had done the work, along with many other jobs about a toun, as part of the agreement that kept a miserable roof over their heads, though there were echoes still of that hardy lifestyle on the crofts that claimed the hillside and the bare edge of the moor. There the crofter women, with their menfolk from home all day, and maybe for the entire week, would spread the muck as they had always done, and often barrow it out to the shift as well. The years had inured them to such drudgery and little they thought of it as they seized the byre-graip in the bygoing, and set off for the field with one of their man's old bonnets over their bunned heads. It is something they would do for as long as the old-style North-east crofting life survived. Mostly they were born to it.

Their byword then was "pairt sma' an' sair a' " (part small and serve all), and that advice had a relevance even about the muck-rich touns, though maybe for somewhat different reasons. Their fetish for having it "broken small" was so that it would be buried by the plough, if for no other reason than to make the work look tidy, though it is true, too, that there were old touns where they cared little about finesse so long as the dung got scattered. And there were some where the farmer-man would not have cared supposing it had stood up and waved to him as he passed on the way to the kirk on the Sabbath.

Some spreaders liked to work with the four-tined fork: it made spreading a lazier job, easier on the back, and maybe for that reason alone there were old grieves who wouldn't countenance its use and insisted always on the ubiquitous graip, which they considered broke the muck smaller.

By the 1930s, most touns were taking to the practice of mucking the stubble, weaned away from the earlier method of mucking the turnip ground in the drill by the time factor at a vital season of the year and maybe by the lunacy of the system associated with the field midden. Yet the field midden was by no means an anomaly of the North-east Lowlands. It was familiar to Tusser. And about the ballad touns it became necessary as the toun midden filled to overflowing. Muck left the autumn toun to be built into middens by the dykes of the appropriate fields, the amount maybe having more to do with the grieve's desire to be rid of it than any accurate forecast of what the "park" would need.

The task was doubly hard, for while the first few loads could be tipped from the cart, the rest had to be forked on to the satellite midden as it grew by the dykeside. Here again, the horseman had a helper to unload the second cart.

Yet when the work of the turnip ground began in the late spring, it was all set at naught, for the muck-loading began again — so that it could be carted to the drills as they were set up. Here the horseman varied his method, mounting his cart to stand on the load to throw the dung in graipfuls over the tail-gate as his Clydesdale obediently walked the drill. In a long field, only one drill would be "muckit" at a time to ensure that the load took the horseman out at the top *fleed* or headland and thus avoid wasted time — or damage caused by the cart crossing the drills. Where the drills were short, two might be "muckit" simultaneously.

In the kind of nicety of language that often existed round the touns, the task of scattering it along the bottoms of the drills — dispersing the horseman's graipfuls — was known as "brakin' muck", subtly distinguishing it from "spreading muck", which related to work on the stubbles of autumn.

Some things though never changed. The men who did the job were the same: the bailies, summoned again from the seclusion of their byres. Nor was the anxiety lessened about the conservation of such a vital constituent in the farming cycle. Still and all (it is said), there were grizzled old farmers of the 1920s and 1930s who slyly managed to have it both ways: to have their muck and spread it.

Theirs was an ingenious stratagem worthy of men who somehow managed to survive in their depressed touns long after they should have gone to the wall. They gave their horseman a well-worn graip, short in the tines, with which to throw the muck into the drills, so that he could not be over-lavish in tossing it into the drill-bottom. The graip given him on the midden head though would nearly always be brand new, long and strong in the prongs so that he could load his cart quickly and not waste time about it.

If the bothy lads took a laugh about such antics, the ploy, for all that, may have been excusable. Few touns now make muck on the grand scale and it is difficult to appreciate the role it once played or to remember its importance in that bare northern landscape.

XIX

Of Byres and Bailies

AT THE HEART of civilisation is the byre, the barn and the midden. The words are those of Edwin Muir, the Orcadian writer and poet; they are from his spare and moving *An Autobiography*. He might well, had he thought of it, have added the plough for it too is close to man, though maybe in a different way, for Muir saw the farmtoun of his Orkney childhood as a carnival of life and death, with its ritualised ceremonies: the mounting of the bull (to male shouts of encouragement); the final killing that was the outcome of the byreman's kindliness. Muir with his sensitive young mind rationalised the contradictions and the seeming cruelty of the farmtoun year: "There was a necessity in the copulation and the killing which took away the sin, or at least by the actual act, transformed it into a sad sanctioned duty."

For all that, Muir, like many another country-born child, was fond of the byre and its docile animals. If it lacked the bustle and contention of the stable it was, as the northern winter drew in, a friendly, welcoming place warmed by the breath of beasts, a refuge from the frosty night outside, its peace punctuated only by the rattle of chains and the rhythmic crunch of turnips in salivating jaws. In its pools of limpid paraffin-lantern light gentle eyes might turn to mark your progress up the *greep*, that central aisle of the byre that gave passage to the stockman's barrow but between times was an animal latrine you trod at your peril. Sunday visitors in patent boots stayed circumspectly by the door, hurling their snippets of talk at the bailie as he passed them, to and fro — a habit that gave prolonged lulls to the conversation and finally silenced it as its thread withered.

Few writers have described the winter byre of the ballad touns as lovingly as John R. Allan in his classic of the region, *Farmer's Boy*:

The byre was the gentlest and sweetest place about the steading,

just as cows are the gentlest and sweetest beasts about a farm. I
have wondered for a long time why men chose to make the dog
their closest friend, for the dog is neither very beautiful in himself
nor is he particularly virtuous. But the cow — there is a thing of
beauty. She is simple, sensuous and impassioned, like a poem,
and she has the Christian virtues as well. She embodies the
maternal impulse magnified to the *n*th degree. She asks but to
give and give and give again. In return for a few turnips and a
handful of straw she gives streams of lovely milk, rich and
health-giving, the very elixir of life.

Accompanying his old grandfather on a last round of the toun before
bedtime, he recalls: ". . . as we stepped quietly through the byre,
we felt a close community with the generous heart of nature."
    And so it always seemed.
    The byre was the bailie's, the stockman's, kingdom. In it he
reigned if not supreme, largely uninterrupted. His realm was
integral to the life of the toun, often its wealth and its pulse-beat; its
rituals were enshrined in the farmtoun year as surely as those of the
plough and the reaper, its cycle irrevocable. Bulls of dairytouns
were brought forth to do the job they were kept for and obliged
unabashed by public gaze and often with the kind of expression that
suggested supreme boredom at nature's unvarying monotony. In
time the calves came and the milk flowed, creamy and once again
abundant.
    The shrewd placing of the byre among the farmtoun's *biggings* —
between the turnip shed, at one end, and the straw-shed at the other
— gave notice of its importance. It was the kind of arrangement that
ensured that the bailie need never put his jacket on (except maybe in
barrowing out muck on a day of blind-drift) and also that the toun
would never have to take on two men where one could be made to
suffice. And the pace at times was such that bailies could work
themselves into a sweat wearing only their *semmits* and trousers.
The layout, indeed, was one that must have delighted the
irrepressible Stephens, with his penchant for the economic
deployment of labour. The great man, incidentally, so that the
stockman would not be offensive to the bull, recommended sombre
dress and the avoidance of red. He was emphatic, too, that the bailie
should own a watch: how else would he be able to ensure that his
beasts got their feed strictly on time?

There were high byres and low byres and dairy byres, each kind with its own peculiar function in the farming year. The first two ran in unison to send prime beef to the grand dinner-tables; the latter gave milk to the cities and the surrounding villages where the folk had long lost their pendicle and cow.

Near the end of the farmtoun era it was the big dairytoun that enjoyed the greatest prestige, its crack bailies (for they were invariably in the plural) seldom being asked to do a hand's turn beyond their own *greeps*, and sometimes not even being made to pull their own turnips let alone help with the *hairst*.

Their day ran to the kind of timetable that would have shamed British Rail. It began at four, before the dawn had sharded the sleep from their eyes. At that hour of the morning they had the toun to themselves, its silences shattered only by the last of the night's marauders and sometimes by the occasional foray of the farmer himself, who would rise early now and then to see fair play on his own behalf. Hungry bellies were quickly filled as the beasts got their first feed of the day: neeps and silage, or maybe draff carted home from some not-too-distant distillery where it had already served a useful purpose. They would have time to "sort the beasts" (i.e., muck them out and tease fresh straw among their hooves) before the band of milkers came in on them, sleepy and sore-headed.

High conversation was never a feature of the morning byre. . . . The milking, as a ritual, began usually at the byre door and moved up the stalls of one side and down those of the other, a kind of leap-frogging of milkmaids played out with pail and stool, each milker taking the next available cow. Its background music was the steady *zing-zing* of milk spurting rhythmically against the sides of the milk pails.

Croft wives with one cow usually milked from the left; in the two-to-a-stall byres of the touns milkers set their stools between beasts and worked from either side. Handle a cow the wrong way and you were in for a disappointment, a poor flow of milk. There were good milkers and bad milkers, their secret success or lack of it a strange unexplainable thing, though it lay not in the "pattern" of pulling the teats for there seems to have been no traditional order, and prosaically, was just a matter of pressure between thumb and fingers.

The job had its hazards. Heifers being milked for the first time could be vicious, and though bailies numbered in their ranks a few chivalrous men who might themselves take on the task, sooner or later a woman milker had to risk injury.

All the same, for good or ill and mainly for the money, cottar wives up and down the country bent their white-capped heads morning and evening into the heaving sides of Ayrshire and Friesian, Shorthorn and Jersey. Each beast took six to eight minutes to milk. If it was swift, it was also relentlessly methodical: each cow's udder would have to be wiped before she was milked, her yield probably weighed before being tipped into the waiting churn. In an hour or little more they would be finished, flying home to put their bairns unwillingly to school or, at the end of the day, to set their man's supper on the table before he stepped in from the stable.

The afternoon milking though was something else again: with folk about the toun it took on the well-rehearsed aspects of urgency and even drama. Bailies came to their roles like actors reborn. It was a kind of second house of the dairying day: between the hours of four and six, the bailies stalked their *greeps* like demigods, stern and ever-vigilant. Their rule was shaken only by the arrival of the milk inspectors. That night the byre was transformed. Electric bulbs were put into all the lights; the milkers marched in, saintly-suited, crisp-capped and wellington-booted. White-coated figures paced the byre floor. It was like Casualty, on a bad night. The bailie himself, for once, was white-overalled above a clean-washed *semmit*. Tonight of nights he wiped udders with ostentatious care and the milk churns gleamed in the glare of unguarded electric. There was a tension about the place that unsettled man and beast; dairymaids in the milk house presided primly over cooler and bottler, neatly serious, banter and lads forgotten. Small boys stumbling in for warmth from the night as they waited for their cottared fathers' nightly flagons of perquisite milk were hustled unceremoniously back into the chill and the dark and went, unresisting.

The evening milking, however, with its congestion of folk and frantic activity, would be diminished by the arrival, in the mid-1930s, of the milking-machine. It largely banished the welling-toned band of women milkers though not the milk inspector. And there were times when the bailie would have to defer not only to him but to the man from the milking-machine company as well, something he did with ill-grace, taking a private revenge:

"Foo's yer aw-tae-matic milker doin', Andra?" somebody, sooner or later, would ask him.

"Oh, nae sae weel, man," he could honestly reply. "It's gey an' often aw-tae-hell."

The feeding of his beasts before he took home to his own supper brought the byre day to a close, though it might still not free the stockman for the night. As dusk came down, were he a conscientious man or with a beast due to calve, he might put away the yard spade and walk up to the toun in the gloam to take a last look round the byre before bedtime.

But not all the dairying places were grand, attested touns. There were smaller "tounies" where, if the milk was just as healthy, the hygiene was somewhat less relentless. David Toulmin, the North-east author who once lived the farmtoun life and has long exposed its harshness in his writing, recalls in *Hard Shining Corn* the ritual of their mornings and his early *fee* as a farmer's boy:

Down in the byre Knowie [the tenant of Knowehead] fed the kye with draff and bruised corn while I mucked them out with barrow and shovel. He scrubbed their hind-quarters with a long-handled broom, dipping it in a pail of cold water as he went along. The cows swished their lithe bushy tails in my face, sprinkling my neck and bare arms with cold icy drops, which soon shook me out of my sleep.

Twenty-four cows stood in a single row, heads to the wall, tails to the greep, licking their food out of rough-faced cement troughs. . . .

At five-thirty, Knowie's wife and two daughters came in for the milking. They brought their cans and pails from the dairy and took down their stools from a shelf. They sat down, each one to a cow, and very soon they had brimming pails between their knees, spurting the hot milk into the rising froth in rhythmic, steady jets, plop-plop, plop-plop. . . .

For the lad newly home to a toun on his first *fee*, his first six-month engagement, it was usually the byre that broke him in to the life. Thus David Fyfe, at nearly seventy, reminiscing a few years ago on his Buchan youth for a northern newspaper:

Being the second oldest of a family of twelve, I was able to leave school at 13½ years in 1921. My father sent me to a dairy farm three miles away. . . .

My first wage was £8 for a six-month period. I remember, my first morning at work, being wakened at five o'clock with a sweaty sock across my face. I leapt out of the chaff-bed and put on my first long breeks, boots, and was about to tie my laces when my senior bed-mate shouted to me: "Come on lad, ye hinna time for that noo." I had to run to keep up with him. When we came to the byre door he said: "In there, I'm going to the stable."

I went to the door and saw the byre lanterns burning brightly over 20 cows and the milkers all sitting tearing the milk from them. On seeing me the boss rose from his cow, fetched a spare pail, and pointed to a large beast.

"Milk that one," he said. Says I: "But I'm sorry, I canna milk."

There was no answer and the boss went back to milking his cow. Terrified, I gave the cow a nervous clap. Wide-eyed now I sat down beside her udder. Only a little milk came. I was still at the same old cow when the others had three or four milked.

That was my start on the farm. . . .

The years and progress would link such landward farms of the North-east Lowlands ever more indissolubly with its seaboard towns. Each morning as dawn broke, and sometimes before it, the silence of their salt-breezy streets would be rent by the sound of a string of milk-gigs, with their spanking high-stepping shelts, clattering their way over the grey cobblestones, their pint and gill stoups (measures), hung from the churn-lugs, adding their own clangour, stirring the sleep of the ungodly and dragging decent folk from their beds. They took the road, those milk-gigs, as though their very life depended on it. And so, in a way, it did. Their milk, hot from the churn, was into townsfolk's jugs before the milkhouse maid had gotten time to sit down to her breakfast. It was those milk-gigs (really spring-carts) that supplied also the small dairy shops tucked away in almost every side-street and congested wynd, and that finally ousted the "toon coo", those anachronistic town-dwelling beasts that had to survive on imported fodder and the poor grazing of a bare town-loaning for milking in their stalls at the point of supply. It was a sad life for any cow, unfair to the often-tubercular beast and to its captive customers.

Those small dairytouns, though, would fall before the bigger, attested touns of the 1930s, where the morning and evening milking scene became ever more sophisticated. There the warmth of the paraffin-lantern's yellow glow would give way, universally, to the hard glare of electric, home-generated and so desperately unreliable that the old lanterns had to remain filled and wick-trimmed at the ready in the engine-house.

By then the little bakery-dairies that had studded the town's street-corners were sliding into eclipse or being annexed as suitable outposts for the larger dairy combines. Theirs was the safer, pasteurised product. Such was the swiftness of advance that the new town depots were often presided over by men, white-coated and wellington-booted, who could remember that time when the town cows had stepped home to their bare lodgings twice daily over the street cobbles.

They brought with them these new milk emporiums, those new citadels of bottle and churn, a grey drabness that chilled the soul. They came to life long before the grey dawn broke and while the city slept for a town's milk, like its post and its newspapers, was a secretive, subterranean business that beat below the city's pulse. The dairies died as daylight broke: their men were home almost as other folk left their beds unaware of how fresh supplies had been spirited into the city.

Today the old dairy's ten-gallon churns have been honourably discharged, an anachronism in our modern time. The old impresarios of the city milk parlours would not have liked that for they were, to a man, virtuosos of the celebrated snatch lift (and the sometimes careless rupture), that two-man art that could make a full and inert ten-gallon milk-churn take flight like a bird from the paving stones on to the platform of waiting cart or lorry.

And their art did not end there for with that ability went an uncanny skill in rolling full churns on their rim-edges. It all dazzled the eye. There were good men in their prime who would let go a spinning churn at six paces, confident that it would crash into the niche in the churn-ranks that the eye had allotted it.

Their pasteurised world coexisted with that of the big dairytouns. About many farmtouns, however, the folk took their milk as

the cow gave it to them. Just a few beasts filled the daily flagons
of the kitchen, the *fee*'d cottars and bothy men, and the kitchen
maid milked the small herd twice a day, helped by the *orra loon*.
The job was a condition of her employment but that didn't
mean she had to like it. Few did: it helped to lengthen their
interminable day, and for some, at least, it was a task fraught
with terror.

John C. Milne in "Fin I cam' hame to Nedderton" bleakly
exposes the plight of a timid lass ordered out to "milk the kye":

> Fin I sat doon by Fitie's side
> My hert was like te brak,
> And lang ere I had milkit her
> I lay upon my back!
>
> Through amang the feeders
> A rottan gid a squeal!
> I left ahin my milkin-pail,
> And a' my wuts as weel!

Round these old touns where the byre was never the mainstay it
was the evening milking that brought the workday to a close, the
last chore of the maid or maybe of the mistress herself. Then the
winter's night folded down on the old touns and the kitchen door
was latched for a moment of ease before bedtime. Many still
remember that moment a little nostalgically, as did the poet
Charles Murray in these lines from "Winter":

> The milkers tak' their cogues at last,
> Draw moggins on, tie mutches fast,
> Syne hap their lantrens fae the blast
>   Maun noo be met;
> An' soon the day's last jot is past,
>   Milk sey'd an' set.

The work of the *orra loon*, a toun's youngest and very humblest
servant, was usually closely linked with the milk byre and its
routine had a monotony that would soon bring him to the point of
rebellion, as in the toun run by "John Bruce of the Corner":

The loon he was fee'd to advance and retire
Atween the neep park and the aul' coo byre,
But he wasna lang hame or he seem'd for to tire
O' aul' Johnny Bruce o' the Corner.

Farmer Bruce in this snatch of bothy ballad was real enough (as were most of the folk named in the songs). The long catechism of the Skene farmer's failings, according to folklorist Gavin Greig, prince of ballad-gatherers, was "superior to most of its kind"; like most of the ballads it spoke "straight and plain and strong". And likely it did, for the *orra loon*'s ambition would almost certainly have been to "have a pair" of Clydesdales. Failing that, though, he might graduate in time to a toun whose business was to raise beef. For finally it was its fatstock not its dairying that brought the ballad countryside its wider fame. A trade that had begun in the Highland hills had coalesced into something better on the Grampian plains, and like everything else about the touns it had its patterns and its hierarchical nuances.

What the farmtouns did was to take the technique of fattening beasts to perfection: they gave the Sunday roast a good name. And, for once, Stephens, in his *Book of the Farm*, is ecstatic:

The fame of Aberdeenshire beef is world-wide. In the attainment of this the people, the land and the cattle have each played a creditable part. To reverse the order, the stock of cattle are of the very best class of beef-producing animals, chiefly crosses between the native black polls and the shorthorn breed. Then the land is peculiarly adapted for the raising of turnips of the highest feeding value. It is well-known that there are turnips and turnips, some much richer than others in feeding properties. The roots grown on the well-farmed granite soils of Aberdeenshire are of exceptionally rich quality. And as to the people, the knack of how to make a bullock hard-fat would seem somehow to have become the special birthright of the Aberdeenshire farmer. He treats his land well and he knows that in so doing he is enriching the raw materials which afterwards go to the production of his annual "crop of beeves" which form such a large portion of the revenue of his farm.

Again, what the stock-fattening touns were about was blindingly simple, and Stephens, as usual, sums it up: "Early maturity at a minimum of expense, with a maximum of meat and manure." Earlier-maturing stock meant a chance to take an earlier profit in the mart and, of course, an opportunity to increase production.

The man who set the pace and brought others at his heels was none other than the Aberdeenshire-Angus king himself, Willie McCombie of Tillyfour, in the upper reaches of Donside, who often fed up 400 beasts a year. But all round the North-east countryside there were touns where the bailies marched in platoons and where there was a constant congestion of barrow-traffic along the *greeps*. In the feeders' byres of the fattening touns the bailies of the old countryside went whey-faced and early bald from trying to contend with their beasts' insatiable appetites. Stripped to their *semmits*, their undervests, they pushed barrowload after barrowload of turnips and dung, feeding one end of the animal and scavenging the spoils of the other.

Like his dairytoun colleague the feeding bailie would rise early and never catch up with himself. He would be expected to tend between 40 and 50 beasts, each capable of getting through one hundredweight (112lb) of turnips a day while looking chidingly over its shoulder, in hurt that he was hungering it. With 50 beasts in the byre, that was two and a half tons a day he had to barrow in from the *neep*-shed, never mind the estimated one and a half tons of dung he daily barrowed out to the midden.

About most of the old touns the bailies, dairymen as well as those in feeders' byres, went to the fields to pull their own turnips. Often, they had to bruise their own corn too. The tasks made the day both long and toilsome and undoubtedly helped to swell the regular ranks of the Scottish regiments each *feeing* market day.

Like the ploughboy, the bailie comes regularly to notice in the bothy ballads — in particular the conscientious stockman who looked after the beasts at that Alford toun "The Guise o' Tough" in "the year o' ninety-one". The song ostensibly, and probably actually, is by the toun's *orra man*:

> We hae a gallant bailie,
>   And Wallace is his name;
> And he can fair redd up the kye
>   When he tak's doon the kaim.

The little bailie though was a lad of lesser worth and did the
Donside toun poorer credit:

> We hae a little bailie,
> And Jamieson's his name,
> And he's gane doon to Alford
> And raised an awfu' fame.

> He's gane doon to Charlie Watt's
> For to get a dram;
> But lang, lang or I got doon
> The laddie couldna stan'.

Wherever cattle were being seriously fattened for market, the
two-tier byre system operated. As winter wore on, the high byre
(the head bailie's domain) gradually lost its beasts. Replacements
came from the stalls of the little bailie's low byre where the
regime was less strict and the diet more mundane, merely *neeps*
and straw. The little bailie's byre in its turn was restocked with
beasts bought in, at eighteen months and as cheaply as possible,
often from the old crofts that once fretted the northern landscape. For the crofter man needing to be rid of his beasts, the
deal could never be favourable. Thus the wily farmer

> On crofter bodies roon aboot
> He aften gie's a ca',
> And buys their bits o' stirkies cheap
> By haudin' on the jaw.

It was a tradition that uniquely brought the lowly crofter man
into the farmtoun circle as a vital link in the production chain, for
with his calf-house again empty, it was to the dairytoun with its
unwanted calves that the smallholder turned for *his* replacements
— in the 1930s, at about £3 each.

In the feeders' byres, as in the old dairytoun byres, the beasts
stood two to a stall, a yard between them so that they could lie
down or, standing, allow the bailie's barrow to pass up between
them to tip the turnips in their troughs. Each steer was tethered

by chain to its own travis, which divided the stall from its neighbour.

Mostly, like those haughty dairytoun queens of the high yield who sauntered home from pasture with tight udders on summer afternoons, the fattening beasts came in from the last of the grass in the fall-of-the-year to a diet of straw and turnips, or the even sweeter sustenance of hay and swedes, going on in their later stages to additional oilcake and bruised corn. Some came in initially to be plumped out on oat-straw, cut while still a bit green, and tares, which bridged an awkward gap for those old farmers unwilling as yet to disturb their *neeps* in the drill. In a landscape of such haggard *hairsts* the green straw was never a problem: it was, most touns believed, more nutritious than straw that had thoroughly ripened.

It was the approach of Christmas that heightened the year's momentum. Black *stots* fed like princes and good bailies came suddenly into their own: there were men, it is said, who could put a bloom on a beast just by speaking to it kindly. McCombie, tenant farmer and Liberal MP, with an eye on the London market, liked to have his fat beasts in and tied up early, by the end of August or early September. Hardly far behind him was James Bruce of Inverquhomery of Longside, whose beef was a lot more chewable than the name of his toun and whose name rang almost as illustriously round London's Smithfield market. He enunciated the three basic principles for success: (a) a good strain of blood, and judicious selection in breeding; (b) feeding the land liberally as well as the cattle; and (c) a good cattleman.

Few touns, however, housed their beasts as early as McCombie. Some took them in for six months, but around most the timing depended on how the grass held out. There were touns where the avowed policy was "early oot, early in" regardless, a view that brought the animals indoors as soon as the first frost of October touched the grass. It would be mid-April at least (and that in a relatively frost-free season) before it would be forward enough to support them again. There were touns where they had their livestock housed before *hairst* was behind them; some went to Whitsunday, the end of May, before letting the beasts back into the fields. And after so long, that moment of freedom evoked a sense of joy even in country folk. What it meant to the animals is described by Lewis Grassic Gibbon in that superb essay, *The Land*:

All winter the cattle were kept to the byres. This morning saw their first deliverance — cows and stirks and stots and calves they grumphed and galumphed from the byre to the park and squattered an astounded delight in the mud, and boxed at each other, and stared a bovine surprise at the world, and went mad with delight and raced round the park, and stood still and mooed: they mooed on a long, devilish note, the whole lot of them, for nearly two minutes on end and for no reason at all but delight in hearing their own moo.

In their summer emptiness the byres would be lime-washed and the cobwebs shaken down from the couples, the rafters, where they had remained unmolested between one year and the next and even, about hard-pressed touns, between one tenant and his in-comer.

You could tell a good bailie, folk said, by the way he kept his *greep* clean: he was a maestro of barrow, graip, fork and broom, the basic handtools of his calling. His barrow — painted the same blue and red as the farmtoun's horse-carts and made by the local joiner or millwright, those country wizards of lathe and spokeshave — carted the beasts' turnips as well as their dung. There were, it is true, touns where the bailie was given *two* barrows, one for each task. Mostly though, the old touns were not the kind of places to be driven to such wanton extravagance.

The "muckin' " of the byre was done with the graip, kin to that ubiquitous four-tined tool that the Home Counties gardener poshly calls a prong — and with a kind of condescension in his voice that is almost an insult to a fine implement. Indeed, it would be impossible to imagine the old farmtouns functioning at all without the graip: it filled dung and dug potatoes, loaded *growth* and delved those odd corners of the cottar's garden when he took it home under his arm at night. Men grew more fond of a good-balanced graip than they did of their wives. Smoothed and polished with months of use, its haft, like that of the well-worn *hairst*-fork, slid through the palm almost without touching.

"Muckin' the byre", in fact, was a skill almost inborn, and certainly encouraged, in every farmtoun boy long before he left school — and there was nobody, then, begging him to stay on, least of all his harassed and often-despairing dominie. Soiled straw was teased from under stubborn hooves and tossed into the *greep*, that central gangway, and then into the barrow, bound for the midden. Great forkfuls of fresh straw were hoisted in (on the four-pronged bailie's fork) to be new bedding — and more manure. The final flourish, the sweep of the besom, bought of the local besom-king — or latterly the stiff bristles of the byre brush — completed an operation that most bailies could do in their sleep, as indeed some of them did, on the morning after a fair-day or the yearly meal-and-ale.

The byre-day had its own immutable pattern, as sacred and predictable as the rituals in the fields. It began in the feeders' byre when the bailie stepped through its door shortly after five and just a fraction before the horsemen fell into the stable. To get quiet for his sore head the stockman first silenced his beasts with their morning *neeps* (thrown into their low concrete troughs) and while they munched he "muckit" them before brushing his *greep* and bedding them down again with the fresh straw, a little of which he also threw into their *hakes* (hay-racks).

The rest of the morning *yoking* would be spent cleaning and perhaps clipping the cattle-beasts, the early part of the afternoon *yoking* being spent in the *neep* park, pulling his turnips. Chilled to the bone, he returned to the byre's warmth in mid-afternoon to repeat the morning performance, returning yet again, after suppertime, to give the selected beasts their oilcake or bruised corn.

Except about the dairytouns whose attested herds gave them a cachet and a special kind of tyranny, their byres constantly besieged by inspectors and milk recordists and farm students avid for experience (of all kinds), and where those priests of the udder and cold churn were expected to do hardly a single chore beyond their byres, bailies lacked lamentably in prestige. They were lonesome men, bound to the steading and somewhat beyond the camaraderie of the ploughmen's ranks. They were men in thrall to beasts for they "sorted their *nowt*" on Sundays as on any other day of the week. The wonder is that not more of them were atheists. Some, against all the odds, went to morning service straight from the *greep*, sneaking in on the last toll of the bell and still in their bicycle clips. Many more never missed the Sacrament though their attendance might be to a late-sitting.

Besides contrary bulls, the bailie's job had other hazards. He was not always popular in the bothy, particularly if he were also the bothy cook, which was sometimes the case. Then the horsemen might plan the most devilish of pranks a bailie could fall foul of.

While the victim's head lay unsuspecting on his bothy pillow a pit would be prepared in his own midden just under the end of the plank that carried the barrow's wheel over the packed dung. The "pit" itself was then hidden by a shallow covering of strawy dung.

Next day the stockman would run his first barrow-load of dung up the plank — to the very end, heave, give the barrow handles that masterly flick that emptied its contents. . . . The plank, unsupported, unsuspected, tilted and down, down would go dung and bailie and barrow and all . . . into the sharny trap set for him.

A bailie's wages never covered such unpopularity nor did they reflect the importance of his place in the pattern of the farmtoun's year or the wealth he created for it. Grieves came always from the horsemen's ranks and even in the late 1920s and through the 1930s £1 a week paid his time and his devotion: his long days in the winter byre, washing bullocks, feeding and combing and brushing them. Few stockmen died rich men and when they retired it was usually with arthritis, with little in the bank, and little knowing what to do socially with the unaccustomed leisure time that life had suddenly thrust upon them.

XX

Laments for a Lost Landscape

THEY ARE GONE from the plough, those men I once knew — and from the harrow and the *hyow* and the sounds of harvest. Their days are already receding, a part of our folk culture; their world has faded before the march of agri-business and agri-technology. All are figures in a far landscape and maybe the land is poorer now: who can say, one way or the other? Theirs was a hard life comforted largely by black twist tobacco and first by the clay pipe and latterly by the famous Stonehaven, which had a following in the land as fervid as any good make of plough. Those men of the bothies — and with them, cottars coming into the same stable — clubbed together to send their *siller* and their combined order to the makers. The evergreen favourite was the "stumpie" model, a stunted apology for a pipe (about four inches long) that slid into the bailie's trouser pocket between barrowed muck-loads and could be as easily resurrected from his cords with the tobacco still glowing. It was just as widely clamped between the horsemen's teeth, leaving them both hands for the reins and the plough.

They were all of them men of the land and with them has gone much of the countryside's old culture, most of the rituals that linked us with the farming past — and the countryside they yearly recreated. The land is something different now, its folk comforming folk that you might meet in any city street, in any suburban environment. War was the watershed, the thing that divided us from our rural yesterdays. Farming marched on increasingly into the province of the engineer and scientist.

The machine-age farming would erode that old affinity of men with the soil and the seasons, or at least sadly diminish it. It would rob the landscape of much of its ancient architecture, the patterns of the hayfield and harvest, and all the rhythms of the horse-drawn age. For all that, it would be churlish to say that today's farming men are less dedicated or knowledgeable. It is only that they are different. It was inevitable that their time would come.

The man who drives today's leviathan of the harvest field is a technician overall-suited, an oily rag in his hand as he walks round his monster machine at the *yoking*'s end. It is a far cry now from the days when the Clydesdale team took the binder round the corn. The combine-harvester ushered in a change in country ways as far-reaching as the early machine-reaper did in its day. It divorced all but a few countrymen from the concerns of the *hairst* field. Old farmtoun men suddenly found themselves disfranchised by a clanking heap of metal that cut and cleaned and threshed the grain for the drier. For some, those grizzled men of the smaller two-pair touns, it took the meaning out of their *hairsts*, sweeping away as it did all the things that were dear to them, the things that justified their lives: the yellow sheaves, the stooks, the autumn glory of the cornyard. They had been fond of their stackyards, walking round them quietly in the end-of-*hairst* gloam as they took a last puff on their pipes before bedtime. The new farming that freed them was something else: less self-sufficient, demanding again some communal involvement, their participation in some new co-operative venture perhaps, in order to get their grain dried. They would not like it, labour-saving though it was: it was not their kind of *hairst*.

Looking back, men will see the coming of the "combine" for what it was: the instrument that severed the landsman's links with those ancestral harvests that knitted the generations and locked rural society in its frame. The language of the *hairst* field would become obsolete; the golden sheaf would lose its heavy symbolism, the Sunday Thanksgiving would become a little more remote in the fabric of the year. Yet the "combine" was a thing of our time: it conveniently displaced men. It had the enviable ability to snatch harvests that the binder might well have lost. It could tackle "laid" crops better than the binder ever could. Men did not have to "*redd* roads" — clear a path — for it. It made its own way in the world, coming in at the field gate to start work at once. Though it was harder on the farmer's purse, it was fine for his blood pressure.

For all that, its timing was crucial: the crop had to be ripe enough for the threshing — some seven to ten days beyond the moment when the binder could have begun to cut. Yet that matters little now: there are not the great fields of oats any more — they went out with the Clydesdales and the kind of hardy folk who took brose for their breakfast, *denner* and supper. And there were other reasons, including the populace's growing distaste for honest porridge against the packaged cereal and the disinclination of suburban wives to make it (except from the packet). *Farls* of oatcakes became the unacceptable proof of country origins and therefore unsuitable for the genteel table. And of course the tractor had no need of bruised corn. Barley now is king in the broad Buchan lands, balmy Moray and in the redlands of the Mearns. It does not cut green but there is a general taste for it, at least in the liquid form. Wheat is again making inroads.

Changes to come in farming and its closed society were already evident in the early 1930s, and Gibbon, ever-observant of the social trends, in *The Land* is aware of it:

> There are fewer children now plodding through the black glaur of the wet summer storms to school, fewer in both farm and cottar house. The ancient, strange whirlimagig of the generations that enslaved the Scots peasantry for centuries is broken.

And so it was. Slowly at first but then with unprecedented pace, the tractor robbed them of their past, broke, finally, their long compact with the land — and the long thread of farmtoun history based on the power of draught animals. What the future would hold would be different entirely, a step into the unknown. Gradually, in every area, the machine would take over, erasing those old patterns that rose from that first streak of brown down the stubble to culminate in the proud stackyards of autumn.

Straw now, once a mainstay of the old touns' agriculture, is left in the bout at the tail of the combine-harvester, the waste of its triumphal but solitary progress and all but an embarrassment. With the "bonnie ricks" but a memory, the old cornyards, where they exist at all, are bleak and weed-grown, as shorn of purpose as of their emblems. Fading too are the skills that once gave them their grandeur.

Silage, but in its modern infancy as the great days of the old touns drew to a close, would take the pressure off dairy-cake and hay and man would not be ungrateful. Milk production would become, increasingly, a mechanised process no longer dependent on the milker's skill, and the old milk churns, lonely sentinels on their road-end perch in the winter-grey dawn, would disappear as milk went from the udder to the bulk carrier beyond the realm of all human agency. Their loss extinguishes that rare piece of dairytoun artistry, the snatch lift.

The mucking of the farmtoun fields would be revolutionised soon after World War Two by the mechanical muck-loader (fitted to the tractor and operated by its hydraulics) and the mechanical muck-spreader. Though they deprived the old-style grieve of the chance to rule the roost, like the farmtoun cock, on his own midden-head, their invention came not a moment too soon for horsemen and bailies. It meant that a few more of the farmtoun men would reach retirement without being irreparably buckled in body.

Now, later in the farmtoun day and with the upsurge of parlour milking, few touns take muck as seriously as once they did. In any case, science and artificial manures now govern the growth of crops and extend and mutate those old cycles of fertility and renewal that demanded the great autumn ritual of muck-spreading by hand.

There are few byres, now — those once-welcoming places. As the old *biggings* fell into disrepair, more cattle courts erupted in their place, with a system that assured the beast of even less dignity since it had to stand still longer in its own dung. Dairy beasts, similarly housed in winter, are ushered in to take their turn in the milking parlour, a term, surely, that shows how far the slick world of advertising has penetrated a world where once it was barely known.

Barley beef, of course, has supplanted turnip beef though the magic circle remains, with the farmtoun feeding its own barley to its own fattening beasts. *Neeps* needed labour, which was always against them, though now there is some suggestion of a turn-round.

Developments in seed germination have done away with the need for the *hyowing* and machine-harvesters have made unnecessary the slow and painful pulling of each turnip individually from the drill. In the slight whiff of revivalist thinking men are going back to the swede in the belief, still, that it can sweeten the milk and maybe boost the yield a little.

Scientific advance, better drainage and improved varieties of grasses and grains and seeds of all kinds are giving today's farming a chance the old touns never had: the means by which to challenge unfavourable climate and conditions with some hope of success.

Seedtime is less a commitment: pest and weed control has immeasurably advanced and a good *hairst* can almost be predetermined. Almost, but not quite. With less need for straw, short-stemmed varieties stand a better chance. Yet the wind can still shake the barley.

It was the dyke, the ditch and the hawthorn hedge that fashioned the old touns' landscape. Now, tragically, these the old margins too are under threat. The hedgerows crash with a kind of inevitability, uprooted on suspicion of harbouring vermin loitering with intent and for the hindrance they may cause to today's modern implements. Their loss is seen in a drabber countryside. Once they were the factors that changed a society and their disappearance poses the important question: whose countryside is it, anyway? Even the fine old drystone dykes, less prone to the ravages of nature, can now be overthrown at the bulldozer's whim, though they at least mainly endure, memorials still to the calloused hands that built them.

But the burn runs past the old mill unmolested. More than most things, the names of the old mills have survived, extrapolated in the name of the toun with which they were once associated, dotting the rural map like the raisins on a rice pudding and clinging still to the stream though the old mill *bigging* now is no more than a rickle of stones. The landscape chimes with their memory: the Uppermills, Mid-mills and Nethermills (among many others), the names that once fixed their pecking order down the waterside. When the dam was high, the mill was put on. . . . A few, sad to say, have come to a bad end as homes of so-called character, or as chi-chi restaurants that take their cachet from the old mill wheel now refurbished but in no danger ever of turning. Mostly though the old mills, where they still stand, are silent now.

About the touns whose meal they ground, the barn mills — the old threshing-mills put on once-weekly — became unloved by all but the millwright who built them. They outwore their time, and in a climate of such uncertainty had to be torn from their moorings to let in the grain-drier. The need was paramount, the logic inescapable.

So there faded from our view the world of Charles Murray, the red land of Lewis Grassic Gibbon, the land from which Flora Garry and John C. Milne distilled their poetry; it went with its seasons and its immutable rhythms, its pace of plodding change suddenly overtaken by the march of machines. As enclosure itself had brought forth the farmtouns so their mechanisation created the world of agri-business. The old cadences of the year — seedtime, summer and harvest and the ploughs of winter — with all the patterns and rituals they brought to the fields would diminish. Traditions and old work practices that had been enshrined in them would be forgotten by a folk who had no further use for them, uncherished by those who had not known them.

So there passed from the land a legion of folk once bound to it, whose destinies were intertwined with it. The hard men have gone. The cottar's house, the tied home of the man who drove a Clydesdale pair, is no longer needed. The old stables stand silent of man and beast. Once they were the centres of bustle morning, noon and night, of pawky argument and occasionally hot disputation.

The bothies above or beyond are as silent, bereft of the men who once lodged there. They were always drifters. Now there is only the smell of the dust gathering in the corners and of rampant woodrot. You will not hear the scrape of a wild fiddle or the wheezy notes of an old melodeon let alone the raucous refrain of a bothy ballad all those miles from Moray to the Mearns.

But if that farming past is beginning to slip away, there are, still and all, concerned men — steeped in the lore of the countryside or those who have fallen into the inheritance of their touns and their memories — who have set aside an old byre or a hayloft as a corner of yesterday, a place where the curious can come to browse; where an old horseman, a man who once strutted the stable cobbles of the proud touns, can pick up the threads of the past and, turning an old tool or implement in the hand, show quietly how it was used.

The moment has its own poignancy, a reminder of how much of the old knowledge has already been lost to us as well as an indicator of the distance farming has come since the 1940s. It is here that one listens to the old voice of the land and marvels at times at its quiet eloquence. The hand that held the plough, that once rolled black twist in the palm, is tremulous now but still gnarled as it packs "ready-rubbed" into the pipe-bowl.

And we are fortunate, too, in another respect: in the later years of last century and the early part of the present one, the folk of the old touns were increasingly photographed for us by the itinerant photographer who, when things were slack in the shop, strapped his tripod to the crossbar of his bicycle (itself a daring innovation) and took away on a round of the touns to drum up business. He has left us a delightful record: what they looked like, those folk who down their generations tilled the soil. Frozen in mid-task or posed in pious black, in dark suits and tight-buttoned bodices and with Adam's apples perched uncomfortably on unaccustomed stiff collars, they gaze at us from under their broad bonnets and frilled mutches with solemn faces, their steely stares for once denying the humour that could convulse them.

There is a belief that such hard-working folk, with their separation from polite town society and with their insular lifestyle, must have been poor in spirit as well as in the material things. With their earthy, vigorous ballads and the cornkister kings to sing them that surely cannot have been so.

They were not all of them fine kirk-going folk; nor were they all outstandingly handsome. They were awkward, thrawn, gley-eyed and splay-footed and some of them would have done you an injury for any injudicious reference to either of these physical imperfections. For others it was a stamp of their character that they took such blemishes through life without being aware of them.

So where did they go, all those sombre-faced folk when the touns no longer had need of them? They went to the city in great numbers, the horsemen to become carters briefly, before that trade died, to drive milk floats and cleansing-department lorries — anything that put a value on their old horseman's skills. They swapped their heavy tacketed boots for the lightweight shoes of summer and sent their children to better schools and even to university. They absorbed the townsman's guile and moved on to become actors in another scenario; and the victims of another lifestyle. Their loss was permanent. Many of the old crofter folk followed them, deeply disillusioned by toil that began before break-of-day and ended only with bedtime.

Then there were the sounds of the old countryside: the *creak* and *jingle* of harness in the plough, the *crunch* of iron-rimmed cart wheels on the stone-metalling of the road, the clean sweet *swish* of the crofter's scythe; the binder's *clack*, the *brumm-brumm* of the travelling mill. All of them now are the sounds of a far landscape, lost to us apart from on the contrived occasion, the staged event of the working museum that purports to take us authentically back in time. That, alas, commendable though the idea is, it can never do.

One is aware of the compromise: the dress is not truly that the old horsemen wore and the threshing, for instance, is not in earnest but a pleasant pastiche — which is not to say that such events lack their value. Far from it; we are indebted to the determined men who stage them.

The sounds of the old bothy songs, however, can be more authentically resurrected: on disc and tape and from the Sound Archives of Broadcasting House, so far from the milieu that begat them. Prominent still is the voice of that *guid-herted* farmer John Strachan, whose satirical songs of protest so vigorously castigated his own class. He had carried a culture over the years. . . .

So there passed the era of the ballad and the plough, of the cattle kings and the men who sang the cornkisters, a folk who lived in the shadow of the seasons and in a deeper harmony with the soil. Murray's quaintly-named Scuttrie Fair, in upcountry Aberdeenshire, faded before the need no longer to hold it. The old smiddies where the Clydesdales came are closed or transformed with the years into emporiums of local engineering, at worst into quick-repair sheds for the assorted ironmongery of today's countryside. The old communion tokens went out, a bit like piety itself, with the upheaval of World War One. When the old elder who gave them out from his village tailor's shop finally quit, the premises were taken over by a man who though a tailor to trade was a draper by inclination and would sooner have sold you a suit ready-made. In that he was but bowing to the inevitable. His customers, too, by then, the cheery ploughmen still whistling in the bout, were men nearing the end of a long tradition.

I know of no work that laments for the old landscape of the farmtouns so tellingly as the lines of John C. Milne's "Tempora Mutantur":

> As I gaed doon by Memsie
> I heard an aul' man speir,
> "Faur's the bonnie dialect
> That aince wis spoken here?
>
> And faur's the weel-faurt fairm
> Wi' a'thing snod and ticht,
> The steadin doors new pintit,
> The harness shinin bricht?

The strappin foreman billy
That chawed the Bogie-Roll?
The hame-owre Memsie menners
Oor gentry cou'dna thole?

The swack and swuppert baillie?
The banie plooman chiel?
The cadger wi' his cairtie?
The fishwife wi' her creel?

The steady fine-gyaun pairie?
The bonnie straucht-plooed rig?
The willin weel-shod sheltie?
The spring-cairt and the gig?

The gweed God-fearin fairmer,
Wi' weel-worn wincey sark,
Wha nivver missed a sermon
For widder or for wark?

. . . .

The brose-caup and the skimmer?
The milkin-steel? The quine
That rose afore the mornin
And beddit efter nine?

. . . .

The weel-kent cornkister?
The dam-brod and the cairts?
And faur's the lowe o' learnin
That made the lad o' pairts?"

In Milne, who died in 1962, one hears the echoes of the bothy ballads; his work at times has some of their metrical thump. But it is Flora Garry, forsaking the Doric in "Decently and in Order", who writes the most moving epitaph for the hardy farmer men who made the land we know today, men short on humour at times, short of friends and sometimes of humanity but never of courage. Death took them ornately away from the simple thing they loved most, the land itself:

They carried him feet first out into the sunlight
(Waste of time, the best hay day all Summer).
The polished cars and the coach's glasswork glittered.
Into the country town they drove decorously.

. . . . . .

It should have been far otherwise for him.
Evening and the clover wet with dew,
The time he used to wander by the whin-dykes,
Eyeing fences, cattle-beasts, and water troughs,
Scythe in hand to snick the seeding thistles.
Then would have been the hour of his own choosing,
He in a plain strong box of his own making,
And the farm lads, their spades well-greased and keen-edged,
In a sheltered corner of the sixteen acre.
Just a natural, necessary field job,
Done with competence and expedition,
Prelude to sleep and tomorrow's work and weather.

When they had housed the old horse ploughs for ever in their old
implement sheds and carted some of them to the museums to have
their clean lines gaped at, there were folk who believed that
something had died in the landscape. The old countryside was filled
with voices; now its emptiness is emphasised by the tractor's
exhaust-crackle. The land has become more solitary. Man hardly
participates. The figure in the heated tractor cab, with radio fitted,
is as remote from the soil as a factory operative at his lathe. The clods
no longer crumble under the soles of his tacketed boots; the plough
when it hits rock no longer wrenches his arms almost out of their
sockets but merely activates the hydraulics to throw his machine out
of damaging gear.

Yet the plough remains, if little else does—although it too may be
abandoned in favour of more minimal cultivation. Already there are
those who are keen for its retirement. And even here there is change:
what was once a careful consummation by the ploughman and his
pair with the single-furrow plough has become a hurried rape with
the machine-drawn multi-furrow. The work itself has changed:
from the sweet symmetry of the flowing unbroken furrow we have

passed into a time when such perfection is bad agriculture. Old ploughmen now, looking over the autumn land of their youth, complain of the "filth" (the unburied trash escaping from the furrows). They shake their heads; there was a time when such work would not have done.

Like the combine-harvester, the forage-harvester and the root-harvester, the tractor has obliterated the old order in the fields. Journey where you will now in the land of those two peerless ballad-singers John Strachan and Willie Kemp, William Duthie, the Cruickshank brothers and the great McCombie, you will not see a man in serious everyday contention between the plough-stilts. You will hardly see a binder between one parish and the next, except perhaps in some upland place where the parks are smaller and they like not to chance their good fortune, cutting a little greener than normal.

Then in the days of early autumn does the corn still sit in the stook in the sough of the wind, a last link with the old rituals. It cannot be so for much longer.

What has changed most of all is that haunting, intangible thing, the "spirit" of the land. The seasons turn now with the stoic inevitability of the digital clock. There is a brisk confidence in the summer parks. The old farmtouns worked *with* nature; today's touns work *on* nature, enormously improving her performance. It may in the end be unwise and there are folk who believe it so. Some of them are the men who once ploughed their lonely furrows in the farmtoun fields and who look back to that time and a life lived closer to the soil. Farming now has no need of their old skills and their artistry. Their day is done, but a bare land remembers them.

GLOSSARY

a, a': all
abeen: above
aboot: about
ae: one
aff: off
afore: before
aft: oft; aften: often; aftimes: oft-
  times
ahingin: hanging
ahint: behind
ain: own
amo', amang: among; among't:
  amongst it
an, an': and
ance, aince: once
ane, anes: one, ones
aneuch: enough
anither: another
approach: avenue
'at: that
a'thing: everything
atween: between
aul', auld: old
awa, awa': away
awfu': awful
aye: always; aye: yes (assent)

bailie: stockman
bairn: child
baith: both
ban': bound
bandwin: sickle-shearing team of 7
  or 9
banie: boney
bargain: agreement on pay and
  conditions struck in hiring fair
beddin: bedding
beddit: gone (went) to bed; in bed

beginnin': beginning
belyve: then, after
ben: through, along
bere: poor, early strain of barley
bide: stay
bield: comfort
bigg: build
biggin, bigging: building
biggit: built
Bill: bull
billy: cheil, man
bin': bind
bit: but
bittie: a small bit
blakes: beats; blakes a': beats all
  (in derogatory sense)
blaw, blaws: blow, blows
blawn: blown
blatter: wild shower (of rain)
bleck: blacking
bledder: bladder
blibberin': dribbling
bodies: folk, people
Bogie-Roll: black-twist tobacco
bone-davie: fertiliser spreader
bothy: squalid accommodation for
  unmarried farmtoun workers
bothy ballad: farmtoun song,
  usually satirical
bowfft: barked
brae: hill
braks: breaks; brakin', brakkin:
  breaking
braw: wonderful, relating usually
  to appearance
bree: liquid
breeks, breekies: trousers
breid: oatcakes

breisted: mounted
bricht: bright
britchin: breeching
brocht: brought
brookie: sooty
broos: brows
brose: oatmeal mixed with water,
   the dish that raised a nation
bruke: broke
burnie: stream
burstin': bursting
byre: cowshed

ca': drive; ca' neeps: to transport
   turnips
ca', ca'd: call; called
cadger: trader in country trifles
caff: chaff
cairry, cairries: carry, carries
cairt: cart; cairtie: small cart;
   cairter: carter
cairtin': carding, playing cards
cam': came
canna: cannot
canny: careful
carlin': lass
caudle: warm mixture
caul', cauld: cold
caup: wooden bowl from which
   brose was traditionally supped
causeys: street cobblestones
chappit-tatties: mashed potatoes
chasin': chasing
chaumer: unmarried men's sleeping quarters
chawed: chewed
cheil, childes: young man, young
   men
claes: clothes
cleekit: hooked, seized
clip: young colt, alas often no
   longer entire
clockin': brooding
cloods: clouds
cloot: cloth
close, closs: steading enclosure

clyack: end of harvest cutting
cogues: wooden pails
coles: haycocks
comin': coming
commen': commend
connached: ruined
consid'rin: considering
convoy: escort
coo: cow
cornkister: bothy ballad
cottar: farm worker in tied cottage
cottie: petticoat
cou'dna, couldnae: could not
countra: country
crap, craps: crop, crops
craws: crows
crofter: smallholder on farming
   fringe
croods: curds
cruive: enclosure of netting wire
cuffins: threshing waste, bits of
   straw, etc.
curran-baps: currant buns
cuttin': cutting

daar't: dared
dae: do; daeing: doing
daen't: doing it
dambrod: draughtboard
dawtit: petted
dearie: sweetheart
deem: lass, girl
deemie: lass, usually kitchen girl
deen: done
deese: long wooden seat in farmtoun kitchen
Deil: Devil
denner: midday meal
dicht: wipe
dinna: do not
dird: thump
disna: does not
dockens: dock-leaf plants
dominie: country headmaster
dool: misery
doon: down

dove, dove in: thrust in (your spoon)

dram: drink (of whisky)

drappie: drop

drappin': dropping

dreeler: drill plough

dreelt: drilled, ordered

dressin': dressing

driech: dreary; driechness: dreariness, bleakness

drivin': driving

drooth: drying wind

drove: a herd

dubbed: muddied; dubby: muddy

duds, duddies: clothes

dune: done

dyke, dykie: stone wall

Dyod: a mild exclamation that avoided taking His name in vain

ear': early

easin's: point at which rick tapered in

echt: eight

e'e, e'en, een: eyes

e'en: evening

engagement: agreement struck in hiring fair; contract between farmer and worker

eildit: elderly

en': end

endrig: headland

eyn: end

fa: who

fa': fall; fa' tae: fall to

fadder: father.

fae: from

fa'en: fallen

faes: foes

fail-dyke: turf wall

fairly: just so; aye fairly: agreement in affirmative

fairm: farm; fairmer: farmer

fame: rage, passion

fan: when

fare-ye-well: farewell

farl: quarter-portion of oatcake

farmin': farming

fat: what

fauld: enclosure

faur: where

fee: farmworker's engagement for 6 or 12 months

feeders: fattening cattle

feeing fair: hiring fair

feering: shallow furrows which begin ploughing

fegs: Doric equivalent of "my goodness"

fichered: tinkered

fin: when

fine-gyaun: easily-going

fire-house: dwelling house

fit: foot

fit: what; fit're: what are

fite: white

Fitie: Whitey

flang: flung

flaughts: binder flashes or sails that carried crop on to platform canvas

fleed: headland

fleer: floor

flittin': moving, removal

flo'er: flower

followin': following

foo: how

foon: foundation

fordel: store

forenicht: early evening

fou: drunk

friens: friends

fu': full; (also) how

funn: the whins

fur: furrow

furth: the outdoors

fye: whey

fyles: whiles

fyow: few

gae: go; gaed: went

gaen, gane: gone
gale: gable
gang, gangs: go; tier of sheaves
gars: makes; gart: made
gaun: going; gaun owre: going
   over
gear: worldly goods, material
   things
gey: very, significant
gid: gave
gie: give; gie's, gies: give us
gin: if
girdin': iron hooping for cart wheel
girdle: griddle; girdled breid:
   oatcakes
girss: grass
gleg: horse-fly
gley-eyed: with a squint
goon: gown
gotten: got
goupin': staring
gowd: gold
granfadder: grandfather
greep: central aisle of cow-byre
grieve: farmtoun bailiff
growin': growing
grun': grind
grun: ground, farming land
gudeman, guidman: farmer
gudewife, guidwife: farmer's wife
guid: good
guidship: treatment, usage
   (usually bad)
gweed: good

hacket: chapped; hacks: chaps
hae: have
hairst: harvest; hairster: harvest
   hand
hale: whole
halflin: young horseman
hame: home; hame-owre: homely;
   hame-spun: homespun
han': hand
hap: cover
harlin': pebble-dashing

harp: mason's screen for cleaning
   sand and gravel
harried, herried: robbed
hasher: machine for slicing turnips
haud: hold
haudin': holding; haudin' on the
   jaw: chatting
hedder: heather
heid: head; heided, beheaded,
   trimming off shaws (of turnips)
heided oot: brought to a head
   (mainly in rick-building)
herdie: herd boy
hert: heart
het: hot
heuk: sickle
hid: had
himsel': himself
hingin': hanging
hinna: have not
hint: end; hint o' hairst: end of
   harvest
holin': digging (usually potatoes)
hoose: house
hose: stockings
howe: shallow valley
hull: hill
hurled: rode; to hurl: to ride
hyow: hoe; hyowing: singling
   turnip plants in drill

i, i': in
ilka: each
ill-trickit: mischievous
ill-will: dislike
ineugh: enough
intae: into
ither: other
ivver: ever

jist: just
jot: chore

kame, kaim: comb
keckl't: cackled
keel: red-earth marking material

keepin': keeping
ken: know; ye ken: you know;
  kent: knew
kirn: churn
kirnin': messing about
kitchie: kitchen; kitchie deem:
  kitchen girl
kittle: tickle; kittle up: liven up
knittal: fabric
kye: milk cows

laft: loft
laich: low
laird: landowner
lampin': striding out
lan, lan's: land, lands
lane, lone: by oneself
lang: long
lantrins: lanterns
lapbuird: lapboard
larick: larch
lat: let
laucht: laughed
leading: carting home sheaves
  from the harvest field
lea's: leaves
leggined: legginged
liftward: skyward
likit: liked
lookin': looking
loon: young lad
losh: Doric equivalent of "gosh"
lowe: flame
lowpin: leaping
lowse: to loosen, unyoke; lowsing
  time: end of work period;
  lowsed: unyoked; lowser: one
  who cut string of sheaves during
  threshing
lowss: spare, horse not properly
  harnessed to implement
lythe: sheltered

maet: food generally
maiden: farmer's eldest daughter
mair: more

mairry: marry
maist: most, almost
mak', maks: make, makes
mannie: man, but usually
  describes farmer
mart: livestock auction market;
  killed animal salted down for
  winter meat
mask: infuse (tea)
maun: must
mebbe: maybe
meenit: minute
meers: mares
menners: manners
micht: might
midden: dung heap in field or
  farmyard
midder: mother
mids: joining of one piece of
  ploughing with neighbouring
  strip
milkin-steel: milking stool
milkit: milked
min': mind, remember
minnen: minnows
mirk: dark, deep dusk
mochy: misty, damp
moggins: boot hose
mony: many
morn: tomorrow
mornin': morning
moss: where peats were dug for
  fuel
mou': mouth
moulter: multure
mowser: moustache; mowsert:
  moustached
muckit: dunged, spread with dung
muckle: large, much
muir: moor
mull: threshing-mill
mutches: frilled headgear for
  women

na, nae: no
naething: nothing

neebour: neighbour
needin': needing
neeperin: neighbouring; a help-
   for-help arrangement
neeps: turnips
ne'er: never
neist: next
neuk: corner
news: gossip, talk
nib: nose
nichert: neighed
nicht: night
nickum: rascal
nives: fists
nivver: never
noo: now
nowt, nowte: cattle

o, o': of
och: exclamation
onding: downpour
onywye: anyway
oor: our
oot: out
orra: spare, but also condemnatory
   as "trashy"
orra loon: youngest member of
   farmtoun crew, despite title
   sometimes a lad of quality
o't: of it
ower, owre: over; owre goudie:
   head over heels
owsen: oxen
oxter: armpit; oxtered: held in
   armpit; more generally, embraced

pairie: Clydesdale pair
pairt: part; pairtin': parting
park: farmtoun field
pat: put
pechin': panting
peesies: peewits, lapwings
Pess-day: Good Friday
pickle: a little
pikit: piked, barbed

pintit: painted
pirn: miller's wheel
pit, pits: put, puts
plash: splash
pleugh: plough
ploo: plough; plooman: ploughman
plukey: pimply; plukey-faced:
   pimply-faced
plyterin: drudging in muddy,
   rainy conditions
pooches, pouches: pockets
pottage: porridge
pottie: deepish part of stream
pow: head
preen: pin; priend: pinned
'prentice: apprentice
pu': pull
puckle: a good many
puir: poor

quaet: quiet
queets: ankles
quine: lass

raikit: raked
raip: rope
rale: real
rampag't: rampaged
rapes: ropes
rarely: wonderfully
ream: cream
redd: clear; redd up: clean up
reekit: smoked, heavily perspired
reel'd: danced the reel
reeshle: rustle
reid: red
reist: arrest motion of horse
richt: right
rick: stack
rig: strip of work, i.e., ploughing
rin, rins: run, runs
roch: rough
rodden: rowan
roon, roun': round
rottan: rat

roup: displenish sale
rowe: to roll, to push
row'n: rowan
rucks: ricks
rundale: strip cultivation in blocks
run-rig: strip cultivation, uncon-
  solidated

Sacrament Sunday: Communion
  Sunday
sae: so
saft: soft
sair: sore
sair't: sick of
san': sand
saps: bread and milk pudding
sark: shirt
saw't: saw it
saxpence: sixpence (old-style)
saxteen: sixteen
scraich: scratch
scrimpin': scrimping
scunnert: fed up with
seen: soon
semmit: undervest
sey'd: sieved
shaeffin': sheafing
sharn: cowshit
sheen: shoes
she'f: sheaf
shelt: light horse for gig or phaeton
shift: patch of ground in yearly
  rotational change
shimming: horse-hoeing
shinin: shining
showd: sway
shune: shoes
sicc-like: such-like
siller: silver, (usually) money
simmer: summer
singin': singing
sittin': sitting
skelp: chunk (of)
skirley: frizzled accompaniment of
  water and oatmeal to boiled
  potatoes as the main midday dish

sklatit: slated; sklates: slates
sklyter: large area
skweel: school
skytit: glanced off
slaes: blackthorn berries
sleepin: sleeping
sma: small
smoor: blizzard
snappert: stumbled
snaw: snow; snaw bree: snow-
  water
snod: tidy
so'ens, sowens: gruel made from
  residual meal left in oat-husks
sonsie: robust
soo: sow
sooter, souter: shoemaker
soughin': sighing
speen: spoon
speirs: asks
sproats: rushes
spullin': spilling
sta': stall
stackit: stacked, ricked
staig: stallion
stamack: stomach
stan': stand; standin', stannin':
  standing
stane: stone
steadin: steading, farmtoun buildings
steens: stones
steer: stir; steerin': thronging
stew: dust
stibble: stubble
stirk: young cattle beast between 1
  and 2 years old
stobs: thistle spines
stoon: twinge
stoppit: stopped
stot: steer, bullock between 2 and 3
  years old
stovies: stoved potatoes
strae: straw; strae soo: straw
  stacked in bulk unit
strang: animal urine, liquid of

dung midden
strapper: man who drove farmer's
    phaeton or gig
strappin': tall, well-built
straucht: straight
styoo: dust
sucker: young sappy branch of
    bush or tree
suppert: suppered
swack: nimble
swacken: loosen, make supple
Swaddish: Swedish
swat: sweated
swingletree: whippletree
swuppert: supple, sinewy
syes: sieves
syne: then

tackety: tacketed
tae: to
taen: taken
tak's: takes
tapner: turnip knife
tay: tea
te: to
teem: empty
Term Day: May 28 and November
    28 (in earlier time the 26th of the
    month) when men left the farm-
    touns or re-engaged for a further
    6 or 12 months
teuchat: lapwing
thackit: thatched
thae: those
than: then
theets: traces
thiggin': begging for seed to sow
thocht: thought
thole: endure
thon: that
thooms: thumbs
thrang: throng, state of intensive
    activity
thraw: dire strait
throu: through
tichened: tightened

ticht: tight
til't: to it
timmer: timber
tire't: tired
tirr: strip
tither: the other
toon: town
toun: farmtoun; tounie: small
    toun
traivelled, traivelt: walked
trampin', trumpin: tramping;
    trumpit: tramped
troot: trout
truffs: turves
tull: till
tummle: tumble
tummlin tam: implement for
    raking hay-swaths together
twa: two
twal: twelve
tweezlelock: thrawcrook, winder
    for making straw ropes
'twid: it would
twine: sheaf-binding string, a com-
    modity that served many farm-
    toun purposes and sometimes
    held the shepherd's coat shut
    and kept the bailie's breeks
    attached to his galluses.
twinin', twining: twisting

unco: very; unco weel: very well

vrapper: long jacket garment worn
    by girls and women

wacht, waught: swig of large
    measure
wad, wid: would
wadna: would not
waes: woes, woe is
walkit: walked
war, wir: were
wark: work
warst: worst
wasna, wisna: was not

wat: wet
wauk: walk
wee: small
weel: well; weel-faurt: of good
 appearance; weel-kent:
 well-known
weemen: women
weet: wet
wha: who
whip-the-cat: the tailor
wi': with; wi't: with it
widder: weather
willin': willing
win': wind
winlins: windlings, small armfuls
 of straw
winna: won't
winnir: wonder
winnoster: corn-dressing
 machine
wird: word

wis: was
workin': working
wrang: wrong
wun: dry
wye: way
wytin': waiting

yavil broth: second day's broth
ye: you; ye'd: you would
yearn't: curdled
yeldrin: yellowhammer
yell: dry
yer: your
yerning: rennet
yird: earth
yirning: churning
yirnt-milk: curdled milk
yokin': yoking, morning or afternoon work period
yon: that, in particular
yowes: ewes, sheep generally